folded or unfolded. The shiny side is the gummed side. If you use a folded hinge, moisten the short side and press it to the back of a stamp. Then hold the stamp with your tongs and moisten the long side of the hinge. Place the stamp where you want it in the album and secure it by pressing down with a blotter. Using your tongs, gently lift the stamp's corners to make sure none have stuck to the page.

People who collect unused, uncanceled or mint stamps may use mounts instead of hinges to prevent air and dirt from damaging them. A **mount** is a small, clear (usually plastic) envelope that covers the whole stamp. With the first story in place, you'll be ready to add more to your "story-book of stamps."

After a while, you may want to buy a special stamp album. Some feature specific categories with pictures of the stamps that are supposed to appear on each page. It's usually best to select an album with loose-leaf pages so you can add pages easily as your collection expands. A **stock book** is an album with plastic or paper pockets on each page. There are no pictures of stamps—you can organize it *your* way.

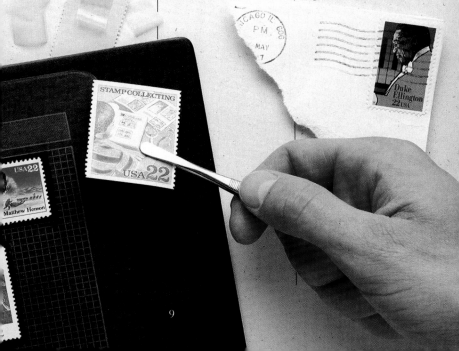

Tools of the Trade

In addition to the tongs, hinges and mounts described above, other equipment that all stamp collectors should have includes:

Glassine (glass-ene) **envelopes** are used to store stamps that you have yet to add to your album. Glassine is a special thin paper that keeps grease and air from damaging stamps.

A **stamp catalog** is a handy reference for every collector. It can help you identify stamps with its many illustrations, and it provides information such as values for used and unused stamps.

A four- or six-power **magnifying glass** helps distinguish stamps that seem to be the same.

A **perforation gauge** measures the jagged cuts or holes, or *perforations*, along the edges of stamps. Size and number of perforations are sometimes needed to identify stamps. "Perfs" make stamps easy to tear apart.

The
Postal Service
Guide to
U.S. Stamps

14TH EDITION

U.S. STAMPS
IN
FULL COLOR

1988
STAMP VALUES

UNITED STATES
POSTAL SERVICE

United States Postal Service
Washington, D.C. 20260-6355
Item No. 862

Definition of
Catalog Prices

The United States Postal Service sells only the commemoratives released during the past few years and current regular and special stamps and postal stationery.

Prices listed in this book are called "catalog prices" by stamp collectors. Collectors use catalog prices as guidelines when they are buying or trading stamps. It is important to remember the prices are simply guidelines to the stamp values. Stamp condition (see pp 11-12) is very important in determining the actual value of a stamp.

The catalog prices are given for unused (mint) stamps and used (cancelled) stamps, which have been hinged and are in Fine condition. Stamps in Superb condition that have never been hinged may cost several times the listed price. Stamps in less than Fine condition may cost less.

The prices for used stamps are based on a light cancellation; a heavy cancellation lessens a stamp's value. Cancelled stamps may be worth more than uncancelled stamps. This happens if the cancellation is of a special type or for a significant date. Therefore, it is important to study an envelope before removing a stamp and discarding its "cover."

Listed prices are estimates of how much you can expect to pay for a stamp from a dealer. If you sell the same stamp to a dealer, he may offer you much less than the catalog price. Dealers pay based on their interest in owning that stamp. If they already have a full supply, they will only buy more at a low price.

Prices in regular type for single unused and used stamps are taken from the *Scott 1988 Standard Postage Stamp Catalogue, Volume 1* © 1987, whose editors have based these values on the current stamp market. Prices quoted for unused and used stamps are for "Fine" condition, except where Fine is not available. If no value is assigned, market value is individually determined by condition of the stamp, scarcity and other factors.

Prices for Plate Blocks and First Day Covers are taken from *Scott's Specialized Catalogue of U.S. Stamps,* 1987 Edition, © 1986. The Scott numbering system for stamps is used in this book.

Prices for Souvenir Cards are taken from the *Catalog of United States Souvenir Cards,* by Franklin R. Bruns, Jr. and James H. Bruns, published by Washington Press. Prices for American Commemorative Panels are from The American Society of Philatelic Pages and Panels, an organization specializing in Commemorative Panels. Souvenir Pages are from Charles D. Simmons of Buena Park, California.

Table of Contents

A Great Way to Collect... and to Learn

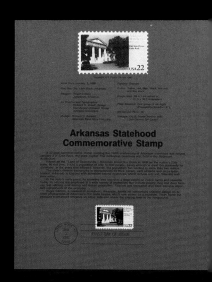

Arkansas Statehood Commemorative Stamp

Colorful Keepsakes of 1987 U.S. Issues

The U.S. Postal Service Souvenir Page Program is an informative, inexpensive way to obtain all the year's stamp issues. These display pages are printed in a limited edition for every definitive and commemorative U.S. stamp issued in a given year, including airmails, coil pairs and booklet panes.

Each Souvenir Page includes the featured stamp, postmarked with a "FIRST DAY OF ISSUE" cancellation and mounted on a brightly colored, 8½" by 10½" page. A black-and-white enlargement of the stamp and its technical specifications (designer, engraver, date of issue and printing information) precede a lively historical narrative about its subject and issuance. All this at an average cost of $1.00 per page.

However, Souvenir Pages are not available at post offices or Philatelic Centers—they are only available by advanced subscription on a first-come first-served basis. Subscribers also receive monthly letters with information on upcoming issues, new designs and other postal products.

Money-back guarantee! If you are ever dissatisfied, return your Souvenir Pages for a *full* refund. For more information and an order form, write to:

USPS Guide
Souvenir Page Program
Philatelic Marketing Division
Washington, D.C. 20260-6755

Once upon a time... Nursery rhymes and fairy tales were the first stories that made us laugh, cry and sit on the edge of our chairs. Then we learned the adventures of Dick, Jane and Spot. Today we continue to excite our senses with mystery, drama, romance and science fiction stories. From Mother Goose and Dr. Seuss to Mark Twain and Stephen King, a good story is something we can all appreciate.

Postage stamps are storytellers, too. There is more to a stamp than a picture—there is his-

The "Penny Black," the world's first postage stamp (circa 1840), depicts Queen Victoria of Great Britain.

tory. Each one tells a true story, from famous individuals to important events, of interest to people of all ages. In the United States alone there are more than 19 million stamp collectors.

The stories behind stamps have intrigued people for nearly a century and a half. Because mail with U.S. stamps on it is delivered all over the world, people around the globe learn about celebrated Americans as well as historic and current events and contemporary social issues in the United States.

The first formal stamps appeared in England in May of 1840. A private postal service in New York City, run by Alexander Greig, issued the first American adhesive stamp two years later. The first two *official* U.S. postage stamps, featuring Benjamin Franklin and George Washington, date back to July 1, 1847. When

the U.S. federal government took sole control of postage stamps in 1861, these small pictorial squares had become the world's window on America.

This close-up of George Washington is from one of the very first U.S. stamps—a 10¢ denomination issued on July 1, 1847.

What Is Philately?

Collecting stamps is easier than pronouncing the technical word that describes it. **Philately** (fi-lat′-el′lee) is the collection and study of postage stamps and other postal materials. Stamp collectors are called **philatelists** (fi-lat′-el′lists). There are two basic ways to collect stamps. You can collect a variety, **general**

collecting, or you can collect specific topics, **topical collecting**.

Saving as many stamps as possible is a good way to start. Many new philatelists find it interesting to have a wide range of stamps. They're similar to beginning readers who want to get their hands on all kinds of stories. Have your family and friends tear off the upper right-hand corners of envelopes they receive in the mail. Ask them to be careful not to rip the stamps or peel them off the envelopes (a careful procedure for this is described on page 8). Neighborhood businesses that get a lot of mail—banks, stores, city halls or telephone companies—may be sources of envelopes for you, as well.

The second, more popular way to collect is to choose one or two stamp topics that really interest you—birds, flowers or sports, for instance.

For those of you seeking variety first, stamps are classified into five major categories:

- **Regular** or **definitive** stamps are found on most mail. Printed in unlimited quantities, they are available for several years.
- **Commemorative** stamps are issued to honor important people, events or special subjects. They are usually larger and more colorful than definitives. Printed in limited quantities, they are available only for two to three months at most post offices.
- **Coil** stamps are issued in rolls. Each one has two straight and two perforated edges.
- **Airmail** stamps are used for sending mail overseas.
- **Postage Due** stamps were used by the U.S. Postal Service until late 1986 when the postage on a letter or package did not cover the cost to mail it.

Definitive

Commemorative

Coil

Airmail

Postage Due

Storing Your Valuables

Just as you may store your favorite books or video tapes on a shelf so they won't get damaged or lost, you'll want to protect your stamps. As they accumulate, it is a good idea to put them in some kind of order. You can organize your first album using a simple three-ring binder with loose-leaf paper.

Before mounting a stamp on an album page, you must carefully remove it from its envelope, or **cover**. Three tools are needed for this: 1) a small pan of warm (not hot) water, 2) paper towels and 3) tongs.

Place the stamp face down in the water, then wait until it floats off the paper and sinks to the bottom of the pan. As soon as that happens, lift it out with your **tongs**, a metal grasping device similar to tweezers. (Never touch stamps with your fingers. Even if your hands are clean, oil from your skin can damage them.) To keep the stamp from curling while it dries, put it between two paper towels and apply pressure with a heavy object, such as a book. Leave

the stamp there overnight, and it will be flat and ready to put in an album the next day.

Do not use tape or glue to attach the stamp to an album page. That could destroy its value. A small strip of thin plastic, gummed on one side, may be used to put the stamp in the album. Called a **hinge**, this strip can be either

A **watermark tray** and **watermark fluid** are used to make more visible the designs or patterns (called *watermarks*) that are pressed into stamp paper during its manufacture. To make the marks show up, simply place a stamp face down on a watermark tray made of black glass or plastic, then cover the stamp with a few drops of watermark fluid. The fluid can be dangerous, so please follow directions and be careful.

Stamp Condition

Like an old book, the value of a stamp depends on two factors: how rare it is—that is, how few of them there are—and what condition it is in. You can get an idea of how rare a stamp is by the price listed for it in a catalog. Depending on its condition, however, a stamp may sell for more or less than the catalog price. A very rare stamp may be quite expensive even though it is in poor condition. At first, you'll probably be collecting stamps that are not very expensive, but you should still try to get them in the best condition you can find. Here are some things to look for when judging stamp condition.

Examine the front of the stamp. Are the colors bright or faded? Is the stamp dirty, stained or clean? Is the design in the center of the paper, or is it a little crooked or off to the side? Are the edges in good condition, or are some of the perforations missing? A stamp with a light cancellation mark is in better condition than one with heavy marks across it.

Now look at the back of the stamp. Is there a thin spot in the paper? It may have been caused by careless removal from an envelope or a hinge. Can you see hinge marks? Stamps that have the original gum and have never been hinged are more valuable.

Stamp dealers put stamps into categories according to their condition. The worst is "Poor" or "Space-filler." Most stamps you see will be in the categories "Superb," "Fine"

or "Good." (Look at the examples to see the differences in these categories.)

A stamp listed as **mint** is in the same condition as when purchased from the post office. An **unused** stamp has not been canceled; it may not have any gum on it, or it may be damaged in some way. Stamps in mint condition are usually more valuable than unused stamps.

Catalog prices listed in *The Postal Service Guide to U.S. Stamps* are for used and unused stamps in Fine condition that have been hinged. A stamp that has not been hinged and has excellent centering and color will cost more; a stamp in less than Fine condition that has been heavily canceled will cost less than the catalog price.

Light Cancel-Very Fine

Medium Cancel-Fine

Heavy Cancel

Superb

Very Fine

Fine

Good

How Stories Become Stamps

In addition to being powerful devices for education and communication, stamps and their stories often function as a public service, stimulating people to take worthwhile action. Similar to other mass mediums, such as television, radio, magazines and newspapers, postage stamps bring important messages to a large audience.

Who decides what goes on stamps? Almost all subjects are suggested by the general public. The Stamp Information Branch receives hundreds of suggestions every week, but only a few are selected. By law, only the Postmaster General has the authority to select stamp subjects, but he relies heavily on the recommendations of the Citizens' Stamp Advisory Committee.

Established 30 years ago, the Committee meets six times a year. It consists of historians, artists, businesspeople, philatelists and others interested in American history and culture. Keeping all postal customers in mind, they use a set of eligibility guidelines to aid in their difficult task. Once a recommended subject receives the Postmaster General's "stamp of approval," a Committee design coordinator assists in selecting a professional artist to design the stamp. The Committee reviews preliminary artwork and may request changes before a final version is submitted to the Postmaster General.

If you think a story should be told on a stamp, submit your idea at least 36 months before its logical date of issue. Suggestions, along with helpful background information, may be sent to:

United States Postal Service
Citizens' Stamp
Advisory Committee
Room 5800
475 L'Enfant Plaza West, SW
Washington, D.C.
20260-6352

It is recommended that artwork not be submitted; unsolicited art is seldom used because stamp designing is an exacting task requiring extraordinary skill.

Other Postal Collectibles

Stories come in many forms—novels, short stories, poems, movies— and so do stamps. In addition to their regular form, stamps are printed or embossed (made with a raised design) directly on envelopes, postal cards, aerogrammes and wrappers. Available at post offices, these **postal stationery** products are particularly popular among more serious collectors:

Stamped envelopes are made in several sizes and styles, including the window type. First issued in 1853, more than one million stamped envelopes are now issued every year.

Postal cards are made of a heavier paper than envelopes. Plain and simple, one-color postal cards were first issued in 1873. They stayed plain and simple until the first U.S. commemorative postal card came out in 1956. Several different postal cards are usually issued during a year and approximately 800 million are printed annually.

An **aerogramme** (air letter) is a flat sheet of paper that is a letter and an envelope all in one. It is specially stamped, marked for folding and gummed. After you write your letter, fold up the aerogramme and seal it. Meant for foreign airmail only, an aerogramme will carry your message anywhere in the world at a lower postage rate than regular airmail.

postal card

aerogramme

1835 · Mark Twain · 191

" I came in with Halley's Comet in 1835. It is coming again next year, and I expect to go out with it. It will be the greatest disappointment of my life if I don't go out with Halley's Comet. "

AEROGRAMME · VIA AIRMAIL · PAR AVION

① Seal top flap last
② Second fold

Additional

There are other, more specialized ways to collect. A **specialty collection**, for example, usually features a particular form of stamps, such as:

- **Blocks of Four** used or unused, unseparated stamps have two stamps above and two below. A block of four is the easiest block to collect.
- **Plate Blocks** are usually four stamps, from a corner of a pane with the printing plate number in the margin, or **selvage**, of the pane. The USPS began a new plate numbering system in 1981. Each color plate used first in stamp production is represented by a number 1 in the group of numbers in the margin. When a plate wears out and is replaced, a number 2

takes the place of the 1. The color of the number is the same as the color of the plate it represents.

- **Copyright Blocks** feature the copyright symbol © followed by "United States Postal Service" or "USPS" and the year in the margin of each pane of stamps. Since the USPS began copyrighting new stamp designs in 1978, most copyright symbols have been collected as part of blocks of four stamps.
- **Booklet Panes** are pages with usually four or more of the same stamps. Several panes of stamps are affixed inside a thin cardboard cover to form a booklet. Most booklet pane

A 111

stamped envelope

collections are devoted to entire panes. (Stamp booklets were first issued in 1898.)

- **First Day Covers** (FDCs) are envelopes

Jean Baptiste Pointe DuSable
AMERICAN PIONEER
BLACK HERITAGE SERIES 1987

with new stamps on them that have been canceled with their respective dates of issue.

- **Souvenir Cards** (6" x 8") are issued as keepsakes of philatelic (stamp collecting) exhibits. Distributed by the USPS or the Bureau of Engraving and Printing, souvenir cards cannot be used for postage; some, however, are available canceled. Of special interest is the annual souvenir card for National Stamp Collecting Month each October that was first issued in 1981.

Ordering First Day Covers

For each new postal stamp or stationery issue, the USPS selects one town or city related to the stamp's story as the site of the "first day" dedication ceremony. First day covers (FDCs) are envelopes with new stamps canceled with the "FIRST DAY OF ISSUE" date and city.

The quickest way to receive a first day cover is to buy the stamp yourself (new stamps usually go on sale the day after the first day of issue), attach it to your own cover and send it to the first day post office for cancellation. You may submit up to 50 envelopes per order. Write your address in the lower right-hand corner of each first day envelope, at least ⅝" from the bottom; use a peel-off label if you prefer. Leave plenty of room for the stamp(s) and the cancellation. Fill each envelope with cardboard about the thickness of a postal card. You can tuck in the flap or seal it.

Put your first day envelope(s) inside another envelope and mail it to "Customer Affixed Envelopes" in care of the postmaster of the first day city. Your envelope(s) will be canceled and returned. First day envelopes may be mailed up to 30 days after the stamp's issue date.

Or, you can send an envelope addressed to yourself, but without a stamp attached. Put the self-addressed envelope(s) into another envelope. Address this outside envelope to the name of the stamp, in care of the postmaster of the first day city. Send a check, bank draft or U.S. Postal money order (made out to the United States Postal Service) to pay for the stamp(s) that are to be put on your envelope(s).

If a new stamp has a denomination less than the First-Class rate, add postage or payment to bring each first day envelope up to the First-Class rate. Do not send requests more than 60 days prior to the issue date. If you receive a damaged first day cover, return it to the postmaster for a replacement.

For Young Beginners:
Benjamin Franklin Stamp Clubs

A Greeting to First-Time Collectors

Whatever your age, the USPS welcomes you to the fascinating world of stamps. We hope this introduction has provided you with the basics to get under way. You are about to write your own chapter in the history of American philately, and we're sure your experience will be unique, enjoyable and longlasting. Stamp collecting is the most popular hobby in the world, and you are just beginning to realize the universal moral of its story: Nearly one in ten Americans collect stamps for one primary reason—for the fun of it!

People of all ages can learn from stamps and the stories they tell. Statistics show, however, that most of America's 19 million stamp collectors were introduced to stamps before they were 16 years old, with the vast majority exposed to stamps before age 12. And where better for children to learn from stamps—and *about* stamps—than in school?

The United States Postal Service (USPS) currently supports some 20,000 Benjamin Franklin Stamp Clubs (BFSCs) in public and private elementary schools and libraries throughout the nation. And the number is growing!

Named after our first Postmaster General and leader in organizing the U.S. postal system, the Benjamin Franklin Stamp Club program was organized in 1974 to create an awareness of

The clubs' namesake, Benjamin Franklin, appeared in July of 1847 on one of the first two U.S. stamps ever issued.

stamps and to demonstrate their educational and entertaining benefits to students in the fourth through seventh grades. Stamp collecting is an enjoyable experience that teaches important skills applicable to everyday life (for example, organization, appreciation of valuable objects, the value of money and how to manage money).

American educators agree that studying stamps is a great way to learn. Stamps have been used as teaching tools in schools for more than 100 years. In the

February 1987 edition of its monthly newsletter, *Communicator*, the National Association of Elementary School Principals called stamp collecting "…a unique teaching tool…" The BFSC program, in its first 13 years of existence, has introduced

more than seven million students and teachers to the fascination and pleasures of the hobby of philately.

BFSC Activities
Thirty-one students at the Eugene Field public elementary school in Chicago have dis-

covered the fun of stamp collecting through their Ben Franklin Stamp Club. The up-and-coming Field School Stamp Club, beginning its second full year, is one of 6,000 new BFSCs established during the 1986-'87 school year. The club was organized by Ms. Valentina Halliday, a fourth- and fifth-grade teacher.

The Postal Service supplies Ms. Halliday, the club's adviser, with teaching materials that enable her to use stamps as educational aids. These materials are provided as a public service at no cost to all BFSC advisers and members.

At the beginning of the school year, the Field Club received an organizational kit and a reprint of selected sections of *The Postal Service Guide to U.S. Stamps*. Two BFSC newsletters, *Stamp fun* (for members) and *Leader feature* (for leaders), are sent five

times during the school year; they suggest activities, such as games, puzzles and class projects. In addition to the newsletter, a *Treasury of Stamps Album* helps members organize the current year's stamps. There is also a pen pal program, as well as eight different films about stamp collecting (available on a loan basis from the USPS).

The Field Stamp Club meets during school hours every six to eight weeks, using two 45-minute periods. Every meeting offers something new and exciting to its members. During one meeting last year, the class spent approximately 30 minutes discussing *Stamp fun* in a language arts setting.

Ben Franklin Stamp Club members at Chicago's Field School eagerly add to their growing collections during a meeting.

The front page of the spring edition featured the Special Occasions booklet of stamps (# 2267-2274) that was issued April 20, 1987. The newsletter used illustrations of "special occasions" in a matching/letter scramble combination exercise. Oral reading skills were developed by reading directions out loud, then students worked on spelling and vocabulary.

A crossword puzzle of great American women involved history, literature, science, social science and vocabulary development. Students tested their visual perception and their ability to categorize while observing similarities in stamps. The variety of subjects motivated the class. When a stamp subject arises that the class knows little about, Ms.

Halliday pairs students and sends them to the library to conduct research after the *Stamp fun* exercises; they report their findings before the meeting closes. After finishing *Stamp fun*, students come to the front of the room to trade stamps.

Some club members enter their collections in exhibits at local stamp shows and school district annual stamp fairs. There are other activities too, such as the Chicago Division's Du Sable Stamp Design and Essay Contest, which was held in February 1987. Area BFSC members helped commemorate Chicago's first settler, Jean Baptiste Pointe Du Sable (#2249), by acting as stamp designers and essayists for a day.

Of 130 entries submitted in the exhibit, 30 of the Field Club's 31 members were recognized: 25 honorable mentions and five winners.

Starting a BFSC

Teachers or administrators interested in starting clubs can call their local postmaster, or, for more information on the BFSC program, they can write to:

*U.S. Postal Service
Benjamin Franklin
    Stamp Club Program
Washington, D.C.
20260-6755*

The Field story is just one example of how a Ben Franklin Stamp Club can be started. A committed, enthusiastic adviser and an interested student body are big first steps. More than 500,000 BFSC members share the excitement of learning from stamps and their stories, and many of them will continue to do so as they mature. No matter how old you are, you are never too old to learn.

Stamp Collecting
Words and Phrases

Adhesive A gummed stamp made to be attached to mail.

Aerophilately The hobby of collecting airmail stamps, covers and other postal materials that are delivered by airplane, balloon or other types of aircraft.

Approvals Stamps sent by a dealer to a collector for examination. Approvals must either be bought or returned to the dealer within a certain time.

Autographed Cover A cover sheet or envelope signed by a person who had something to do with the commemorated event (for example, the pilot of the plane that carried the material), or an envelope addressed to a famous person and signed by that person.

Block An attached group of stamps at least two stamps high and two stamps wide.

Booklet Pane A small sheet of stamps specially cut and printed to be sold in booklets.

Cachet (ka-shay') A design on a first day cover (envelope).

Cancellation A mark placed on a stamp to show that it has been used.

Centering The position of the design on a postage stamp. On perfectly centered stamps the design is exactly in the middle.

Coils Stamps issued in rolls for use in dispensers, affixers or vending machines.

Commemoratives Stamps that honor anniversaries, important people or special events. Commemoratives are usually sold for only a certain length of time.

Condition The state of a stamp in regard to such things as centering, freshness, color, gum and hinge marks.

Cover The envelope or wrapping in which a letter has been sent through the mail.

Definitives Regular issues of stamps—not commemoratives. Regular issues are usually sold over long periods of time.

Face Value The monetary value of a stamp as printed on it.

First Day Cover (FDC) An envelope with a new stamp and a cancellation showing the date the stamp was first issued.

Gum The adhesive on the back of a stamp.

Hinges Small strips of thin plastic gummed on one side and used by collectors to put stamps in albums.

Imperforate Stamps Stamps printed in sheets without perforations or other means of separating them. Usually early issues, users had to cut the stamps apart with scissors or a knife.

Mint Sheet One of the four panes of unused stamps that make up the flat sheet that comes off the printing press. The selvage (margin) usually contains information such as plate block numbers, copyrights and other data.

Mint Stamp A postage stamp that is in the same condition as when it was purchased from a post office.

Overprint A regular issue stamp that has some printing on top of the original design. Sometimes stamps are overprinted when there has been a change of government or when one country takes over another in a war.

Pane Part of an original large printed sheet of stamps. Sheets are cut into panes so they are easier to handle and sell at post offices.

Pen Cancellation A cancellation made before modern post office equipment was used. Postmasters drew a line in ink across stamps and initialed them or wrote their names on them. Used in modern times by postal employees to obliterate stamps from further use.

Perforations Lines of small cuts or holes between two rows of stamps that make them easy to separate.

Philately (fi-lat'-el'lee) The collection and study of postage stamps and other postal materials.

Plate Block (or **plate number block**) A block of stamps with the plate number or numbers in the margin.

Postal Stationery Envelopes, postal cards, aerogrammes and wrappers with stamps printed or embossed on them.

Postmark A mark put on envelopes and other mailing pieces showing the date and the name of the post office where it was mailed.

Postmaster Provisionals Stamps made by local postmasters that were used before the government began issuing stamps or when the post office ran out of regular stamps.

Precancels Stamps with cancellations applied before the material was mailed.

Reissue An official reprinting of a stamp that was no longer being printed.

Revenue Stamps Stamps issued for use in collecting taxes on special papers or products. Not permitted for postal use.

Selvage The paper around panes of stamps, sometimes called the margin.

Coils

Se-tenant An attached pair, strip or block of stamps that differ in value, design or surcharge.

Surcharge An overprint that alters or restates the face value or denomination of the stamp to which it is applied.

Tagging Marking stamps with chemicals to be read by machines that sort mail and turn letters face-up for cancellation.

Thin Spot A thinning of the paper on the back of a stamp where a hinge was carelessly removed.

Tied On A stamp is "tied on" when the cancellation or postmark goes from the stamp to the envelope.

Topicals A group of stamps all with the same subject—space travel, for example.

Unused A stamp with or without original gum that has no cancellation or other sign of use.

Used A stamp that has been canceled.

Want List A list of stamp numbers or philatelic items needed by a collector.

Watermark A design or pattern pressed into stamp paper during its manufacture.

Overprint

Precancel

Perforate

Imperforate

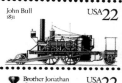

Se-tenant

Surcharge

Peer Into the imeless Wind of a Great Nation Soul

ative Mint Set contains:
nmemorative stamps issued in a given
ustrated folder
to protect, preserve and display stamps

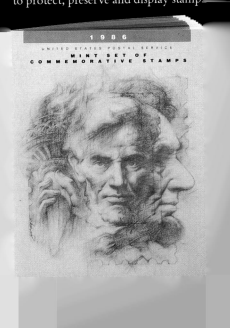

Capture the spirit of America's past and present with Commemorative Mint Sets. The USPS issues stamps honoring historically important people, places, events and ideals. These commemorative stamps are assembled annually in mint sets that are popular with stamp collectors and the general public alike.

The Story Behind the Stamp

Commemorative Mint Sets serve as educational tools, too. They provide details about each stamp, as well as its designer, modeler and engraver.

Stamp collectors have known the pleasure of philately for years, and new enthusiasts are joining them regularly. Whether you are a veteran or a newcomer, the ongoing series of Commemorative Mint Sets will add to your collecting enjoyment.

1986 Commemorative Mint Set—Consists of all 32 commemorative issues from last year, including: the Statue of Liberty joint issue with France; one randomly selected stamp from the Presidents souvenir sheet; T.S. Eliot, Duke Ellington and Sojourner Truth; Arkansas and Texas statehood issues; Fish block of four; and the first commemorative booklet featuring Stamp Collecting, which was also a joint issue with Sweden. ($11.00)

1987 Commemorative Mint Set—Contains all the new commemorative and special issues, including a pane of the Special Occasions, U.S. Constitution and Locomotive booklets, and a random selection from North American Wildlife. ($12.95)

Philatelic Societies & Publications

Philatelic Exhibition

AAPE
Box 7088
Shawnee Mission, KS
66207-7088

Philatelic Societies

American Air Mail Society
102 Arbor Rd.
Cinnaminson, NJ 08077-3859
Specializes in aerophilately, and periodically presents the Conrath Award to a member of the society in the name of Walter Conrath, one of its founders.

American First Day Cover Society
Mrs. Monte Eiserman
Membership Chairman
14359 Chadbourne
Houston, TX 77079-6611
A full-service, not-for-profit, non-commercial Society devoted exclusively to First Day Covers and First Day Cover collecting. Offers information on 300 current cachet producers, expertizing, foreign covers, translation service, color slide programs, and archives covering First Day Covers.

American Philatelic Society
Box 8000
State College, PA 16803-8000
A full complement of services and resources for the philatelist. Membership offers: American Philatelic Research Library; expertizing service; estate advisory service; translation services; a stamp theft committee which functions as a clearing house for stamp theft information; a speakers' bureau and a monthly journal, "The American Philatelist," sent to all members.

American Society For Philatelic Pages and Panels
P.O. Box 64
Hillsdale, NJ 07642

American Stamp Dealer's Association
5 Dakota Dr.
Suite 102
Lake Success, NY 11042-1109
Association of dealers engaged in every facet of philately, with eleven regional chapters

nation wide. Sponsors national and local shows, seminars for member and non-member dealers, credit information service, monthly newsletter and ASDA membership directory.

American Topical Association
P.O. Box 630
Johnstown, PA 15907-0630
A service organization concentrating on the specialty of topical collecting. Offers handbooks on specific topics; an exhibition award; *Topical Time*, a bi-monthly publication dealing with topical interest areas; a slide and film loan service; information, translation, biography and sales services; and an heirs' estate service.

Black American Philatelic Society
C/o Walt Robinson
9101 Taylor Street
Landover, MD 20785-2554
For collectors interested in the study of black Americans on postage stamps.

Bureau Issues Association
834 Devonshire Way
Sunnyvale, CA 94087
The only society devoted to the study of U.S. stamps printed by the Bureau of Engraving and Printing.

Cardinal Spellman Philatelic Museum, Inc.
235 Wellesley Street
Weston, MA 02193

Collectors Club, Inc.
22 East 35th Street
New York, NY 10016-3806
Regular services include library and reading rooms, a publication and lectures on philatelic subjects. The group also honors a great American collector annually and actively supports national and international exhibitions.

Council of Philatelic Organizations
P.O. Box COPO
State College, PA 16803-8340
A non-profit organization comprised of more than 200 national, regional and local stamp clubs, organizations, societies

and philatelic business firms. The objective of COPO is to promote and encourage the hobby of stamp collecting. Membership is open only to organizations; COPO uses a variety of methods to promote stamp collecting including an on-going publicity campaign, a quarterly newsletter and joint sponsorship (with the USPS) of National Stamp Collecting Month.

Errors, Freaks and Oddities Collectors Club
Box 1125
Falls Church, VA 22041-0125
Includes an exhibit critique service.

Junior Philatelists of America
P.O. Box 701010
Central Office
San Antonio, TX 78270-1010
Provides an auction department, library service, tape and slide service, stamp identification and translation services. Publishes a bi-monthly, illustrated publication titled the *Philatelic Observer*.

Maximum Card Study Club
Bill Kelleher
Box 375
Bedford, MA 01730-0375

Mobile Post Office Society
5030 Aspen Drive
Omaha, NE 68157-2267
A non-profit organization concentrating on transit markings and the history of postal transit routes. The Society is engaged in documenting and recording transit postal history by publishing books, catalogs and monographs, as well as a semi-monthly journal.

Modern Postal History Society
Box 258
Thornwood, NY 10594-0258

National Association of Precancel Collectors
5121 Park Blvd.
Wildwood, NJ 08260-1454

The Perfins Club
2163 Cumbre Place
El Cajon, CA 92020-1005
Send SASE for information.

Philatelic Foundation
270 Madison Ave.
New York, NY 10016-0656
A non-profit organization known for its excellent expertization service. The Foundation's broad resources, including extensive reference collections, 5,000-volume library and Expert Committee, provide collectors with comprehensive consumer protection. It also publishes educational information. Slide and cassette programs are available on such subjects as the Pony Express, Provisionals, Confederate Postal History and special programs for beginning collectors.

Plate Block Collector Club
Box 937
Homestead, FL 33090-0937

Plate Number Society
9600 Colesville Rd.
Silver Spring, MD 20901-3144

Postal History Society
Box 20
Bayside, NY 11361-0020

Post Mark Collectors Club
Wilma Hinrichs
4200 SE Indianola Rd.
Des Moines, IA 50320-1555

Precancel Stamp Society
David A. Coates, Secretary
2500 Wisconsin Avenue, N.W. #829
Washington, D.C. 20007-4561

Souvenir Card Collectors Society
P.O. Box 4155
Tulsa, OK 74159-4155

Souvenir Page & Commemorative Panel Society
417 Lanza Avenue
Garfield, NJ 07026-2401

United Postal Stationery Society
Mrs. J. Thomas
Box 48
Redlands, CA 92373-0601

The United States Possessions Philatelic Society
141 Lyford Drive
Tiburon, CA 94920-1652

The Universal Ship Cancellation Society
P.O. Box 127
New Britain, CT 06050-0127
Specializing in naval ship cancellations.

Catalogs

Brookman Price List of U.S. Stamps
91 South 9th Street
Minneapolis, MN 55402-3295

Catalogue of United States Souvenir Cards
The Washington Press
2 Vreeland Rd.
Florham Park, NJ 07932-1587

First Day Cover Catalogue (U.S.-U.N.)
The Washington Press
2 Vreeland Rd.
Florham Park, NJ 07932-1587

Souvenir Pages Price List
(Please send self-addressed stamped envelope to receive current listings.)
Charles D. Simmons
P.O. Box 6238
Buena Park, CA 90622-6238

Noble Official Catalog of United States Bureau Precancels, 64th Edition
P.O. Box 931
Winter Park, FL 32789-0931

Stamps of the World 1982 Catalogue
Stanley Gibbons Publications. Available through dealers only. All the stamps of the world from 1840 to date. Over 1,900 pages feature more than 200,000 stamps (47,900 illustrations) from over 200 issuing countries.

Commemorative Panel Price List
(Please send self-addressed stamped envelope to receive current listings.)
Frank Riolo
P.O. Box 6279
Delray Beach, FL 33484-6279

Fleetwoods Standard First Day Cover Catalog
Unicover Corporation
Cheyenne, WY 82008-0001

Harris Illustrated Postage Stamp Catalog
H.E. Harris & Co., Inc.
Boston, MA 02117-0810

American Air Mail Catalogue
American Air Mail Society
Cinnaminson, NJ 08077-3859

Scott Standard Postage Stamp Catalogue
911 South Vandemark Road
Sidney, OH 45367-8959
The annual five volumes of the Scott Catalogue present listings of all stamps of the world from 1840 through now. Additionally, one of the volumes is a specialized presentation of the stamps of the United States, with emphasis on varieties not normally shown in general catalogues. All stamp entries are priced.

U.S. Postal Card Catalog, 1980
Box 48
Redlands, CA 92373-0061

Magazines and Newspapers

Linn's Stamp News*
Box 29
Sidney, OH 45365-0029
Largest weekly stamp newspaper.

Mekeel's Weekly Stamp News
Box 1660
Portland, ME 04104-1660

Minkus Stamp Journal
41 West 25th Street
New York, NY 10010-2021

Scott Stamp Monthly
911 South Vandemark Road
Sidney, OH 45367-8959
Principally oriented toward presenting information on the new stamp issues of the world, with in-depth articles about stamps of all eras.

Stamps
85 Canisteo Street
Hornell, NY 14843

Stamp Collector
Box 10
Albany, OR 97321-0006

*Introductory Materials
Stamp Collecting Made Easy
For a free copy of an illustrated 96-page booklet write to:
Linn's Stamp News
Box 29
Sidney, OH 45365-0029

Diversity in Richness

American Commemorative Panels are rich—rich in heritage, rich in tradition, rich in beauty. Special intaglio-printed engraving reproductions and exquisite stamp art combine to form a treasured philatelic collectible.

Each Panel is devoted to a separate commemorative stamp and is a work of art in itself, worthy of framing, exhibiting and sharing. A block of four, newly issued, mint-condition stamps are mounted on an 8½" by 11¼" panel of heavy, high-quality paper. The stamps' subject is portrayed in words and pictures. Objects of true workmanship, American Commemorative Panels are becoming increasingly popular with collectors.

Since the series began in 1972, thousands of stamp collectors have become regular subscribers to USPS American Commemorative Panels. Because they are printed in limited editions, the panels are available on an advanced subscription basis *only*. For details, write to:

USPS Guide
Commemorative Panel Program
Philatelic Marketing Division
Washington, D.C. 20260-6755

Philatelic Centers

In addition to the more than 15,000 postal facilities authorized to sell philatelic products, the U.S. Postal Service also maintains more than 400 Philatelic Centers located in major population centers throughout the country.

These Philatelic Centers have been established to serve stamp collectors and make it convenient for them to acquire an extensive range of all current postage stamps, postal stationery and philatelic products issued by the Postal Service.

Centers listed are located at the Main Post Office unless otherwise indicated.

Alabama
351 North 24th Street
Birmingham, AL 35203

101 Holmes N.W.
Huntsville, AL 35804

250 St. Joseph
Mobile, AL 36601

Downtown Station
135 Catoma Street
Montgomery, AL 31604

1313 22nd Avenue
Tuscaloosa, AL 35401

Alaska
Downtown Station
3rd & C Street
Anchorage, AK 99510

College Branch
3350 College Road
Fairbanks, AK 99708

Arizona
Osborn Station
3905 North 7th Avenue
Phoenix, AZ 85013

General Mail Facility
4949 E. Van Buren
Phoenix, AZ
85026-9998

1501 South Cherrybell
Tucson, AZ 85726

Arkansas
30 South 6th Street
Fort Smith, AR 72901

100 Reserve
Hot Springs National
Park, AR 71901

310 East Street
Jonesboro, AR 72401

600 West Capitol
Little Rock, AR 72201

Rogers, AR
72756-9998

California
Holiday Station
1180 W. Ball Road
Anaheim, CA
92802-9998

Cerritos Branch Office
18122 Carmencita
Artesia, CA 90701

General Mail Facility
3400 Pegasus Drive
Bakersfield, CA
93380-9998

200 Allston Way
Berkeley, CA 94504

135 East Olive St.
Burbank, CA 91502

Main Post Office
2121 Meridian Park Blvd.
Concord, CA 94520

2020 Fifth Street
Davis, CA 95616

8111 East Firestone
Downey, CA 90241

Cutten Station
3901 Walnut Drive
Eureka, CA 95501

1900 E Street
Fresno, CA 93706

313 E. Broadway
Glendale, CA 91209

Hillcrest Station
303 E. Hillcrest
Inglewood, CA 90311

5200 Clark Avenue
Lakewood, CA
90712-9998

Main Post Office
Lakewood, CA 90712

300 Long Beach Blvd.
Long Beach, CA 90801

300 N. Los Angeles St.
Los Angeles, CA 90012

Terminal Annex
900 N. Alameda
Los Angeles, CA 90052

Village Station
11000 Wilshire Blvd.
Los Angeles, CA 90024

El Viejo Station
1125 I Street
Modesto, CA 95354

565 Hartnell St.
Monterey, CA
93940-9998

Civic Center Annex
201 13th Street
Oakland, CA 94612

211 Brooks
Oceanside, CA 92054

281 E. Colorado Blvd.
Pasadena, CA 91109

1647 Yuba St.
Redding, CA 96001

1201 North Catalina
Redondo Beach,
CA 90277

Downtown Station
3890 Orange St.
Riverside, CA 92501

2000 Royal Oaks Drive
Sacramento, CA 95813

Base Line Station
1164 North E Street
San Bernardino,
CA 92410

2535 Midway Drive
San Diego, CA 92199

7th and Mission Sts.
San Francisco, CA 94101

1750 Meridian Drive
San Jose, CA 95101

Simms Station
41 Simms Street
San Rafael, CA 94901

Spurgeon Station
615 North Bush
Santa Ana, CA 92701

836 Anacada Street
Santa Barbara,
CA 93102

120 W. Cypress St.
Santa Maria, CA
93454-9998

Main Post Office
730 Second Street
Santa Rosa, CA 95404

4245 West Lane
Stockton, CA 95208

15701 Sherman Way
Van Nuys, CA 91408

Channel Islands
Ventura, CA 93001

396 South California St.
West Covina, CA 91790

Colorado
1905 15th St.
Boulder, CO 80302

201 E. Pikes Peak
Colorado Springs,
CO 80901

1823 Stout Street
Denver, CO 80202

Main Post Office
222 West Eighth Street
Durango, CO 81301

241 N. 4th St.
Grand Junction,
CO 81501

5733 South Prince Street
Littleton, CO 80120

421 N. Main Street
Pueblo, CO 81003

Connecticut
141 Weston Street
Hartford, CT 06101

11 Silver Street
Middletown, CT 06457

141 Church Street
New Haven, CT 06510

27 Masonic Street
New London, CT 06320

421 Atlantic Street
Stamford, CT 06904

Stratford Branch
3100 Main Street
Stratford, CT 06497

135 Grand Street
Waterbury, CT 06701

Delaware
55 The Plaza
Dover, DE 19801

Federal Station
110 E. Main St.
Newark, DE 19711

11th and Market Streets
Wilmington, DE 19850

District of Columbia
Harriet Tubman
Philatelic Center
North Capitol Street and
Massachusetts Avenue
Washington, DC 20066

Headsville Station
National Museum of
American History
Smithsonian Institution
Washington, DC 20560

L'Enfant Pl. Philatelic Ctr.
U.S.P.S. Hdqtrs.
475 L'Enfant Pl., SW
Washington, DC 20260

National Visitors Center
Union Station
50 Massachusetts, NE
Washington, DC 20002

Pavilion Postique
Old Post Office Bldg.
1100 Pennsylvania, NW
Washington, DC 20004

Florida
824 Manatee Ave. West
Bradenton, FL 33506

100 South Belcher Road
Clearwater, FL 33515

27

Downtown Station
220 North Beach Street
Daytona Beach, FL 32015

1900 West Oakland Park
Fort Lauderdale, FL
33310

Fort Myers, FL
33906-9998

401 S.E. 1st Avenue
Gainesville, FL 32601

1801 Polk Street
Hollywood, FL 33022

1110 Kings Road
Jacksonville, FL 32203

210 North Missouri Ave.
Lakeland, FL 33802

118 North Bay Drive
Largo, FL 33540

2200 NW 72nd Avenue
Miami, FL 33101

Philatelic Center
Naples, FL 33940

1200 Goodlette Rd.
North Naples, FL 33940

400 Southwest First Ave.
Ocala, FL 32678

Main Post Office
1335 Kingsley Avenue
Orange Park, FL 32073

46 East Robinson Street
Orlando, FL 32801

1400 West Jordan St.
Pensacola, FL 32501

Main Post Office
99 King Street
St. Augustine, FL 32084

3135 First Avenue
North Saint Petersburg,
FL 33730

Open Air Station
76 4th St. N.
Saint Petersburg, FL
33701

1661 Ringland Blvd.
Sarasota, FL 33578

Main Post Office
2800 South Adams Street
Tallahasee, FL 32301

5201 Spruce Street
Tampa, FL 33630

801 Clematis Street
West Palm Beach, FL
33401

Georgia
115 Hancock Avenue
Athens, GA 30601

Downtown Station
101 Marietta Street
Atlanta, GA 30301

Perimeter Branch
4400 Ashford-
Dunwoody Road
Atlanta, GA 30346

Downtown Station
3916 Milgen Road
Columbus, GA 31908

364 Green Street
Gainesville, GA 30501

451 College Street
Macon, GA 31201

2 North Fahm Street
Savannah, GA 31401

Hawaii
3600 Aolele Street
Honolulu, HI 96819

Idaho
770 South 13th Street
Boise, ID 83708

Collectors' Corner
Philatelic Center
Main Post Office
Moscow, ID 83843

Main Post Office
Pocatello, ID 83201

Illinois
909 West Euclid Ave.
Arlington Heights, IL
60004

Moraine Valley Station
7401 100th Place
Bridgeview, IL 60455

1301 East Main Street
Carbondale, IL
62901

433 West Van Buren St.
Chicago, IL 60607

Loop Station
211 South Clark Street
Chicago, IL 60604

1000 East Oakton
Des Plaines, IL 60018

1101 Davis St.
Evanston, IL 60204

2350 Madison Ave.
Granite City, IL 62040

2000 McDonough St.
Joliet, IL 60436

901 Lake Street
Oak Park, IL 60301

123 Indianwood
Park Forest, IL 60466

5225 Harrison Ave.
Rockford, IL 61125

211-19th Street
Rock Island, IL 61201

Schaumburg Station
450 W. Schaumburg Rd.
Schaumburg, IL 60194

2105 E. Cook St.
Springfield, IL 62703

Edison Square Station
1520 Washington
Waukegan, IL 60085

Indiana
North Park Branch
44923 1st Avenue
Evansville, IN 47710

Fort Wayne Postal
Facility
1501 S. Clinton Street
Fort Wayne, IN 46802

5530 Sohl Street
Hammond, IN 46320

125 West South Street
Indianapolis, IN 46206

2719 South Webster
Kokomo, IN 46901

3450 State Road 26, E.
Lafayette, IN 47901

424 South Michigan
South Bend, IN 46624

30 N. 7th Street
Terre Haute, IN 47808

Iowa
615 6th Avenue
Cedar Rapids, IA 52401

1165 Second Avenue
Des Moines, IA 50318

320 6th Street
Sioux City, IA 51101

Kansas
1021 Pacific
Kansas City, KS 66110

6029 Broadmoor
Shawnee Mission,
KS 66202

434 Kansas Avenue
Topeka, KS 66603

Downtown Station
401 North Market
Wichita, KS 67202

Kentucky
1088 Nadino Blvd.
Lexington, KY 40511

St. Mathews Station
4600 Shelbyville Road
Louisville, KY 40207

Louisiana
1715 Odom St.
Alexandria, LA 71301

750 Florida Street
Baton Rouge, LA 70821

1105 Moss Street
Lafayette, LA 70501

3301 17th Street
Metairie, LA 70004

501 Sterlington Road
Monroe, LA 71201

701 Loyola Avenue
New Orleans, LA 70113

Vieux Carre Station
1022 Iberville Street
New Orleans, LA 70112

2400 Texas Avenue
Shreveport, LA 71102

Maine
40 Western Avenue
Augusta, ME 04330

202 Harlow Street
Bangor, ME 04401

125 Forest Avenue
Portland, ME 04101

Maryland
900 E. Fayette Street
Baltimore, MD 21233

201 East Patrick Street
Frederick, MD 21701

6411 Baltimore Avenue
Riverdale, MD 20840

U.S. Route 50 and
Naylor Road
Salisbury, MD 21801

Massachusetts
Post Office and
Courthouse Bldg.
Boston, MA 02109

120 Commercial Street
Brockton, MA 02401

7 Bedford Street
Burlington, MA 01803

Center Station
Chicopee, MA 01014

Main Post Office
2 Government Center
Fall River, MA 02722

Main Post Office
Fitchburg, MA 01420

330 Cocituate Road
Framingham, MA 01701

385 Main Street
Hyannis, MA 02601

Post Office Square
Lowell, MA 01853

212 Fenn Street
Pittsfield, MA 01201

Long Pond Road
Plymouth, MA 02360

Quincy Branch
47 Washington Street
Quincy, MA 02169

2 Margin Street
Salem, MA 01970

1883 Main Street
Springfield, MA 01101

462 Washington St.
Woburn, MA 01888

4 East Central Street
Worcester, MA 01603

Michigan
2075 W. Stadium Blvd.
Ann Arbor, MI 48106

26200 Ford Road
Dearborn Heights,
MI 48127

1401 West Fort Street
Detroit, MI 48233

250 East Boulevard Dr.
Flint, MI 48502

225 Michigan Avenue
Grand Rapids, MI 49501

200 South Otsego
Jackson, MI 49201

GMF
4800 Collins Road
Lansing, MI 48924

1300 Military Street
Port Huron, MI 48060

30550 Gratiot Street
Roseville, MI 48066

200 West 2nd Street
Royal Oak, MI 48068

1233 South Washington
Saginaw, MI 48605

Minnesota
2800 West Michigan
Duluth, MN 55806

297 Baker Building
706 Second Avenue, S
Minneapolis, MN 55402

Downtown Station
102 S. Broadway
Rochester, MN 55904

The Pioneer Postal
Emporium
133 Endicott Arcade
St. Paul, MN 55101

Mississippi
2421-13th Street
Gulfport, MS 39501

La Fleur Station
1501 Jacksonian Plaza
Jackson, MS 39211

500 West Miln Street
Tupelo, MS 38801

Missouri
315 Pershing Road
Kansas City, MO 64108

Northwest Plaza Station
500 Northwest Plaza
St. Ann, MO 63074

8th and Edmond
St. Joseph, MO 64501

Clayton Branch
7750 Maryland
St. Louis, MO 63105

H. S. Jewell Station
870 Boonville Ave.
Springfield, MO 65801

28

Montana
841 South 26th
Billings, MT 59101

215 First Ave., North
Great Falls, MT
59401-9998

1100 W. Kent
Missoula, MT
59801-9998

Nebraska
204 W. South Front St.
Grand Island, NE 68801

700 R Street
Lincoln, NE 68501

300 East Third Street
North Platte, NE 69101

1124 Pacific
Omaha, NE 68108

Nevada
1001 Circus Circus Dr.
Las Vegas, NV 89114

200 Vassar Street
Reno, NV 89510

New Hampshire
Main Post Office
15 Mount Forest Avenue
Berlin, NH 03570

South Main Street
Hanover, NH 03755

955 Goffs Falls Road
Manchester, NH 03103

80 Daniel Street
Portsmouth, NH 03801

New Jersey
1701 Pacific Avenue
Atlantic City, NJ 08401

Main Post Office
Veterans Plaza
Bergenfield, NJ 07621

3 Miln Street
Cranford, NJ 07016

General Mail Facility
Edison, NJ 08899

Main Post Office
229 Main Street
Fort Lee, NJ 07024

Belimawr Branch
Haag Ave. & Benigno
Gloucester, NJ 08031

Route 35 & Hazlet Ave.
Hazlet, NJ 07730

Main Post Office
Island Heights, NJ 08732

Main Post Office
160 Maplewood Avenue
Maplewood, NJ 07040

150 Ridgedale
Morristown, NJ 07960

Federal Square
Newark, NJ 07102

86 Bayard Street
New Brunswick,
NJ 08901

Nutley Branch
372 Franklin Avenue
Nutley, NJ 07110

194 Ward Street
Paterson, NJ 07510

171 Broad Street
Red Bank, NJ 07701

757 Broad Ave.
Ridgefield, NJ 07657

76 Huyler Street
South Hackensack,
NJ 07606

680 Highway #130
Trenton, NJ 08650

155 Clinton Road
West Caldwell,
NJ 07006

41 Greenwood Avenue
Wykoff, NJ 07481

New Mexico
1135 Braodway NE
Albuquerque,
NM 87101

200 E. Las Cruces Ave.
Las Cruces, NM 88001

415 N. Pennsylvania Ave.
Roswell, NM
88201-9998

New York
General Mail Facility
30 Old Karner Road
Albany, NY 12212

Empire State Plaza
Albany, NY 12220

115 Henry Street
Binghampton,
NY 13902

Bronx General P.O.
149th Street &
Grand Concourse
Bronx, NY 10451

Parkchester Station
1449 West Avenue
Bronx, NY 10462

Riverdale Station
5951 Riverdale Avenue
Bronx, NY 10471

Throggs Neck Station
3630 East Tremont Ave.
Bronx, NY 10465

Wakefield Station
4165 White Plains Rd.
Bronx, NY 10466

Bayridge Station
5501 7th Avenue
Brooklyn, NY 11220

Brooklyn General P.O.
271 Cadman Plaza East
Brooklyn, NY 11201

Greenpoint Station
66 Meserole Avenue
Brooklyn, NY 11222

Homecrest Station
2002 Avenue U
Brooklyn, NY 11229

Kensington Station
421 McDonald Avenue
Brooklyn, NY 11218

1200 William Street
Buffalo, NY 14240

Rte. 9
Clifton Park, NY 12065

Downtown Station
255 Clemens Ave.
Elmira, NY 14901

1836 Mott Avenue
Far Rockaway, NY 11691

41-65 Main Street
Flushing, NY 11351

Ridgewood Station
869 Cypress Avenue
Flushing, NY 11385

Old Glenham Road
Glenham, NY 12527

16 Hudson Avenue
Glens Falls, NY 12801

185 West John Street
Hicksville, NY 11802

88-40 164th Street
Jamaica, NY 11431

Main Post Office
Corner Main & Hunt Street
Oneonta, NY 13820

Ansonia Station
1980 Broadway
New York, NY 10023

Bowling Green Station
25 Broadway
New York, NY 10004

Church Street Station
90 Church Street
New York, NY 10007

Empire State Station
350 Fifth Avenue
New York, NY 10001

F.D.R. Station
909 Third Avenue
New York, NY 10022

Grand Central Station
45th St. & Lexington
New York, NY 10017

Madison Square Station
149 East 23rd Street
New York, NY 10010

New York General P.O.
33rd and 8th Avenue
New York, NY 10001

Rockefeller Center
610 Fifth Avenue
New York, NY 10020

Times Square Station
340 West 42nd Street
New York, NY 10036

Franklin & S. Main Sts.
Pearl River, NY 10965

Main Post Office
10 Miller Street
Plattsburgh, NY 12901

55 Mansion Street
Poughkeepsie, NY 12601

1335 Jefferson Road
Rochester, NY 14692

Rockville Centre
250 Merrick Road
Rockville Centre,
NY 11570

Main Post Office
110 East Garden Street
Rome, NY 13440

Main Post Office
29 Jay Street
Schenectady, NY 12305

25 Route 11
Smithtown, NY 11787

550 Manor Road
Staten Island, NY 10314

New Springville Station
2843 Richmond Ave.
Staten Island, NY 10314

5640 East Taft Road
Syracuse, NY 13220

10 Broad Street
Utica, NY 13503

100 Fisher Avenue
White Plains, NY 10602

78-81 Main Street
Yonkers, NY 10701

North Carolina
West Asheville Station
1300 Patton Avenue
Asheville, NC 28806

Eastway Station
3065 Eastway Drive
Charlotte, NC 28205

301 Green Street
Fayetteville, NC 28302

310 New Bern Avenue
Raleigh, NC 27611

North Dakota
657 2nd Avenue North
Fargo, ND 58102

Ohio
675 Wolf Ledges Pkwy.
Akron, OH 44309

2650 N. Cleveland Ave.
Canton, OH 44701

Fountain Square Station
5th and Walnut Street
Cincinnati, OH 45202

301 W. Prospect Ave.
Cleveland, OH 44101

850 Twin Rivers Drive
Columbus, OH 43216

1111 East 5th Street
Dayton, OH 45401

200 North Diamond St.
Mansfield, OH 44901

200 North 4th Street
Steubenville, OH 43952

435 S. St. Clair Street
Toledo, OH 43601

99 South Walnut Street
Youngstown, OH 44503

Oklahoma
101 East First
Edmond, OK 73034

115 West Broadway
Enid, OK 73701

102 South 5th
Lawton, OK 73501

525 West Okmulgee
Muskogee, OK 74401

129 West Gray
Norman, OK 73069

76320 SW 5th
Oklahoma City,
OK 73125

333 West 4th
Tulsa, OK 74101

12 South 5th
Yukon, OK 73099

Oregon
520 Willamette Street
Eugene, OR 97401

751 N.W. Hoyt
Portland, OR 97208

Williamette Valley
Salem, OR 97301

Pennsylvania
442-456 Hamilton St.
Allentown, PA 18101

535 Wood St.
Bethlehem, PA 18016

115 Boylston Street
Bradford, PA 16701

Beaver Dr. Industrial Pk.
Dubois, PA 15801

Griswold Plaza
Erie, PA 16501

238 S. Pennsylvania
Greensburg, PA 15601

10th and Markets Sts.
Harrisburg, PA 17105

West Avenue and
Cedar Street
Jenkintown, PA 19046

111 Franklin Street
Johnstown, PA 15901

Downtown Station
48-50 W. Chestnut St.
Lancaster, PA 17603

980 Wheeler Way
Langhorne, PA 19047

Lehigh Valley Branch
Airport Rd. & Route 22
Lehigh Valley, PA 18001

Monroeville Mall Branch
439 Northern Pike
Monroeville, PA 15146

1 W. Washington Street
Kennedy Square
New Castle, PA 16101

28 East Airy Street
Norristown, PA 19401

30th and Market Sts.
Philadelphia, PA 19104

B. Free Franklin Station
316 Market Street
Philadelphia, PA 19106

Penn Center Station
2 Penn Center Plaza
Philadelphia, PA 19102

William Penn Annex
9th and Chestnut Sts.
Philadelphia, PA 19107

Castle Shannon Branch
307 Castle Shannon Blvd.
Pittsburgh, PA 15232

McKnight Branch
McKnight and Seibert
Pittsburgh, PA 15237

Seventh Avenue &
Grant Street
Pittsburgh, PA 15219

59 North 5th Street
Reading, PA 19603

North Washington Ave.
& Linden St.
Scranton, PA 18503

237 South Frazer Street
State College, PA 16801

7th and Ann Streets
Stroudsburg, PA 18360

South and West Wayne
Wayne, PA 19087

300 S. Main St.
Wilkes Barre, PA 18701

Center City Finance St.
240 West Third Street
Williamsport, PA 17703

200 S. George Street
York, PA 17405

Puerto Rico
San Juan General P.O.
Roosevelt Avenue
San Juan, PR 00936

Plaza Las Americas
San Juan, PR 00938

Rhode Island
24 Corliss Street
Providence, RI 02904

South Carolina
4290 Daley Avenue
Charleston, SC 29402

1601 Assembly Street
Columbia, SC 29201

600 West Main Street
Greenville, SC 29602

South Dakota
500 East Boulevard
Rapid City, SD 57701

320 S. 2nd Avenue
Sioux Falls, SD 57101

Tennessee
General Mail Facility
6050 Shallowford Road
Chattanooga, TN 37401

Tom Murray Station
133 Tucker Street
Jackson, TN 38301

501 West Main Avenue
Knoxville, TN 37901

Colonial Finance Unit
4695 Southern Avenue
Memphis, TN 38124

555 South Third
Memphis, TN 38101

Crosstown Finance Unit
1520 Union Street
Memphis, TN 38174

901 Broadway
Nashville, TN 37202

Texas
2300 South Ross
Amarillo, TX 79105

300 East South Street
Arlington, TX 76010

300 East 9th
Austin, TX 78710

300 Willow
Beaumont, TX 77704

Main Post Office
1535 Los Ebanos
Brownsville, TX 78520

809 Nueces Bay
Corpus Christi, TX
78408

400 North Ervay Street
Dallas, TX 75221

5300 East Paisano Dr.
El Paso, TX 79910

251 West Lancaster
Fort Worth, TX 76101

408 Main Street
Hereford, TX 79045

401 Franklin Avenue
Houston, TX 77201

411 "L" Avenue
Lubbock, TX 79408

601 E. Pecan
McAllen, TX 78501

100 East Wall
Midland, TX 79702

Downtown Station
615 East Houston
San Antonio, TX 78205

10410 Perrin Beitel Road
San Antonio, TX 78284

Main Post Office
1411 Wunsche Loop
Spring, TX 77373

2211 North Robinson
Texarkana, TX 75501

221 West Ferguson
Tyler, TX 75702

800 Franklin
Waco, TX 76701

1000 Lamar Street
Wichita Falls, TX 76307

Utah
Main Post Office
Ogden, UT 84401

Main Post Office
Provo, UT 84601

1760 West 2100 South
Salt Lake City, UT 84119

Vermont
Main Post Office
Brattleboro, VT 05301

1 Elmwood Avenue
Burlington, VT 05401

151 West Street
Rutland, VT 05701

Virginia
111 Sixth Street
Briston, VA 24201

1155 Seminole Trail
Charlottesville,
VA 22906

1425 Battlefield Blvd., N.
Chesapeake, VA 23320

700 Main Street
Danville, VA 24541

Merrifield Branch
8409 Lee Highway
Fairfax, VA 22116

809 Aberdeen Road
Hampton, VA 23670

300 Odd Fellows Road
Lynchburg, VA 24506

Tyson's Corner
Shopping Center
McLean VA 22103

Denbigh Station
14104 Warwick
Newport News,
VA 23602

600 Granby Street
Norfolk, VA 23501

Thomas Corner Station
6274 East Virginia
Beach Blvd.
Norfolk, VA 23502

1801 Brook Road
Richmond, VA 23232

419 Rutherford Ave. NE
Roanoke, VA 24022

1430 North Augusta
Staunton, VA 24401

London Bridge Station
550 1st Colonial Road
Virginia Beach,
VA 23454

Washington
Main Post Office
Auburn, WA 98071

Crossroads Station
15800 N.E. 8th
Bellevue, WA 98008

315 Prospect St.
Bellingham, WA 98225

Main Post Office
Everett, WA 98201

2828 West Sylvester
Pasco, WA 99301

Main Post Office
Port Angeles, WA 98362

301 Union Street
Seattle, WA 98101

West 904 Riverside
Spokane, WA 99210

1102 A Street
Tacoma, WA 98402

205 West Washington
Yakima, WA 98903

West Virginia
301 North Street
Bluefield, WV 24701

Lee and Dickinson St.
Charleston, WV 25301

500 West Pike Street
Clarksburg, WV 26301

1000 Virginia Street, West
Huntington, WV 25704

217 King Street
Martinsburg, WV 25401

Wisconsin
325 East Walnut
Green Bay, WI 54301

3902 Milwaukee St.
Madison, WI 53707

345 West St. Paul Ave.
Milwaukee, WI 53203

Main Post Office
Wausau, WI 54401

Wyoming
Main Post Office
150 East B Street
Casper, WY 82601

2120 Capitol Avenue
Cheyenne, WY 82001

FOREIGN CENTERS

Australia
Max Stern & Co.
Port Phillip Arcade
234 Flinders Street
Melbourne 3000

France
Theodore Champion
13 Rue Drouot
75009 Paris

**Federal Republic
of Germany**
Hermann W. Sieger
Venusberg 32-34
D-7073
Lorch Wurttemberg

Netherlands
J.A. Visser
P.O. Box 184
3300 Ad Dordrecht

Sweden
Frimarkshuset AB
S-793 01 Leksand

Switzerland
De Rosa International
S.A. Av Du Tribunal
Federal 34
CH-1005 Lausanne
Telex No. 25524

England
Stanley Gibbons
International, Ltd.
391 Strand
London WC2R OLX

Japan
Japan Philatelic Co., Ltd.
P.O. Box 2
Suginami-Minami
Tokyo 168-91

Hand Picked for Quality

...taking advantage of a special subscription service, U.S. pane collectors will ...eive mint-condition panes of exceptional quality — from paper, color and ...rforations to gum, centering, marginal markings and registration. The U.S. Bureau of Engraving and Printing selects each pane individually. ...ey are delivered with attractive acetate album sheets. Most importantly, ... Postal Service guarantees *superior* panes. If not completely satisfied with ...ane, simply return it within 30 days for a full refund or replacement. ...Subscribers may choose the type of service they want. Order commemoratives ...definitives or both. *Service A* includes one full pane of each stamp issued ...your category (commemoratives or definitives or both, $66 deposit). ...*vice B* includes four panes with matching plate block numbers ($264 ...posit). *Service C*, for the exacting collector, includes four panes with ...r-position matching plate block numbers for each plate block number ...de available to the Philatelic Sales Division ($264 deposit). ...You may subscribe any time and receive top quality panes for one full year. ...dvance deposits are for the first six stamp issues. Subsequent issues are ...billed at stamp face value.) For more detailed information, write to:

...PS Guide
...l Panes Program, Philatelic Marketing Division
...shington, D.C. 20260-6755

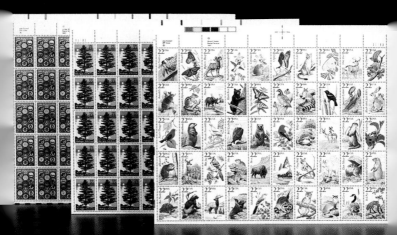

Tracking American Railroad History

The 1987 Locomotive Booklet, issued on October 1, signaled the start of National Stamp Collecting Month.

"I've been working on the railroad,
All the live-long day,..."

"She'll be comin' 'round the mountain when she comes,...
She'll be breathin' smoke an' fire when she comes,..."

"Come, all you rounders, for I want you to hear
The story of a brave engineer;
Casey Jones was the rounder's name
On a heavy eight wheeler he rode to fame..."

These lyrics from old railroad songs reveal America's love affair with trains and locomotives. Music tells the story of the railroads, and so do postage stamps. On October 1, 1987 the USPS kicked off National Stamp Collecting Month by issuing a booklet of stamps recognizing five locomotives that helped launch the railroad era in America: the *Stourbridge Lion*, the *Best Friend of Charleston*, the *John Bull*, the *Brother Jonathan* and the *Gowan & Marx*.

Those Old Iron Horses

The *Stourbridge Lion*, the first actual locomotive (as distinguished from experimental engines) to run in the United States, got its name from the city where it was built—Stourbridge, England—and a painting of a fierce lion on its front. It was intended to replace horse-drawn carts on an inclined "gravity" railroad between the coal mines of the Delaware & Hudson Canal Company and its canal terminal at Honesdale, Pennsylvania.

There, on August 8, 1829, Horace Allen, the company's chief engineer who had ordered it in England, set the engine up for its first run. It was more than twice as heavy as specified, appearing far too heavy for a trestle over a creek, but Allen had the steam up and drove away at a good speed.

This picture shows the historic run of the Stourbridge Lion, *the first locomotive in America.*

A crowd gathered to watch, fireworks were set off, a cannon was fired and the locomotive rolled down the tracks, over the shaky trestle and disappeared beyond nearby hills. After making a three-mile forward run, the engineer completed the round trip in reverse, already convinced the engine would not do.

Too heavy for the iron-covered wooden tracks, the *Stourbridge Lion* was relegated to providing steam for the company shop. It was shown at the National Railway Exposition of 1883 and acquired, minus many of its parts, by the Smithsonian Institution six years later.

The *Best Friend of Charleston* is credited with a number of "famous firsts:" On Christmas Day 1830 it became the *first* locomotive to run that was designed and built in the U.S.; it also was the *first* engine to pull a train in America; the *Best Friend* holds the *earliest record* of carrying mail by railroad, unofficially hauling a sack of mail to

Bamberg, South Carolina on January 15, 1831; and it was blown up five months later in the *first* explosion of a locomotive boiler in the United States. For reasons he did not live to explain, an inexperienced fireman tied down the safety valve lever.

During its short life, *The Best Friend of Charleston* carried an average of 40 to 50 passengers at speeds of up to 21 miles per hour (mph). Future trains had a flat "barrier" car loaded with bales of cotton placed behind the locomotive to protect passengers in case of explosion. For night travel, a flat car with a bright fire burning on a bed of sand was placed ahead of the engine to illuminate the track.

The *John Bull* was put into regular service in New Jersey on November 12, 1831. Built by the British firm of Robert Stephenson & Co., then the world's leading locomotive maker, the *Bull* was improved by Isaac Dripps, boss mechanic of the Camden & Amboy line. He added a tender car to carry fuel and a whiskey barrel with water for the engine. To help negotiate curves, Dripps attached a truck on two swiveling wheels ahead of the engine. It also had projecting bars a little above track level to clear the way, if necessary—the earliest version of the cowcatcher or "pilot."

The durable *John Bull* was brought out of retirement in 1893 to haul a train from Washington, D.C. to the Chicago World's Fair. It gave tens of thousands of passengers a ride as part of the exhibition attractions. It was under steam again in 1927 for the Baltimore & Ohio's (B&O) centennial pageant, in 1980 for a test run on a rural track in Maryland and in 1981 for a run through Washington's Georgetown on its 150th anniversary. The

A steam locomotive (believed to be the Baldwin *of about 1857) was pictured on one of the first U.S. pictorial stamps in 1869 (#114).*

The first engine designed and built in America, the Best Friend of Charleston *pulled a train of 40 to 50 passengers at 21 miles per hour in the early 1830s.*

engine can still be seen at the Smithsonian. As the oldest locomotive preserved in the U.S., "The *Bull* goes on forever."

The *Brother Jonathan*, built in 1832, was the world's fastest locomotive at that time, reaching reported speeds up to 60 mph. New York's Mohawk and Hudson Railroad, proud owner of the *Jonathan*, established a route from Troy to Schenectady, which also was served by the Utica and Schenectady line. This created an opportunity and a problem: how to coordinate a schedule so passengers and mail could make connections between the two lines. On August 1, 1836, with the encouragement of the Post Office Department, a joint timetable was published.

The *Gowan & Marx*, named for the London banking firm on which the Philadelphia and Reading Railroad relied for its financing, was one of the most powerful early locomotives. Designed by Joseph Harrison, Jr. of Philadelphia and built in 1839 by Eastwick and Harrison, the 11-ton engine pulled 101 freight cars weighing 423 tons—nearly 40 times its own weight—the full length of the line, averaging just under 10 mph. The railroad's owners were so impressed that they ordered 10 more engines like it.

By 1840 more than 2,800 miles of railroad were in operation along the Atlantic coast. The advantage of year-round service made the railroads superior to stagecoaches and steamboats for passenger, freight and mail service. By the late 1840s growth had spread to the Midwest, where rail links were especially important to land-locked cities, such as Indianapolis, Indiana. In the years after 1850 construction was so rapid that U.S. rail mileage was nearly equal to the rest of the world's combined.

The Pony Express preceded rail mail delivery. Its 100th anniversary was commemorated in 1960 with a 4¢ stamp (#1154).

When the Civil War erupted in 1861, railroads played an important role: Both sides made massive movements of troops and supplies by train.

Helping a Nation Communicate

For years, mail going to the western territories took weeks and even months to deliver. Then the Post Office Department offered a lucrative contract to the company that could deliver mail from Missouri to California in 10 days. The Central Overland and Pikes Peak Express Company had a plan to meet this challenge. The experiment, begun on April 3, 1860, became known as the Pony Express. Thousands of miles of wilderness, mountain trails and the great plains were conquered by young, adventurous riders who changed horses at relay stations about 15 miles apart. This romantic era of America's early mail delivery system drew to a close in 1862, when Congress passed the Pacific Railroad Act.

The act assured governmental support for a railroad spanning the entire nation, from East to West Coast. Two newly chartered companies were authorized to build this railroad that would extend into the wild, undeveloped regions west of the Mississippi River: the Union Pacific Railroad and the Central Pacific Railroad.

The Central Pacific started laying track in Sacramento, California in 1863 and pushed eastward. Progress was slow because locomotives, rails, ties and tools had to be shipped by boat around Cape Horn, at the tip of South America. The Sierra Nevada mountain range made construction difficult and dangerous for the crew. Seven tunnels were dug for a single two-mile stretch; explosives were often planted by workers suspended in baskets. To complicate matters, "gold fever" lured away 1,900 out of 2,000 men working on the track. They, however, were rapidly replaced with Chinese laborers.

The Union Pacific began heading west from Omaha, Nebraska in 1865. Rail lines already linked the East Coast to the Midwest, but it would be

The Empire State Express of the New York Central and Hudson River Railroad (#295) was the first train clocked at better than a mile a minute. On May 18, 1893 it made the run from Syracuse to Buffalo in the record time of 112.5 mph.

East meets west... Nearly 1,800 miles of track laid by the Central Pacific Railroad and the Union Pacific Railroad came together in 1869 (above), and the first transcontinental railroad was complete. For a stamp commemorating the 75th anniversary of the golden spike ceremony, the Post Office Department selected a mural painting by John McQuarrie in the Union Pacific Station in Salt Lake City, Utah (#922 below).

two more years before Chicago hooked up with Omaha. In the meantime, a crew of 10,000 men and an equal number of draught animals moved tons of supplies by wagon and canal boat, often up the Missouri River. Union Pacific track crossed the Rocky Mountains, where rock sometimes had to be chipped away by hand at a tedious rate of about two inches per day. As they advanced through Indian territory, the men frequently had to lay down their tools and take up guns to fend off attacks.

The whole country watched what had, by 1868, turned into a race between the Central and Union Pacific Railroads. Each company wanted to build as much track as possible to get the government subsidy and the land grants of territory near the railroad lines. In the spirited competition, the two lines actually passed and continued building parallel tracks. It took an act of Congress to name the contact spot: Promontory Point, near Ogden, in northern Utah. On May 10, 1869 a ceremonial golden spike joined the two sets of track. The first transcontinental railroad in the world, covering nearly 1,800 combined miles, had physically united America.

This 1952 issue (#1006), commemorating the 125th year of the Baltimore & Ohio (B&O) Railroad, illustrates the evolution of rail transportation with a horse-drawn "Pioneer Car," the B&O's first steam locomotive, the Tom Thumb *and a 1950s streamlined diesel locomotive.*

The railroads' expansion meant greater speed in transporting mail. A new job category appeared in the Post Office Department—postal transportation clerk. On the old stagecoach lines, the local postmaster took the mail pouch upon arrival, opened it and "exchanged mails" while the driver changed horses. And when a steamboat came into port, there was plenty of time for mail sacks to be opened and sorted while freight was unloaded. This luxury of time, however, was not available to the railroads, so a clerk was assigned to accompany the mail on the train.

W. A. Davis of St. Louis, Missouri, a postal clerk, is credited with the idea of sorting mail on a moving train, for which he reportedly received $100 from the Post Office Department. The "traveling post office" made its first *official* run on August 28, 1864 from Chicago to Clinton, Iowa, and the U.S. Railway Mail Service was born. As the idea proved itself, post office mail cars were built, and the first one was put into service in 1867. Six years later there were 862 *route agents*, as they became known, sorting mail on trains. At one point after World War II, more than 30,000 mail clerks worked on trains as they crisscrossed the United States.

The early mail clerk had a difficult job as the train sped through towns. He had to snare the mail pouch with a steel "catcher" arm as it hung from a crane and, at the same time, throw out a pouch for the town's residents. The clerk also carried a postmarking stamp for canceling letters along the way. In addition, route agents kept track of the mail pouches on board, the distance carried and the speed of delivery.

These transportation clerks worked in wooden cars heated by potbellied stoves, and fires were a common hazard. Bandits who robbed mail cars are legendary; many stories have been written about trains being stopped and railway clerks forced to give up their precious cargo.

The Post Office Department can be partially credited with the innovation of the "Through Train." Mail was being handled efficiently on short runs, but valuable time was lost at connecting points between railroads. On September 16, 1875 the "Fast Mail" train between New York and Chicago carried more than 33 tons of mail in a record-breaking 26 hours—about half the former time. The event was a milestone for the railroads and the Post Office. The first transcontinental Fast Mail service left Omaha on November 15, 1889.

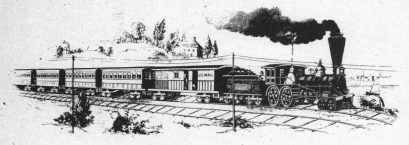

Steady improvements continued as new speed records were set, met and broken. Eventually, entire Fast Mail trains were made up solely of mail cars that carried no passengers.

The railroads faced another problem as their trains went from city to city: Each city had its own "Sun Time," which was based on the transit of the sun across the meridian. Travelers had to reset their watches once every 13 minutes on a trip from Boston to Chicago during the 1880s. Philadelphia's time was five minutes slower than New York's but five minutes faster than Baltimore's; Illinois had 27 different local times. It was an impossible situation for making connecting train schedules. After 11 years of campaigning, the nation's railroads met in Chicago on November 18, 1883 and adopted

Mail cars and trains have come in all shapes and sizes through the years (left and above).

39

the four standard time zones we observe today. All railroad clocks were reset accordingly.

Locomotives moved ahead at a rapid pace to meet the increased demand for longer, more powerful trains. The obsession with speed continued. On May 18, 1893 the *Empire State Express* pulled out of Syracuse, New York. The engineer was expected to set a new speed record of 100 mph with the brand new engine. When the train arrived in Buffalo, it had achieved a speed of 112.5 mph. It then headed to the Chicago World's Fair, where it was put on display. Later, it served passengers for many years.

The Post Office Department was constantly striving for faster delivery of its mail. Profitable contracts were offered to railroad lines that could meet its demands. Several railroads raced to see which could deliver the mail between two cities in the shortest time, with the winner getting the Post Office contract.

Before standard time zones were adopted in late 1883, engineers and conductors had to synchronize their watches several times during a single trip.

Decline and Preservation

The "Golden Era" of railroading peaked nearly a century ago. Compared with the railroad's steady 60-year climb, its fall was abrupt. The industry's heyday became part of America's past as the transportation spotlight shone on improved means of travel: The advent of the automobile marked the end of the passenger trains' prime years, and airplanes soon stripped freight and mail trains of their "fastest service" claim.

The locomotive did, however, revolutionize America; it brought settlers to the middle and western parts of the nation, and it served as a reliable mode of transportation to these and other growing areas. Train station sounds of steam engine chugs and shouts of "All Aboard!" are not so familiar any more. But while memories of great American rail days may gradually fade like a high-pitched train whistle blowing in the distance, their heritage is preserved in the stories told by songs… and stamps. In a way, stamps carry the trains that once carried them.

Collecting Railroad Philately

Just as the American public seems to have a love affair with trains, so do American *stamp collectors*. Two specialized philatelic societies, both organized in 1950, service the cravings of railroad/transportation stamp enthusiasts.

Devoted specifically to the advancement of railway philately, the Casey Jones Railroad Unit is affiliated with the American Topical Association. Its 309 members span the globe, coming from the United States, Canada and 15 other foreign countries. For a fee of only $5.00 per year, members receive a bimonthly, illustrated publication, *The Dispatcher*, which lists all the new railway issues (U.S. and foreign), events of interest, stamp descriptions and historical information on trains. For more information, contact:

Oliver C. Atchison, Treasurer
Casey Jones Railroad Unit
P.O. Box 31631
San Francisco, CA 94131

On the broader topic of transportation, the Mobile Post Office Society (MPOS) is devoted to the collection of worldwide transit markings of all types, including railway, highway and waterway. Its 600 members receive the bimonthly *Transit Postmark Collector*, which includes all society news and articles of interest. The MPOS, an affiliate member of the American Philatelic Society (APS), is also active in the publication of books and monographs relating to its interests. For more information, contact:

Charles Towle, Director
Mobile Post Office Society
4621 E. Don Jose Dr.
Tucson, AZ 85718

Railway philately is popular in foreign countries as well. Two groups, the Railway Philatelic Group in England and the Railway Stamp Club from Taipei, Taiwan, regularly exchange bulletins and information with the Casey Jones Railway Unit.

"Casey" Jones, an engineer on the Illinois Central Main Line, volunteered to make the run of the Cannon Ball Express when the regular engineer called in sick. Trying to bring the overdue train in on time, he crashed into a stationary freight train. Before the collision, Casey ordered his fireman to jump, applied the brakes and saved the passengers. He was the only person to die in the accident. The central design (above) of stamp #993 is a portrait of the engineer superimposed on a locomotive wheel.

Organize Your Collection... Efficiently, Conveniently

Created in 1984 for new collectors, the Commemorative Stamp Club makes sure you get all the commemoratives issued in 1987 (usually between 30 and 40 stamps each year). The Club has expanded to include definitive stamps as an option. Specially designed Commemorative Stamp Club Album pages include illustrations and space for two issues. They give information about the stamp, including dates, places and general history.

Annual membership for the 1987 Commemorative Stamp Club program costs just $19.95 and offers you these benefits:

- Advance announcements of *every* U.S. commemorative stamp
- Commemorative stamps mailed directly to you
- Automatic shipment of custom-printed album pages for current commemorative issues
- Mounts to hold and protect the stamps
- A *free* one-year subscription to *The Philatelic Catalog*, a bimonthly publication with full-color illustrations of all stamps, cards, aerogrammes, stationery and other collectibles available through mail order
- A complimentary, gold-imprinted Commemorative Stamp Club Album ($3.95 value) for enrolling now
- Special offers for definitive stamps, album pages and annual commemorative sets issued in previous years.

How to Get Involved

A no-risk, money-back guarantee assures your satisfaction. If you discontinue your membership within 90 days, simply return the album pages and stamps with a label from one of your shipments, and we'll send you a complete refund; the album is yours to keep. For more information and an order form, write to:

USPS Guide
Commemorative Stamp Club
Philatelic Marketing Division
Washington, D.C. 20260-6755

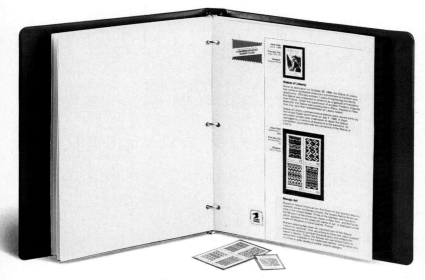

Early Stamp Details

1¢ Franklin Types I-IV of 1851-56

5

Bust of **5**

Detail of **7** Type II
Lower scrollwork incomplete (lacks little balls).
Side ornaments are complete.

11

Bust of **5**

Detail of **6** Type Ia
Top ornaments and outer line partly cut away.
Lower scrollwork is complete.

Bust of **5**

Detail of **8** Type III
Outer lines broken in the middle.
Side ornaments are complete.

Detail of **8A** Type IIIa
Outer lines broken top or bottom but not both.

Detail of **11**
THREE CENTS.
Type I. There is an outer frame line at top and bottom.

Bust of **5**

Detail of **5** Type I
Has curved, unbroken lines outside labels.
Scrollwork is complete, forms little balls at bottom.

Detail of **5A** Type Ib
Lower scrollwork is incomplete, the little balls are not so clear.

Bust of **5**

Detail of **9** Type IV
Outer lines recut top, bottom, or both.

12

Detail of **12**
FIVE CENTS.
Type I. There are projections on all four sides.

10¢ Washington Types I-IV of 1855

15

Bust of **15**
↓   ↓

↑   ↑

Detail of **13**
Type I. The "shells" at the lower corners are practically complete. The outer line below the label is very nearly complete. The outer lines are broken above the middle of the top label and the "X" in each upper corner.

Bust of **15**
↓

Detail of **14**
Type II. The design is complete at the top. The outer line at the bottom is broken in the middle. The shells are partly cut away.

↓

Detail of **15**
Type III. The outer lines are broken above the top label and the "X" numerals. The outer line at the bottom and the shells are partly cut away, as in Type II.

Bust of **15**
↓

Detail of **16**
Type IV. The outer lines have been recut at top or bottom or both.
Types I, II, III, and IV have complete ornaments at the sides of the stamps and three pearls at each outer edge of the bottom panel.

Bust of **5**

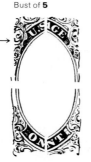

Detail of **24**
ONE CENT FRANKLIN
Type V. Similar to Type III of 1851-56 but with side ornaments partly cut away.

Bust of **11**

↑

Detail of **26**
THREE CENTS WASHINGTON
Type II. The outer frame line has been removed at top and bottom. The side frame lines were recut so as to be continuous from the top to the bottom of the plate.

30A

↑

Detail of **30A**
FIVE CENTS JEFFERSON
Type II. The projections at top and bottom are partly cut away.

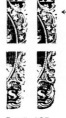
←

Detail of **35**
TEN CENTS WASHINGTON
(Two typical examples).
Type V. Side ornaments slightly cut away. Outer lines complete except over right X.

55   **57**

Detail of **67**
5¢. A leaflet has been added to the foliated ornaments at each corner.

Detail of **64**
3¢. Ornaments at corners have been enlarged and end in a small ball.

Issue of 1861

Detail of **55**

56   **58**   **68**   **69**

Detail of **57**

Detail of **56**

Detail of **68**
10¢. A heavy curved line has been cut below the stars and an outer line has been added to the ornaments above them.

63   **67**

Detail of **58**

Issue of 1861-62

Detail of **63**
1¢. A dash has been added under the tip of the ornament at right of the numeral in upper left corner.

62   **64**

Detail of **69**
12¢. Ovals and scrolls have been added to the corners.

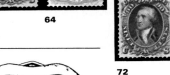

72

Detail of **62**

46

Detail of **72**
90¢. Parallel lines form an angle above the ribbon with "U.S. Postage"; between these lines a row of dashes has been added and a point of color to the apex of the lower pair.

Detail of **134**

Detail of **138**

118

135   **136**   **139**   **140**

Detail of **118**
FIFTEEN CENTS.
Type I. Picture unframed.

Detail of **135**

Detail of **139**

Detail of **119**
Type II. Picture framed.
Type III. Same as Type I but without fringe of brown shading lines around central vignette.

Detail of **136**

Detail of **140**

Issue of 1870-71:
Printed by the National Bank
Note Company.
Issued without secret marks (see Nos. 156-163).

137   **138**   **141**

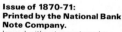

134

Detail of **137**

Detail of **141**

1873: Printed by the Continental Bank Note Co.

Designs of the 1870-71 Issue with secret marks on the values from 1¢ to 15¢ as described and illustrated below.

159   **160**

Detail of 159
6¢. The first four vertical lines of the shading in the lower part of the left ribbon have been strengthened.

Detail of 160
7¢. Two small semi-circles are drawn around the ends of the lines which outline the ball in the lower right hand corner.

161   **162**

Detail of 161
10¢. There is a small semi-circle in the scroll, at the right end of the upper label.

Detail of 162
12¢. The balls of the figure "2" are crescent shaped.

163

Detail of 163
15¢. In the lower part of the triangle in the upper left corner two lines have been made heavier forming a "V". This mark can be found on some of the Continental and American (1879) printings, but not all stamps show it.
Secret marks were added to the dies of the 24¢, 30¢, and 90¢ but new plates were not made from them. The various printings of these stamps can be distinguished only by the shades and paper.

206   **207**

Detail of 206
1¢. Upper vertical lines have been deepened, creating a solid effect in parts of background. Upper arabesques have lines of shading.

Detail of 207
3¢. Shading at sides of central oval is half its previous width. A short horizontal dash has been cut below the "TS" of "CENTS"

208   **209**

Detail of 208
6¢. Has three vertical lines instead of four between the edge of the panel and the outside of the stamp.

Detail of **209**
10¢. Has four vertical lines instead of five between left side of oval and edge of the shield. Horizontal lines in lower part of background have been strengthened.

2¢ Washington
Types I-III of 1984

Triangle of **248-250**
Type I. Horizontal lines of uniform thickness run across the triangle.

248

Triangle of **251**
Type II. Horizontal lines cross the triangle, but are thinner within than without.

Triangle of **252**
Type III. The horizontal lines do not cross the double frame lines of the triangle.

$1 Perry
Types of 1894

261

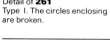 ←

Detail of **261**
Type I. The circles enclosing $1 are broken.

 ←

Detail of **261A**
Type II. The circles enclosing $1 are complete.

282C

 ←

Detail of **282C**
TEN CENTS
Type I. The tips of the foliate ornaments do not impinge on the white curved line below "TEN CENTS."

283

 ←

Detail of **283**
Type II. The lips of the ornaments break the curved line below the "E" of "TEN" and the "T" of "CENTS."

Watermark **190**

Watermark **191**

USPS
Watermark **191**

49

Commemorative and
Definitive Stamps

1847-1875

1   2   3   4   5   11

12   15   17   30A   37   39

Issues of 1847-94 are Unwatermarked, Issues of 1847, Imperf.

		Un	U
1	5¢ Benjamin		
	Franklin, July 1	4,000.00	650.00
2	10¢ George		
	Washington,		
	July 1	18,500.00	2,000.00

Issues of 1875, Reproductions of 1 & 2

		Un	U
3	5¢ Franklin	1,300.00	—
4	10¢ Washington	1,700.00	—

Reproductions. The letters R. W. H. & E. at the bottom of each stamp are less distinct on the reproductions than on the originals.

5¢. On the original the left side of the white shirt frill touches the oval on a level with the top of the "F" of "Five." On the reproduction it touches the oval about on a level with the top of the figure "5."

10¢. On the reproduction, line of coat at left points to right of "X" and line of coat at right points to center of "S" of CENTS. On the original, line of coat points to "T" of TEN and between "T" and "S" of CENTS.

On the reproduction the eyes have a sleepy look, the line of the mouth is straighter and in the curl of hair near the left cheek is a strong black dot, while the original has only a faint one.

Issues of 1851-56, Imperf.

		Un	U
5	1¢ Franklin, type I	100,000.00	22,500.00
5A	1¢ Same, type Ib	13,000.00	4,750.00

#6-9: Franklin (5)

		Un	U
6	1¢ dark blue,		
	type Ia	15,500.00	5,500.00
7	1¢ blue, type II	450.00	85.00
8	1¢ blue, type III	5,250.00	1,450.00
8A	1¢ pale blue,		
	type IIIA	1,750.00	575.00
9	1¢ blue, type IV	300.00	75.00
10	3¢ orange brown Washington,		
	type I (11)	1,200.00	45.00
11	3¢ Washington, type I	130.00	7.00

		Un	U
12	5¢ Jefferson, type I	9,500.00	1,300.00
13	10¢ green Washington,		
	type I (15)	8,500.00	700.00
14	10¢ green, type II (15)	1,700.00	275.00
15	10¢ Washington, type III	1,750.00	285.00
16	10¢ green, type IV (15)	10,000.00	1,450.00
17	12¢ Washington	1,850.00	250.00

Issues of 1857-61, Perf. 15

		Un	U
	#18-24: Franklin (5)		
18	1¢ blue, type I	700.00	375.00
19	1¢ blue, type Ia	9,500.00	2,400.00
20	1¢ blue, type II	425.00	135.00
21	1¢ blue, type III	4,250.00	1,250.00
22	1¢ blue, type IIIa	650.00	250.00
23	1¢ blue, type IV	1,750.00	300.00
24	1¢ blue, type V	110.00	22.50

		Un	U
	#25-26: Washington (11)		
25	3¢ rose, type I	650.00	27.50
26	3¢ dull red, type II	45.00	2.75
	#27-29: Jefferson (12)		
27	5¢ brick red, type I	7,500.00	1,000.00
28	5¢ red brown, type I	1,350.00	275.00
28A	5¢ Indian red, type I	9,000.00	1,500.00
29	5¢ brown, type I	750.00	225.00
30	5¢ orange brown		
	Jefferson, type II (30A)	750.00	900.00
30A	5¢ Jefferson, type II	450.00	175.00
	#31-35: Washington (15)		
31	10¢ green, type I	5,000.00	525.00
32	10¢ green, type II	1,650.00	170.00
33	10¢ green, type III	1,750.00	180.00
34	10¢ green, type IV	15,000.00	1,550.00
35	10¢ green, type V	175.00	57.50
36	12¢ black Washington		
	(17)	325.00	85.00
37	24¢ Washington	600.00	200.00
38	30¢ Franklin	750.00	285.00
39	90¢ Washington	1,450.00	2,750.00
	90¢ Same, with pen cancel	—	1,000.00

Note: Beware of forged cancellations of #39. Genuine cancellations are rare.

Issues of 1875: Government Reprints, Perf. 12, White Paper, Without Gum

		Un	U
40	1¢ bright blue Franklin (5)	550.00	—
41	3¢ scarlet Washington (11)	2,850.00	—
42	5¢ orange brown		
	Jefferson (30A)	950.00	—
43	10¢ blue green		
	Washington (15)	2,250.00	—

	1875 continued, Reprints, Perf. 12	Un	U
44	12¢ greenish black		
	Washington (17)	2,600.00	—
45	24¢ blackish violet		
	Washington (37)	2,850.00	—
46	30¢ yel. org. Franklin		
	(38)	2,850.00	—
47	90¢ deep blue		
	Washington (39)	4,250.00	—
48-54 not assigned			

Issues of 1861

Following the outbreak of the Civil War, the U.S. Government demonetized all previous issues.

55	1¢ Franklin	17,000.00	—
56	3¢ Washington	700.00	—
57	5¢ brown Jefferson	12,500.00	—
58	10¢ Washington	5,500.00	—
59	12¢ Washington	35,000.00	—
60	24¢ dk. vio. Washington		
	(70)	6,000.00	—
61	30¢ red org. Franklin		
	(71)	16,000.00	—
62	90¢ dull blue		
	Washington (72)	20,000.00	—
62B	10¢ dark green		
	Washington (58)	5,500.00	450.00

#55-62 were not used for postage and do not exist in a canceled state. The paper they were printed on is thin and semi-transparent, that of the following issues is more opaque.

Issues of 1861-62

63	1¢ Franklin	110.00	17.50
64	3¢ Washington	3,500.00	250.00
65	3¢ rose Washington (64)	50.00	1.10
66	3¢ lake Washington (64)	1,650.00	—
67	5¢ Jefferson	4,000.00	375.00
68	10¢ Washington	250.00	27.50
69	12¢ Washington	450.00	50.00
70	24¢ Washington	500.00	75.00
71	30¢ Franklin	450.00	65.00
72	90¢ Washington	1,200.00	250.00

Issues of 1861-66

73	2¢ Andrew Jackson		
	("Black Jack")	100.00	20.00

		Un	U
74	3¢ scarlet Washington		
	(64)	4,000.00	—
75	5¢ red brown Jefferson		
	(67)	1,200.00	200.00
76	5¢ brn. Jefferson (67)	300.00	50.00
77	15¢ Abraham Lincoln	450.00	60.00
78	24¢ lilac Washington (70)	265.00	47.50

#74 was not regularly issued.

Grills on U.S. Stamps

Between 1867 and 1870 postage stamps were embossed with grills to prevent people from reusing canceled stamps. The pyramid-shaped grills absorbed cancellation ink, making it virtually impossible to remove a postmark chemically.

Issues of 1867, With Grills

Grills A, B, C: Points Up

A. Grill Covers Entire Stamp

79	3¢ rose Washington		
	(64)	1,650.00	425.00
80	5¢ brn. Jefferson (67)	40,000.00	—
81	30¢ org. Franklin (71)	—	32,500.00

B. Grill about 18 x 15mm.

82	3¢ rose Washington (64)	—	45,000.00

C. Grill about 13 x 16mm.

83	3¢ rose Washington (64)	1,600.00	375.00

Grills, D, Z, E, F: Points Down

D. Grill about 12 x 14mm.

84	2¢ blk. Jackson (73)	3,000.00	900.00
85	3¢ rose Washington (64)	1,350.00	425.00

Z. Grill about 11 x 14mm.

85A	1¢ bl. Franklin (63)		—110,000.00
85B	2¢ blk. Jackson (73)	1,200.00	350.00
85C	3¢ rose Washington (64)	3,500.00	950.00
85D	10¢ green Washington		
	(68)	—	25,000.00
85E	12¢ black Washington		
	(69)	1,550.00	525.00
85F	15¢ blk. Lincoln (77)	—	35,000.00

E. Grill about 11 x 13mm.

86	1¢ blue Franklin (63)	750.00	240.00
87	2¢ black Jackson (73)	325.00	65.00
88	3¢ rose Washington (64)	225.00	9.50
89	10¢ grn. Washington (68)	1,100.00	175.00
90	12¢ blk. Washington (69)	1,300.00	185.00

55 56 57 58 59

62 63 64 67 68 69

70 71 72 73 77

112   113   114   115   116

117   118   120   121   122

134   135   136   137   138

139   140   141   142

		Un	U
	1867 continued, With Grill, Perf. 12		
91	15¢ black Lincoln (77)	2,750.00	425.00
	F. Grill about 9 x 13 mm.		
92	1¢ blue Franklin (63)	300.00	100.00
93	2¢ black Jackson (73)	110.00	22.50
94	3¢ red Washington (64)	85.00	2.50
95	5¢ brown Jefferson (67)	800.00	200.00
96	10¢ yellow green		
	Washington (68)	600.00	100.00
97	12¢ black Washington		
	(69)	625.00	105.00
98	15¢ black Lincoln (77)	625.00	110.00
99	24¢ gray lilac		
	Washington (70)	1,150.00	450.00
100	30¢ orange Franklin (71)	1,300.00	350.00
101	90¢ blue Washington		
	(72)	4,000.00	900.00
	Reissues of 1861-66 in 1875, Without Grill		
102	1¢ blue Franklin (63)	*500.00*	*800.00*
103	2¢ black Jackson (73)	*2,500.00*	*4,000.00*
104	3¢ brown red		
	Washington (64)	*3,250.00*	*4,250.00*
105	5¢ brown Jefferson (67)	*1,800.00*	*2,250.00*
106	10¢ grn. Washington (68)	*2,100.00*	*3,750.00*
107	12¢ blk. Washington (69)	*3,000.00*	*4,500.00*
108	15¢ black Lincoln (77)	*3,000.00*	*4,750.00*
109	24¢ deep violet		
	Washington (70)	*4,000.00*	*6,000.00*
110	30¢ brownish orange		
	Franklin (71)	*4,500.00*	*7,000.00*
111	90¢ blue		
	Washington (72)	*5,750.00*	*18,500.00*
	Issues of 1869, With Grill Measuring 9½ x 9 mm.		
112	1¢ Franklin	225.00	60.00
113	2¢ Post Horse & Rider	160.00	25.00
114	3¢ Locomotive	135.00	5.50
115	6¢ Washington	775.00	90.00
116	10¢ Shield and Eagle	850.00	95.00
117	12¢ S. S. Adriatic	750.00	90.00
118	15¢ Columbus		
	Landing, type I	1,750.00	250.00
119	15¢ brown and blue		
	Columbus Landing,		
	type II (118)	850.00	120.00

		Un	U
119b	Center		
	inverted	*130,000.00*	*17,500.00*
120	24¢ Declaration of		
	Independence	2,500.00	450.00
120b	Center		
	inverted	*110,000.00*	*16,500.00*
121	30¢ Shield, Eagle		
	and Flags	2,250.00	225.00
121b	Flags inverted	*105,000.00*	*45,000.00*
122	90¢ Lincoln	7,000.00	1,200.00
	Reissues of 1869 in 1875, Without Grill, Hard, White Paper		
123	1¢ Buff (112)	325.00	225.00
124	2¢ brown (113)	375.00	325.00
125	3¢ blue (114)	2,750.00	1,400.00
126	6¢ blue (115)	850.00	550.00
127	10¢ yellow (116)	1,400.00	1,200.00
128	12¢ green (117)	1,500.00	1,200.00
129	15¢ brown and blue		
	Columbus Landing,		
	type III (118)	1,300.00	550.00
130	24¢ grn. & vio. (120)	1,250.00	550.00
131	30¢ bl. & car. (121)	1,750.00	1,000.00
132	90¢ car. & blk. (122)	5,500.00	*6,000.00*
	Reissue of 1869 in 1880, Soft, Porous Paper		
133	1¢ buff (112)	200.00	135.00
	Issues of 1870-71, With Grill, White Wove Paper		
134	1¢ Franklin	475.00	55.00
135	2¢ Jackson	325.00	35.00
136	3¢ Washington	265.00	10.00
137	6¢ Lincoln	1,500.00	250.00
138	7¢ Edwin M. Stanton	1,000.00	225.00
139	10¢ Jefferson	1,350.00	400.00
140	12¢ Henry Clay	*12,000.00*	1,500.00
141	15¢ Daniel Webster	1,700.00	675.00
142	24¢ General Winfield		
	Scott	—	*10,500.00*

It is generally accepted as fact that the Continental Bank Note Co. printed and delivered a quantity of 24¢ stamps. They are impossible to distinguish from those printed by the National Bank Note Co.

	1870-71 continued, With Grill, Perf. 12	Un	U
143	30¢ Alexander		
	Hamilton	3,750.00	800.00
144	90¢ Commodore Perry	5,000.00	700.00
	Without Grill, White Wove Paper		
145	1¢ ultra. Franklin (134)	150.00	6.50
146	2¢ red brn. Jackson		
	(135)	50.00	4.50
147	3¢ green Washington		
	(136)	100.00	.50
148	6¢ carmine Lincoln (137)	200.00	12.00
149	7¢ verm. Stanton (138)	300.00	50.00
150	10¢ brown Jefferson (139)	200.00	12.00
151	12¢ dull violet Clay (140)	500.00	55.00
152	15¢ bright orange Webster		
	(141)	475.00	55.00
153	24¢ purple W. Scott (142)	550.00	75.00
154	30¢ black Hamilton (143)	900.00	90.00
155	90¢ carmine Perry (144)	1,200.00	175.00
	Issues of 1873, Without Grill, White Wove Paper, Thin to Thick		
156	1¢ Franklin	50.00	1.75
157	2¢ Jackson	130.00	7.00
158	3¢ Washington	40.00	.15
159	6¢ Lincoln	190.00	8.00
160	7¢ Stanton	375.00	55.00
161	10¢ Jefferson	190.00	9.00
162	12¢ Clay	550.00	60.00
163	15¢ Webster	525.00	55.00
164	not assigned		
165	30¢ Hamilton (143)	550.00	55.00
166	90¢ Perry (144)	1,250.00	175.00
	Issues of 1875, Special Printing, Hard, White Wove Paper, Without Gum		
167	1¢ ultra. Franklin (156)	7,500.00	—
168	2¢ dark brown		
	Jackson (157)	3,500.00	—
169	3¢ blue green		
	Washington (158)	9,500.00	—
170	6¢ dull rose Lincoln		
	(159)	8,500.00	—
171	7¢ reddish vermilion		
	Stanton (160)	2,100.00	—
172	10¢ pale brown		
	Jefferson (161)	7,750.00	—

		Un	U
173	12¢ dark violet Clay		
	(162)	2,750.00	—
174	15¢ bright orange		
	Webster (163)	7,750.00	—
175	24¢ dull purple		
	W. Scott (142)	1,850.00	—
176	30¢ greenish black		
	Hamilton (143)	7,000.00	—
177	90¢ violet car. Perry		
	(144)	7,000.00	—

Although perforated, these stamps were usually cut apart with scissors. As a result, the perforations are often much mutilated and the design is frequently damaged.

	Yellowish Wove Paper		
178	2¢ vermilion Jackson		
	(157), June 21	135.00	4.50
179	5¢ Zachary Taylor,		
	June 21	150.00	8.00
	Special Printing, Hard, White Wove Paper, Without Gum		
180	2¢ carmine verm.		
	Jackson (157)	17,000.00	—
181	5¢ bright blue Taylor		
	(179)	32,500.00	—
	Issues of 1879, Printed by the American Bank Note Co. Soft, Porous Paper, Thin to Thick		
182	1¢ dark ultramarine		
	Franklin (156)	100.00	1.20
183	2¢ vermilion Jackson		
	(157)	47.50	1.20
184	3¢ green Washington		
	(158)	40.00	.10
185	5¢ blue Taylor (179)	200.00	7.50
186	6¢ pink Lincoln (159)	400.00	11.00
187	10¢ brown Jefferson (139)		
	(no secret mark)	700.00	14.00
188	10¢ brown Jefferson (161)		
	(with secret mark)	400.00	15.00
189	15¢ red orange		
	Webster (163)	150.00	14.00
190	30¢ full black Hamilton		
	(143)	450.00	27.50
191	90¢ carmine Perry (144)	1,000.00	150.00

143   144   156   157   158

159   160   161   162   163

179

205

206

207

208

209

210

211

212

219

220

221

222

223

224

225

226

227

228

229

	Un	U
Issues of 1880,		
Special Printing,		
Perf. 12, Soft,		
Porous Paper, Without Gum		
192 1¢ dark ultramarine		
Franklin (156)	9,000.00	—
193 2¢ black brown		
Jackson (157)	5,750.00	—
194 3¢ blue green		
Washington (158)	13,500.00	—
195 6¢ dull rose Lincoln		
(159)	9,500.00	—
196 7¢ scarlet vermilion		
Stanton (160)	2,100.00	—
197 10¢ deep brown		
Jefferson (161)	8,750.00	—
198 12¢ blackish purple		
Clay (162)	4,000.00	—
199 15¢ orange Webster		
(163)	8,250.00	—
200 24¢ dark violet		
W. Scott (142)	2,750.00	—
201 30¢ greenish black		
Hamilton (143)	7,000.00	—
202 90¢ dull car. Perry (144)	7,000.00	—
203 2¢ scarlet vermilion		
Jackson (157)	16,000.00	—
204 5¢ deep blue Taylor		
(179)	28,500.00	—
Issue of 1882		
205 5¢ yellow brown		
Garfield, Apr. 10	90.00	4.00
Special Printing, Soft, Porous Paper,		
Without Gum		
205C 5¢ gray brown (205)	16,500.00	—
Issues of 1881-82, Designs of 1873		
Re-engraved		
206 1¢ Franklin	30.00	.40
207 3¢ Washington	35.00	.12
208 6¢ Lincoln	210.00	45.00
209 10¢ Jefferson	70.00	2.25
Issues of 1883		
210 2¢ Washington, Oct. 1	28.50	.08
211 4¢ Jackson, Oct. 1	130.00	7.50
Special Printing, Soft, Porous Paper		
211B 2¢ pale red brown		
Washington (210)	700.00	—

	Un	U
211D 4¢ deep blue green		
Jackson (211) no gum	12,500.00	—
Issues of 1887		
212 1¢ Franklin	50.00	.65
213 2¢ green Washington		
(210)	20.00	.08
214 3¢ vermilion		
Washington (207)	42.50	37.50
Issues of 1888		
215 4¢ carmine Jackson		
(211)	130.00	11.00
216 5¢ indigo Garfield (205)	120.00	6.50
217 30¢ orange brown		
Hamilton (143)	300.00	70.00
218 90¢ purple Perry (144)	675.00	130.00
Issues of 1890-93		
219 1¢ Franklin	18.50	.10
219D 2¢ lake Washington	135.00	.45
220 2¢ carmine	15.00	.05
221 3¢ Jackson	47.50	4.50
222 4¢ Lincoln	47.50	1.50
223 5¢ Ulysses S. Grant	47.50	1.50
224 6¢ Garfield	50.00	15.00
225 8¢ William T. Sherman	40.00	8.50
226 10¢ Webster	90.00	1.75
227 15¢ Clay	135.00	15.00
228 30¢ Jefferson	200.00	18.50
229 90¢ Perry	325.00	90.00

	1893 continued	Un	U	PB/LP	#	FDC	Q
	Columbian Exposition Issue, Jan. 2 (8¢ March), Perf. 12						
230	1¢ Columbus Sights Land	21.00	.30	350.00	(6)	3,000.00	449,195,550
231	2¢ Landing of Columbus	20.00	.06	300.00	(6)	2,400.00	1,464,588,750
232	3¢ The Santa Maria	45.00	15.00	650.00	(6)	6,000.00	11,501,250
233	4¢ ultramarine Fleet of Columbus	65.00	6.00	950.00	(6)	6,000.00	19,181,550
233a	4¢ blue (error) (233)	6,500.00	2,500.00				
234	5¢ Columbus Seeking Aid	75.00	7.00	1,350.00	(6)	6,250.00	35,248,250
235	6¢ Columbus at Barcelona	65.00	20.00	1,050.00	(6)	6,750.00	4,707,550
236	8¢ Columbus Restored to Favor	50.00	8.00	650.00	(6)		10,656,550
237	10¢ Columbus Presenting						
	Indians	110.00	6.50	3,000.00	(6)	7,500.00	16,516,950
238	10¢ Columbus Announcing						
	His Discovery	200.00	65.00	4,750.00	(6)		1,576,950
239	30¢ Columbus at La Rabida	275.00	90.00	7,000.00	(6)		617,250
240	50¢ Recall of Columbus	325.00	140.00	9,500.00	(6)		243,750
241	$1 Isabella Pledging						
	Her Jewels	1,000.00	550.00	19,500.00	(6)		55,050
242	$2 Columbus in Chains	1,100.00	500.00	21,000.00	(6)	15,000.00	45,550
243	$3 Columbus Describing His						
	Third Voyage	2,300.00	1,100.00	45,000.00	(6)		27,650
244	$4 Isabella and Columbus	3,100.00	1,450.00	90,000.00	(6)		26,350
245	$5 Portrait of Columbus	3,250.00	1,700.00	100,000.00	(6)		27,350

The Columbians

Since they were issued in 1893, the series of Columbian stamps (#230-245) have been of interest to stamp collectors and connoisseurs. As a result, they have come under close scrutiny. Look carefully at the "Columbus in Sight of Land" stamp (#230) — Columbus is clean shaven. Yet in the following stamp, "Landing of Columbus" (#231), he is sporting a full beard. According to historians, Columbus first sighted land shortly after midnight on October 12, 1492 and landed in El Salvador later that day, which hardly gave him enough time to grow a beard. Did the artist make a mistake? Maybe not. Supposedly, Columbus and his crew **thought** they sighted land as early as September 25, which might have given him enough time to grow a beard.

230

231

232

233

234

235

236

237

238

239

240

241

242

243

244

245

246   251   253   254   255   256

257   258   259   260   261   262

263

Watermark 191

Bureau Issues Starting in 1894, the Bureau of Engraving and Printing at Washington has produced all U.S. postage stamps except #909-921 (Overrun Countries), 1335 (Eakins painting), 1355 (Disney), 1410-1413 (Anti-Pollution), 1414-1418 (Christmas, 1970), 1789 (John Paul Jones), 1804 (Banneker), 1825 (Veterans Administration), 1833 (American Education), 2023 (Francis of Assisi), 2038 (Priestley), 2065 (Martin Luther), 2066 (Alaska Statehood), 2073 (Woodson), 2080 (Hawaii Statehood), 2087 (Health Research), 2091 (Seaway), 2093 (Roanoke Voyages), 2102 (Crime Prevention), 2110 (Kern), 2137 (Bethune), 2138-41 (Duck Decoys), 2153 (Social Security), 2159 (Public Education), 2160-63 (Youth), 2164 (Help End Hunger), 2167 (Arkansas Statehood), 2203 (Sojourner Truth), 2204 (Republic of Texas), 2210 (Hospitals), 2211 (Ellington), 2220-23 (Polar Explorers) and 2240-43 (Woodcarved Figurines).

	Issues of 1894, Perf. 12, Unwmkd.	Un	U	PB/LP	#	FDC	Q
246	1¢ Franklin	22.50	3.00	300.00	(6)		
247	1¢ blue Franklin (246)	52.50	1.25	600.00	(6)		
248	2¢ pink Washington, type I	17.50	2.00	200.00	(6)		
	#249-252: Washington (248)						
249	2¢ carmine lake, type I	125.00	1.35	1,250.00	(6)		
250	2¢ carmine, type I	21.00	.25	300.00	(6)		
251	2¢ carmine, type II	165.00	2.50	2,100.00	(6)		
252	2¢ carmine, type III	90.00	3.25	1,200.00	(6)		
253	3¢ Jackson	80.00	6.25	1,000.00	(6)		
254	4¢ Lincoln	90.00	2.50	1,250.00	(6)		
255	5¢ Grant	75.00	3.50	875.00	(6)		
256	6¢ Garfield	140.00	15.00	1,500.00	(6)		
257	8¢ Sherman	100.00	10.00	1,000.00	(6)		
258	10¢ Webster	175.00	7.50	2,400.00	(6)		
259	15¢ Clay	250.00	45.00	3,750.00	(6)		
260	50¢ Jefferson	325.00	75.00	6,000.00	(6)		
261	$1 Commodore Perry, type I	850.00	250.00	*15,000.00*	(6)		
261A	$1 black Perry, type II (261)	1,850.00	500.00	*25,000.00*	(6)		
262	$2 James Madison	2,100.00	650.00	*35,000.00*	(6)		
263	$5 John Marshall	3,250.00	1,150.00	—	(6)		
	Issues of 1895, Wmkd. (191)						
264	1¢ blue Franklin (264)	5.00	.10	175.00	(6)		
	#265-267: Washington (248)						
265	2¢ carmine Washington, type I	22.50	.65	350.00	(6)		
266	2¢ carmine, type II	20.00	2.50	325.00	(6)		
267	2¢ carmine, type III	4.50	.05	125.00	(6)		
268	3¢ purple Jackson (253)	35.00	1.00	575.00	(6)		
269	4¢ dk. brown Lincoln (254)	37.50	1.10	600.00	(6)		
270	5¢ chocolate Grant (255)	35.00	1.75	600.00	(6)		
271	6¢ dull brn. Garfield (256)	65.00	3.50	1,100.00	(6)		
272	8¢ vio. brn. Sherman (257)	40.00	1.00	700.00	(6)		
273	10¢ dk. green Webster (258)	60.00	1.20	1,150.00	(6)		
274	15¢ dark blue Clay (259)	160.00	8.25	3,000.00	(6)		
275	50¢ orange Jefferson (260)	235.00	20.00	6,000.00	(6)		
276	$1 black Perry, type I (261)	550.00	65.00	*10,000.00*	(6)		
276A	$1 blk. Perry, type II (261)	1,200.00	125.00	*20,000.00*	(6)		
277	$2 brt. blue Madison (262)	900.00	275.00	*18,500.00*	(6)		
278	$5 dk. grn. Marshall (263)	2,000.00	425.00	*60,000.00*	(6)		

	Issues of 1898, Perf. 12	Un	U	PB/LP	#	FDC	Q
279	1¢ dp. green Franklin (246)	10.00	.06	175.00	(6)		
279B	2¢ red Washington,						
	type III (248)	9.00	.05	160.00	(6)		
279Be	Booklet pane of 6	350.00	*200.00*				
280	4¢ rose brn. Lincoln (254)	30.00	.70	600.00	(6)		
281	5¢ dark blue Grant (255)	35.00	.65	650.00	(6)		
282	6¢ lake Garfield (256)	45.00	2.00	900.00	(6)		
282C	10¢ Webster, type I	160.00	2.00	2,500.00	(6)		
283	10¢ Webster, type II	90.00	1.75	1,500.00	(6)		
284	15¢ olive green Clay (259)	125.00	7.50	2,250.00	(6)		
	Trans-Mississippi Exposition Issue, June 17						
285	1¢ Marquette on the						
	Mississippi	27.50	5.50	325.00	(6)	*4,500.00*	70,993,400
286	2¢ Farming in the West	25.00	1.50	300.00	(6)	*4,000.00*	159,720,800
287	4¢ Indian Hunting Buffalo	140.00	22.50	1,700.00	(6)		4,924,500
288	5¢ Freemont on the Rocky Mts.	125.00	20.00	1,500.00	(6)	*5,000.00*	7,694,180
289	8¢ Troops Guarding Train	165.00	40.00	2,650.00	(6)	*7,500.00*	2,927,200
290	10¢ Hardships of Emigration	185.00	20.00	3,500.00	(6)		4,629,760
291	50¢ Western Mining						
	Prospector	725.00	165.00	*20,000.00*	(6)	*9,000.00*	530,400
292	$1 Western Cattle in Storm	1,750.00	625.00	*52,500.00*	(6)		56,900
293	$2 Mississippi River Bridge						
	at St. Louis	2,650.00	875.00	*115,000.00*	(6)		56,200
	Issue of 1901, Pan-American Exposition Issue, May 1, Wmkd. (191)						
294	1¢ Great Lakes Steamer	20.00	4.00	275.00	(6)	*3,500.00*	91,401.500
294a	Center inverted	*10,000.00*	*4,500.00*	*44,000.00*	(3)		
295	2¢ An Early Locomotive	20.00	1.10	275.00	(6)	*3,000.00*	209,759,700
295a	Center inverted	*45,000.00*	*13,500.00*				
296	4¢ Closed Coach Automobile	110.00	20.00	2,500.00	(6)	*4,250.00*	5,737.100
296a	Center inverted	*13,000.00*	—	*67,500.00*	(4)		
297	5¢ Bridge at Niagara Falls	125.00	20.00	2,750.00	(6)	*4,500.00*	7,201,300
298	8¢ Sault Ste. Marie						
	Canal Locks	150.00	75.00	4,750.00	(6)		4,921,700
299	10¢ American Line Steamship	225.00	35.00	7,500.00	(6)		5,043,700

282C   283   285   286

287   288   289

290   291   292

293   294   294a   295

295a   296   296a   297

 300

 301

 302

 303

 304

 305

 306

 307

 308

 309

 310

311

 312

313

 319

 323

 324

325

 326

327

	Issues of 1902-03, Perf. 12, Wmkd. (191)	Un	U	PB/LP	#	FDC	Q
300	1¢ Franklin, 1903	10.00	.05	185.00	(6)		
300b	Booklet pane of 6	500.00	250.00				
301	2¢ Washington, 1903	12.50	.05	200.00	(6)	2,750.00	
301c	Booklet pane of 6	425.00	250.00				
302	3¢ Jackson, 1903	45.00	3.00	850.00	(6)		
303	4¢ Grant, 1903	45.00	1.00	850.00	(6)		
304	5¢ Lincoln, 1903	55.00	1.00	950.00	(6)		
305	6¢ Garfield, 1903	60.00	2.25	1,000.00	(6)		
306	8¢ Martha Washington, 1902	35.00	2.00	700.00	(6)		
307	10¢ Webster, 1903	60.00	1.50	1,150.00	(6)		
308	13¢ Benjamin Harrison, 1902	35.00	8.50	650.00	(6)		
309	15¢ Clay, 1903	135.00	6.00	3,000.00	(6)		
310	50¢ Jefferson, 1903	450.00	25.00	7,500.00	(6)		
311	$1 David G. Farragut, 1903	800.00	60.00	16,500.00	(6)		
312	$2 Madison, 1903	1,050.00	200.00	25,000.00	(6)		
313	$5 Marshall, 1903	2,750.00	650.00	62,500.00	(6)		

For listings of #312 and 313 with Perf. 10, see #479 and 480.

	Issues of 1906-08, Imperf.						
314	1¢ bl. grn. Franklin (300), 1906	30.00	21.00	275.00	(6)		
314A	4¢ brown Grant (303), 1908	17,500.00	9,000.00				
315	5¢ blue Lincoln (304), 1908	550.00	250.00	4,750.00	(6)		

#314A was issued imperforate, but all copies were privately perforated with large oblong perforations at the sides. (Schermack type III).

	Coil Stamps, Perf. 12 Horizontally						
316	1¢ blue green pair						
	Franklin (300), 1908	22,500.00		55,000.00			
317	5¢ blue pair Lincoln (304), 1908	5,500.00		7,000.00			
	Perf. 12 Vertically						
318	1¢ blue green pair Franklin						
	(300), 1908	4,250.00	—	6,000.00			
	Issue of 1903, Perf. 12, Shield-shaped Background						
319	2¢ Washington, Nov. 12	6.00	.05	100.00	(6)		
319g	Booklet pane of 6	110.00	20.00				
	Issue of 1906, Washington (319), Imperf.						
320	2¢ carmine, Oct. 2	30.00	21.00	300.00	(6)		
	Issues of 1908, Coil Stamps (319), Perf. 12 Horizontally						
321	2¢ carmine pair, Feb. 18	35,000.00	—				
	Perf. 12 Vertically						
322	2¢ carmine pair, July 31	5,500.00	—	7,500.00			
	Issues of 1904, Louisiana Purchase Exposition Issue, Apr. 30, Perf. 12						
323	1¢ Robert R. Livingston	27.50	5.00	275.00	(6)	3,000.00	79,779,200
324	2¢ Thomas Jefferson	25.00	1.50	275.00	(6)	2,750.00	192,732,400
325	3¢ James Monroe	95.00	35.00	950.00	(6)	3,250.00	4,542,600
326	5¢ William McKinley	110.00	25.00	1,100.00	(6)	4,250.00	6,926,700
327	10¢ Map of Louisiana Pur.	190.00	35.00	2,500.00	(6)	6,500.00	4,011,200

	Issues of 1907	Un	U	PB/LP	#	FDC	Q
	Jamestown Exposition Issue, Apr. 26, Perf. 12						
328	1¢ Captain John Smith	20.00	4.00	300.00	(6)	*3,250.00*	77,728,794
329	2¢ Founding of Jamestown	27.50	3.00	425.00	(6)	*4,000.00*	149,497,994
330	5¢ Pocahontas	125.00	30.00	2,900.00	(6)		7,980,594
	Issues of 1908-09, Wmkd. (191)						
331	1¢ Franklin, Dec. 1908	8.00	.05	80.00	(6)		
331a	Booklet pane of 6	150.00	*35.00*				
332	2¢ Washington, Nov. 1908	7.50	.05	80.00	(6)		
332a	Booklet pane of 6	120.00	*35.00*				
333	3¢ Washington, type I,						
	Dec. 1908	30.00	3.00	350.00	(6)		
	#334-342: Washington (333)						
334	4¢ orange brown, Dec. 1908	35.00	1.00	375.00	(6)		
335	5¢ blue, Dec. 1908	47.50	2.00	600.00	(6)		
336	6¢ red orange, Jan. 1909	55.00	4.50	900.00	(6)		
337	8¢ olive green, Dec. 1908	40.00	2.50	475.00	(6)		
338	10¢ yellow, Jan. 1909	70.00	1.50	1,000.00	(6)		
339	13¢ blue green, Jan. 1909	37.50	25.00	475.00	(6)		
340	15¢ pale ultramarine,						
	Jan. 1909	60.00	5.75	650.00	(6)		
341	50¢ violet, Jan. 13, 1909	300.00	15.00	*7,500.00*	(6)		
342	$ 1 violet brown,						
	Jan. 29, 1909	450.00	90.00	*12,500.00*	(6)		
	Imperf.						
343	1¢ green Franklin (331), 1908	8.00	3.50	80.00	(6)		
344	2¢ car. Washington (332), 1908	11.00	3.00	145.00	(6)		
	#345-347: Washington (333)						
345	3¢ deep violet, type I, 1909	25.00	13.50	300.00	(6)		
346	4¢ orange brown, 1909	40.00	20.00	400.00	(6)		
347	5¢ blue, 1909	60.00	35.00	650.00	(6)		
	Issues of 1908-10, Coil Stamps, Perf. 12 Horizontally						
	#350-351, 354-356: Washington (333)						
348	1¢ green Franklin (331), 1908	22.50	13.00	175.00			
349	2¢ car. Washington (332), 1909	45.00	6.00	225.00			
350	4¢ orange brown, 1910	110.00	65.00	750.00			
351	5¢ blue, 1909	130.00	80.00	800.00			
	Issues of 1909, Coil Stamps, Perf. 12 Vertically						
352	1¢ green Franklin (331)	55.00	18.50	275.00			
353	2¢ car. Washington (332)	45.00	6.00	275.00			
354	4¢ orange brown	120.00	50.00	750.00			
355	5¢ blue	130.00	70.00	800.00			
356	10¢ yellow	1,300.00	375.00	7,500.00			
	Issues of 1909, Bluish Paper, Perf. 12						
	#359-366: Washington (333)						
357	1¢ green Franklin (331), Feb. 16	110.00	100.00	1,150.00	(6)		
358	2¢ car. Washington (332), Feb. 16	100.00	75.00	1,100.00	(6)		

328   329   330

331   332   333   334

335   336   337   338   342

367

368

370

371

372

373

		Un	U	PB/LP	#	FDC	Q
	1909 continued, Bluish Paper, Perf. 12						
359	3¢ deep violet, type I	1,650.00	1,250.00	16,500.00	(6)		
360	4¢ orange brown	14,000.00	—	60,000.00	(3)		
361	5¢ blue	3,500.00	4,000.00	35,000.00	(6)		
362	6¢ red orange	1,000.00	650.00	11,000.00	(6)		
363	8¢ olive green	14,000.00	—	55,000.00	(3)		
364	10¢ yellow	1,050.00	700.00	12,000.00	(6)		
365	13¢ blue green	2,100.00	1,100.00	17,500.00	(6)		
366	15¢ pale ultramarine	1,000.00	700.00	9,500.00	(6)		
	Lincoln Memorial Issue, Feb. 12						
367	2¢ Lincoln, Perf. 12	7.50	2.75	160.00	(6)	350.00	148,387,191
368	2¢ Lincoln, Imperf.	35.00	30.00	300.00	(6)	1,900.00	1,273,900
369	2¢ Lincoln, bluish paper, Perf. 12	275.00	200.00	4,250.00	(6)		637,000
	Alaska-Yukon Exposition Issue, June 1						
370	2¢ William Seward, Perf. 12	12.00	2.25	300.00	(6)	1,800.00	152,887,311
371	2¢ William Seward, Imperf.	50.00	35.00	400.00	(6)		525,400
	Hudson-Fulton Celebration Issue, Sept. 25						
372	2¢ Half Moon & Clermont, Perf. 12	16.00	4.75	350.00	(6)	850.00	72,634,631
373	2¢ Half Moon & Clermont, Imperf.	55.00	35.00	450.00	(6)	2,000.00	216,480
	Issues of 1910-13, Wmkd. (190)						
	#376-382: Washington (333)						
374	1¢ green Franklin (331), 1910	7.50	.06	85.00	(6)		
374a	Booklet pane of 6	135.00	30.00				
375	2¢ car. Washington (332), 1910	7.00	.05	85.00	(6)		
375a	Booklet pane of 6	110.00	25.00				
376	3¢ deep violet, type I, 1911	17.50	1.50	165.00	(6)		
377	4¢ brown, 1911	25.00	.50	250.00	(6)		
378	5¢ blue, 1911	25.00	.50	275.00	(6)		
379	6¢ red orange, 1911	35.00	.75	500.00	(6)		
380	8¢ olive green, 1911	115.00	13.50	1,250.00	(6)		
381	10¢ yellow, 1911	110.00	4.00	1,300.00	(6)		
382	15¢ pale ultramarine, 1911	260.00	15.00	2,500.00	(6)		
	Imperf.						
383	1¢ green Franklin (331), 1911	4.00	3.00	65.00	(6)		
384	2¢ car. Washington (332), 1911	6.00	2.00	200.00	(6)		
	Coil Stamps, Perf. 12 Horizontally						
385	1¢ green Franklin (331), 1910	25.00	12.00	200.00			
386	2¢ car. Washington (332), 1910	45.00	11.00	375.00			
	Perf. 12 Vertically						
387	1¢ green Franklin (331), 1910	75.00	22.50	350.00			
388	2¢ car. Washington (332), 1910	550.00	75.00	3,750.00			
389	3¢ dp. vio. Washington, type I (333), 1911	13,000.00	5,000.00	—			
	Perf. 8½ Horizontally						
390	1¢ green Franklin, (331), 1910	5.00	3.25	27.50			

	1910-13 continued, Perf. 8½ Horizontally, Wmkd. (190)	Un	U	PB/LP	#	FDC	Q
391	2¢ car. Washington (332), 1910	32.50	8.50	175.00			
	Perf. 8½ Vertically						
	#394-396: Washington (333)						
392	1¢ green Franklin (331), 1910	20.00	15.00	110.00			
393	2¢ car. Washington (332), 1910	40.00	6.00	200.00			
394	3¢ deep violet, type I, 1911	50.00	27.50	300.00			
395	4¢ brown, 1912	50.00	27.50	300.00			
396	5¢ blue, 1913	50.00	27.50	300.00			
	Issues of 1913, Panama Pacific Exposition Issue, Perf. 12						
397	1¢ Balboa	17.50	1.75	175.00	(6)	3,250.00	167,398,463
398	2¢ Locks, Panama Canal	20.00	.50	300.00	(6)		251,856,543
399	5¢ Golden Gate	80.00	11.00	2,250.00	(6)	4,000.00	14,544,363
400	10¢ Discovery, San Fran. Bay	150.00	25.00	3,000.00	(6)		8,484,182
400A	10¢ orange (400)	250.00	20.00	9,500.00	(6)		
	1914-15, Perf. 10						
401	1¢ green Balboa (397), 1914	27.50	6.50	375.00	(6)		167,398,463
402	2¢ carmine Canal Locks						
	(398), 1915	90.00	1.50	1,850.00	(6)		251,856,543
403	5¢ blue Golden Gate (399), 1915	190.00	17.50	4,500.00	(6)		14,544,363
404	10¢ orange Discovery of						
	San Francisco Bay (400), 1915	1,400.00	70.00	15,000.00	(6)		8,484,182
	Issues of 1912-14, Perf. 12						
	#405-413: Washington (333)						
405	1¢ green, 1912	7.50	.06	115.00	(6)		
405b	Booklet pane of 6	65.00	7.50				
406	2¢ carmine, type I, 1912	6.00	.05	140.00	(6)		
406a	Booklet pane of 6	70.00	17.50				
407	7¢ black, 1914	100.00	8.00	1,250.00	(6)		
408	1¢ green, Imperf., 1912	1.50	.60	25.00	(6)		
409	2¢ carmine, type I, Imperf., 1912	1.65	.60	50.00	(6)		
	Coil Stamps. Perf. 8½ Horizontally						
410	1¢ green, 1912	6.25	3.50	35.00			
411	2¢ carmine, type I, 1912	7.75	3.75	42.50			
	Perf. 8½ Vertically						
412	1¢ green, 1912	21.00	5.00	90.00			
413	2¢ carmine, type I, 1912	35.00	.60	165.00			
	Perf. 12						
	#414-423: Franklin (414)						
414	8¢ Franklin, 1912	37.50	1.50	475.00	(6)		
415	9¢ salmon red, 1914	50.00	15.00	750.00	(6)		
416	10¢ orange yellow, 1912	37.50	.30	525.00	(6)		
417	12¢ claret brown, 1914	45.00	4.50	550.00	(6)		
418	15¢ gray, 1912	75.00	3.50	850.00	(6)		
419	20¢ ultramarine, 1914	175.00	16.00	2,000.00	(6)		
420	30¢ orange red, 1914	120.00	16.00	1,750.00	(6)		

397   398   399   400

405   406   414   420

	1912-14 continued, Perf. 12	Un	U	PB/LP	#	FDC	Q
	#421-423: Franklin (414), Wmkd. (190)						
421	50¢ violet, Apr. 29, 1914,	500.00	17.50	9,000.00	(6)		
	Wmkd. (191)						
422	50¢ violet, Feb. 12, 1912	250.00	17.50	5,500.00	(6)		
423	$1 violet brown, Feb. 12, 1912	575.00	70.00	*12,500.00*	(6)		
	Issues of 1914-15, Perf. 10, Wmkd. (190)						
	#424-430: Washington (333)						
424	1¢ green, Sept. 5, 1914	2.75	.06	45.00	(6)		
424d	Booklet pane of 6	4.00	.75				
425	2¢ rose red, type I, Sept. 5, 1914	2.50	.05	30.00	(6)		
425e	Booklet pane of 6	15.00	*3.00*				
426	3¢ deep violet, type I,						
	Sept. 18, 1914	12.50	1.25	135.00	(6)		
427	4¢ brown, Sept. 7, 1914	35.00	.40	400.00	(6)		
428	5¢ blue, Sept. 14, 1914	27.50	.40	285.00	(6)		
429	6¢ red orange, Sept. 28, 1914	37.50	1.20	350.00	(6)		
430	7¢ black, Sept. 10, 1914	90.00	4.25	850.00	(6)		
	#431-440: Franklin (414)						
431	8¢ pale olive green,						
	Sept. 26, 1914	37.50	1.50	400.00	(6)		
432	9¢ salmon red, Oct. 6, 1914	47.50	.25	550.00	(6)		
433	10¢ orange yellow, Sept. 9, 1914	45.00	.25	550.00	(6)		
434	11¢ dark green, Aug. 11, 1915	22.50	7.00	200.00	(6)		
435	12¢ claret brown, Sept. 10, 1914	25.00	4.50	250.00	(6)		
437	15¢ gray, Sept. 16, 1914	115.00	7.25	850.00	(6)		
438	20¢ ultramarine, Sept. 19, 1914	225.00	4.00	2,500.00	(6)		
439	30¢ orange red, Sept. 19, 1914	275.00	20.00	3,500.00	(6)		
440	50¢ violet, Dec. 10, 1914	800.00	20.00	11,000.00	(6)		
	Issues of 1914, Coil Stamps, Perf. 10 Horizontally						
	#441-459: Washington (333)						
441	1¢ green, Nov. 14	1.00	.90	7.50			
442	2¢ carmine, type I, July 22	10.00	7.50	55.00			
	Perf. 10 Vertically						
443	1¢ green, May 29	22.50	6.00	110.00			
444	2¢ carmine, type I, Apr. 25	30.00	1.50	175.00			
445	3¢ violet, type I, Dec. 18	225.00	110.00	1,100.00			
446	4¢ brown, Oct. 2	130.00	35.00	650.00			
447	5¢ blue, July 30	45.00	22.50	225.00			
	Issues of 1915-16, Coil Stamps, Perf. 10 Horizontally						
448	1¢ green, Dec. 12, 1915	8.50	3.00	45.00			
449	2¢ red, type I, Dec. 5, 1915	1,600.00	160.00	7,500.00			
450	2¢ carmine, type III, Feb., 1916	12.00	3.00	60.00			
	Issues of 1914-16, Coil Stamps, Perf. 10 Vertically						
452	1¢ green, Nov. 11, 1914	12.00	1.75	72.50			
453	2¢ red, type I, July 3, 1914	120.00	4.50	575.00			

	1914-16 continued, Coil Stamps, Perf. 10 Vertically	Un	U	PB/LP	#	FDC	Q
454	2¢ carmine, type II, June 1915	115.00	13.50	575.00			
455	2¢ carmine, type III, Dec. 1915	10.00	1.00	60.00			
456	3¢ violet, type I, Feb. 18, 1916	300.00	95.00	1,300.00			
457	4¢ brown, Feb. 18, 1916	30.00	18.00	165.00			
458	5¢ blue, Mar. 9, 1916	30.00	18.00	165.00			
	Issue of 1914, Imperf., Coil						
459	2¢ carmine, type I, June 30	450.00	*600.00*	2,100.00			
	Issues of 1915, Perf. 10, Wmkd. (191)						
460	$1 violet black Franklin						
	(414), Feb. 8	975.00	95.00	*12,500.00*	(6)		
	Perf. 11						
461	2¢ pale carmine red, type I,						
	Washington (333), June 17	100.00	85.00	950.00	(6)		
	Privately perforated copies of #409 have been made to resemble #461.						
	From 1916 to date, all postage stamps except #519 and #832b are on unwatermarked paper.						
	Issues of 1916-17, Perf. 10, Unwmkd.						
	#462-469: Washington (333)						
462	1¢ green, Sept. 27, 1916	8.50	.20	150.00	(6)		
462a	Booklet pane of 6	12.00	*1.00*				
463	2¢ carmine, type I, Sept. 25, 1916	4.25	.10	120.00	(6)		
463a	Booklet pane of 6	85.00	*20.00*				
464	3¢ violet, type I, Nov. 11, 1916	80.00	11.00	1,350.00	(6)		
465	4¢ orange brown, Oct. 7, 1916	40.00	1.75	650.00	(6)		
466	5¢ blue, Oct. 17, 1916	75.00	1.75	900.00	(6)		
467	5¢ carmine						
	(error in plate of 2¢) Mar. 7, 1917	750.00	525.00	135.00	(6)		
468	6¢ red orange, Oct. 10, 1916	95.00	7.50	1,150.00	(6)		
469	7¢ black, Oct. 10, 1916	125.00	13.00	1,350.00	(6)		
	#470-478: Franklin (414)						
470	8¢ olive green, Nov. 13, 1916	55.00	6.50	525.00	(6)		
471	9¢ salmon red, Nov. 16, 1916	60.00	16.00	650.00	(6)		
472	10¢ orange yellow, Oct. 17, 1916	110.00	1.00	1,350.00	(6)		
473	11¢ dark green, Nov. 16, 1916	30.00	17.50	325.00	(6)		
474	12¢ claret brown, Oct. 10, 1916	50.00	5.00	550.00	(6)		
475	15¢ gray, Nov. 16, 1916	175.00	12.00	2,500.00	(6)		
476	20¢ light ultramarine,						
	Dec. 5, 1916	250.00	12.50	3,500.00	(6)		
477	50¢ light violet, Mar. 2, 1917	1,400.00	75.00	*25,000.00*	(6)		
478	$1 violet black, Dec. 22, 1916	950.00	20.00	*13,000.00*	(6)		
	Issues of 1917, Perf. 10, Mar. 22						
479	$2 dark blue Madison (312)	500.00	45.00	6,000.00	(6)		
480	$5 light green Marshall (313)	400.00	47.50	4,500.00	(6)		

	Issues of 1916-17, Imperf., Unwmkd.	Un	U	PB/LP	#	FDC	Q
	#481-496: Washington (333)						
481	1¢ green, Nov. 1916	1.00	.75	15.00	(6)		
482	2¢ carmine, type I, Dec. 8, 1916	1.25	1.25	25.00	(6)		
482a	2¢ deep rose, type 1a	—	6,000.00				
483	3¢ violet, type I, Oct. 13, 1917	15.00	8.50	175.00	(6)		
484	3¢ violet, type II, Oct. 13, 1917	11.00	4.00	135.00	(6)		
485	5¢ carmine (2¢ error), Mar. 1917	13,000		300.00	(6)		
	Issues of 1916-19, Coil Stamps, Perf. 10 Horizontally						
486	1¢ green, Jan. 1918	1.00	.15	4.50			
487	2¢ carmine, type II, Nov. 15, 1916	18.00	2.50	135.00			
488	2¢ carmine, type III, 1919	3.00	1.50	20.00			
489	3¢ violet, type I, Oct. 10, 1917	6.00	1.00	35.00			
	Issues of 1916-22, Coil Stamps, Perf. 10 Vertically						
490	1¢ green, Nov. 17, 1916	.75	.15	4.75			
491	2¢ carmine, type II,						
	Nov. 17, 1916	1,450.00	225.00	7,000.00			
492	2¢ carmine, type III, 1916	10.00	.15	55.00			
493	3¢ violet, type I, July 23, 1917	21.00	3.00	140.00			
494	3¢ violet, type II, Feb. 4, 1918	11.50	.60	75.00			
495	4¢ orange brown, Apr. 15, 1917	12.50	3.50	85.00			
496	5¢ blue, Jan. 15, 1919	4.50	.60	30.00			
497	10¢ or. yel. Franklin						
	(414), Jan. 31, 1922	26.50	8.50	150.00		1,750.00	
	Issues of 1917-19, Perf. 11						
	#498-507: Washington (333)						
498	1¢ green, Mar. 1917	.25	.05	15.00	(6)		
498e	Booklet pane of 6, Apr. 6, 1917	1.75	.35				
498f	Booklet pane of 30	550.00					
499	2¢ rose, type I, Mar. 1917	.25	.05	14.00	(6)		
499e	Booklet pane of 6, Mar. 31, 1917	2.00	.50				
499f	Booklet pane of 30	8,500.00					
500	2¢ deep rose, type Ia, 1917	275.00	130.00	2,250.00	(6)		
501	3¢ light violet, type I, Mar. 1917	17.50	.10	175.00	(6)		
501b	Booklet pane of 6,						
	Oct. 17, 1917	75.00	15.00				
502	3¢ dark violet, type II, 1917	20.00	.25	210.00	(6)		
502b	Booklet pane of 6,						
	Feb. 25, 1918	50.00	10.00				
503	4¢ brown, Mar. 1917	13.00	.20	175.00	(6)		
504	5¢ blue, Mar. 1917	10.00	.08	140.00	(6)		
505	5¢ rose (error in plate of 2¢)						
	Mar. 23, 1917	550.00	400.00	35.00	(6)		
506	6¢ red orange, Mar. 1917	15.00	.30	210.00	(6)		
507	7¢ black, Mar. 1917	32.50	1.50	325.00	(6)		

	1917-19 continued, Unwmkd., Perf. 11	Un	U	PB/LP	#	FDC	Q
	#508-518: Franklin (414)						
508	8¢ olive bistre, Mar. 1917	13.50	.70	200.00	(6)		
509	9¢ salmon red, Mar. 1917	17.50	2.75	190.00	(6)		
510	10¢ orange yellow, Mar. 1917	20.00	.10	250.00	(6)		
511	11¢ light green, May 1917	10.00	3.75	120.00	(6)		
512	12¢ claret brown, May 1917	10.50	.45	140.00	(6)		
513	13¢ apple green, Jan. 10, 1919	12.00	7.00	135.00	(6)		
514	15¢ gray, May 1917	47.50	1.00	650.00	(6)		
515	20¢ light ultramarine, May 1917	60.00	.30	750.00	(6)		
516	30¢ orange red, May 1917	47.50	.95	575.00	(6)		
517	50¢ red violet, May 1917	90.00	.65	1,350.00	(6)		
518	$1 violet brown, May 1917	75.00	1.75	1,200.00	(6)		
	Issue of 1917, Wmkd. (191)						
519	2¢ carmine Washington						
	(332), Oct. 10	250.00	275.00	2,500.00	(6)		
	Privately perforated copies of #344 have been made to resemble #519.						
520-22 not assigned.							
	Issues of 1918, Aug., Unwmkd.						
523	$2 orange red and black						
	Franklin (547)	1,100.00	200.00	*18,500.00*	(8)		
524	$5 deep green and black						
	Franklin (547)	450.00	30.00	*6,000.00*	(8)		
	Issues of 1918-20						
	#525-535: Washington (333)						
525	1¢ gray green, Dec. 1918	2.25	.60	30.00	(6)		
526	2¢ carmine, type IV, 1920	30.00	4.00	250.00	(6)	*800.00*	
527	2¢ carmine, type V, 1920	17.50	1.00	150.00	(6)		
528	2¢ carmine, type Va, 1920	8.00	.15	65.00	(6)		
528A	2¢ carmine, type VI, 1920	50.00	1.00	375.00	(6)		
528B	2¢ carmine, type VII, 1920	20.00	.12	160.00	(6)		
529	3¢ violet, type III, 1918	3.00	.10	70.00	(6)		
530	3¢ purple, type IV, 1918	.70	.06	12.00	(6)		
	Imperf.						
531	1¢ green, Jan. 1919	10.00	8.00	100.00	(6)		
532	2¢ car. rose, type IV, 1919	47.50	27.50	350.00	(6)		
533	2¢ carmine, type V, 1919	235.00	70.00	2,000.00	(6)		
534	2¢ carmine, type Va, 1919	12.50	9.00	110.00	(6)		
534A	2¢ carmine, type VI, 1919	40.00	25.00	350.00	(6)		
534B	2¢ carmine, type VII, 1919	1,550.00	425.00	*12,500.00*	(6)		
535	3¢ violet, type IV, 1918	8.50	6.50	70.00	(6)		
	Issues of 1919, Perf. 12½						
536	1¢ gray green Washington						
	(333), Aug.	15.00	13.50	200.00	(6)		

	1919 continued, Perf. 11	Un	U	PB/LP	#	FDC	Q
537	3¢ Allied Victory, Mar. 3	11.00	4.25	150.00	(6)	*700.00*	99,585,200
	#538-546: Washington (333), 1919						
	Perf. 11x10						
538	1¢ green	10.00	9.00	110.00	(4)		
539	2¢ carmine rose, type II	2,350.00	750.00	*15,000.00*	(4)		
540	2¢ carmine rose, type III	11.00	9.00	115.00	(4)		
541	3¢ violet, type II	37.50	35.00	400.00	(4)		
	Issue of 1920, Perf. 10x11						
542	1¢ green, May 26	10.00	1.00	165.00	(6)	*700.00*	
	Issue of 1921, Perf. 10						
543	1¢ green	.60	.06	20.00	(4)		
	Perf. 11						
544	1¢ green, 19x22½ mm	6,500.00	1,500.00				
545	1¢ green, 19½-20x22mm	135.00	110.00	1,150.00	(4)		
546	2¢ carmine rose, type III	100.00	90.00	875.00	(4)		
	Issues of 1920						
547	$2 Franklin	400.00	40.00	7,000.00	(8)		
	Pilgrim Tercentenary, Dec. 21						
548	1¢ Mayflower	5.50	3.00	55.00	(6)	*700.00*	137,978,207
549	2¢ Pilgrims Landing	8.50	2.25	80.00	(6)	*625.00*	196,037,327
550	5¢ Signing of Compact	52.50	18.50	650.00	(6)		11,321,607
	Issues of 1922-25						
551	5¢ Nathan Hale, 1925	.15	.06	7.00	(6)	22.50	
552	1¢ Franklin (19x22mm), 1923	2.25	.05	25.00	(6)	32.50	
552a	Booklet pane of 6	5.50	.50				
553	1½¢ Harding, 1925	3.50	.20	40.00	(6)	35.00	
554	2¢ Washington, 1923	1.75	.05	25.00	(6)	45.00	
554c	Booklet pane of 6	7.00	1.00				
555	3¢ Lincoln, 1923	21.00	1.25	210.00	(6)	37.50	
556	4¢ Martha Washington, 1923	22.50	.20	225.00	(6)	50.00	
557	5¢ Theodore Roosevelt, 1922	22.50	.08	250.00	(6)	*125.00*	
558	6¢ Garfield, 1922	40.00	.85	425.00	(6)	200.00	
559	7¢ McKinley, 1923	10.00	.75	90.00	(6)	100.00	
560	8¢ Grant, 1923	55.00	.85	725.00	(6)	100.00	
561	9¢ Jefferson, 1923	17.00	1.25	210.00	(6)	100.00	
562	10¢ Monroe, 1923	22.50	.10	300.00	(6)	100.00	
563	11¢ Rutherford B. Hayes, 1922	2.00	.25	35.00	(6)	550.00	
564	12¢ Grover Cleveland, 1923	8.50	.08	90.00	(6)	*135.00*	
565	14¢ American Indian, 1923	5.00	.85	60.00	(6)	300.00	
566	15¢ Statue of Liberty, 1922	22.50	.06	275.00	(6)	350.00	
567	20¢ Golden Gate, 1923	25.00	.06	300.00	(6)	*400.00*	
568	25¢ Niagara Falls, 1922	22.50	.50	250.00	(6)	*600.00*	
569	30¢ Buffalo, 1923	45.00	.35	450.00	(6)	*725.00*	

537   547   548   549

550   551   552   553   554

555   556   557   558   559

560   561   562   563   564

565   566   567   568   569

570   571   572   573

610   611

	1922-25 continued, Perf. 11	Un	U	PB/LP	#	FDC	Q
570	50¢ Arlington Amphitheater,						
	1922	75.00	.12	900.00	(6)	1,000.00	
571	$1 Lincoln Memorial, 1923	50.00	.45	500.00	(6)	4,000.00	
572	$2 U.S. Capitol, 1923	145.00	11.00	1,650.00	(6)	10,000.00	
573	$5 Head of Freedom,						
	Capitol Dome, 1923	375.00	15.00	5,500.00	(8)	11,000.00	
574 not assigned							
	Issues of 1923-25, Imperf.						
575	1¢ green Franklin (552), 1923	10.00	3.50	100.00	(6)		
576	1½¢ yel. brown Harding						
	(553), 1925	2.25	1.75	30.00	(6)		45.00
577	2¢ carmine Washington (554)	2.50	2.00	30.00	(6)		
	For listings of other perforated stamps of issues 551-573 see:						
	#578 and 579	Perf. 11x10					
	#581 to 591	Perf. 10					
	#594 and 595	Perf. 11					
	#622 and 623	Perf. 11					
	#632 to 642, 653, 692 to 696	Perf. 11x10½					
	#697 to 701	Perf. 10½x11					
	Perf. 11x10						
578	1¢ green Franklin (552)	80.00	65.00	750.00	(4)		
579	2¢ carmine Washington (554)	57.50	50.00	450.00	(4)		
580 not assigned							

	Issues of 1923-26, Perf. 10	Un	U	PB/LP	#	FDC	Q
581	1¢ green Franklin (552), 1923	9.50	.65	125.00	(4)	*2,000.00*	
582	1½¢ brown Harding (553), 1925	5.00	.60	45.00	(4)	47.50	
583	2¢ car. Washington (554), 1924	2.50	.05	30.00	(4)		
583a	Booklet pane of 6	75.00	*25.00*				
584	3¢ violet Lincoln (555), 1925	27.50	1.75	250.00	(4)	55.00	
585	4¢ yellow brown						
	M. Washington (556), 1925	17.00	.40	175.00	(4)	*55.00*	
586	5¢ blue T. Roosevelt (557), 1925	16.00	.18	165.00	(4)	55.00	
587	6¢ red or. Garfield (558), 1925	7.50	.40	70.00	(4)	70.00	
588	7¢ black McKinley (559), 1926	11.50	5.00	110.00	(4)	70.00	
589	8¢ olive green Grant (560), 1926	26.00	3.00	250.00	(4)	72.50	
590	9¢ rose Jefferson, (561), 1926	4.50	2.25	45.00	(4)	75.00	
591	10¢ or. Monroe (562), 1925	70.00	.10	650.00	(4)	100.00	
	592-93 not assigned.						
	Perf. 11						
594	1¢ green Franklin,						
	19¾x22¼mm (552)	*7,000.00*	1,850.00				
595	2¢ carmine Washington,						
	19¾x22¼mm (554)	200.00	175.00	1,500.00	(4)		
596	1¢ green Franklin,						
	19¼x22¾mm (552)	—	*13,500.00*				
	Issues of 1923-29, Coil Stamps, Perf. 10 Vertically						
597	1¢ green Franklin (552), 1923	.35	.06	2.25		*450.00*	
598	1½¢ br. Harding (553), 1925	.75	.10	5.25		55.00	
599	2¢ carmine Washington,						
	type I (554), 1929	.30	.05	2.00		*850.00*	
599A	2¢ carmine Washington,						
	type II (554), 1929	140.00	12.00	800.00			
600	3¢ violet Lincoln (555)	8.00	.08	35.00		72.50	
601	4¢ yellow brown						
	M. Washington (556), 1923	4.00	.40	27.50			
602	5¢ dark blue						
	T. Roosevelt (557), 1924	1.50	.18	9.00		75.00	
603	10¢ or. Monroe (562), 1924	4.00	.08	27.50		95.00	
	Perf. 10 Horizontally						
604	1¢ yel. grn. Franklin (552), 1924	.25	.08	3.00		85.00	
605	1½¢ yel. brn. Harding (553), 1925	.30	.15	2.75		55.00	
606	2¢ car. Washington (554), 1923	.30	.12	2.00		80.00	
	607-09 not assigned.						
	Issues of 1923, Harding Memorial Issue, Flat Plate Printing (19¼x22¼mm)						
610	2¢ Harding, Perf. 11, Sept. 1	.75	.10	30.00	(6)	40.00	1,459,487,085
611	2¢ Harding Imperf., Nov. 15	12.00	6.00	140.00	(6)	100.00	770,000
	Rotary Press Printing (19¼x22¾mm)						
612	2¢ blk. Perf. 10 (610), Sept. 12	25.00	2.50	350.00	(4)	110.00	99,950,300
613	2¢ black Perf. 11 (610)	—	*13,500.00*				

	Issues of 1924	Un	U	PB/LP	#	FDC	Q
	Huguenot-Walloon 300th Anniversary Issue, May 1, Perf. 11						
614	1¢ Ship *New Netherland*	4.50	4.50	50.00	(6)	27.50	51,378,023
615	2¢ Landing at Fort Orange	7.50	3.50	85.00	(6)	35.00	77,753,423
616	5¢ Huguenot Monument, FL	45.00	22.50	450.00	(6)	70.00	5,659,023
	Issues of 1925						
	Lexington-Concord Issue, Apr. 4						
617	1¢ Washington at Cambridge	4.50	4.50	50.00	(6)	27.50	15,615,000
618	2¢ Birth of Liberty	8.00	7.50	95.00	(6)	35.00	26,596,600
619	5¢ Statue of Minute Man	40.00	20.00	400.00	(6)	50.00	5,348,800
	Norse-American Issue, May 18						
620	2¢ Sloop *Restaurationen*	7.00	5.00	250.00	(8)	25.00	9,104,983
621	5¢ Viking Ship	22.50	21.00	750.00	(8)	45.00	1,900,983
	Issues of 1925-26						
622	13¢ Benjamin Harrison, 1926	17.50	.65	200.00	(6)	35.00	
623	17¢ Woodrow Wilson, 1925	25.00	.35	250.00	(6)	30.00	
	Issues of 1926						
627	2¢ Independence,						
	150th Anniv., May 10	4.00	.60	50.00	(6)	14.00	307,731,900
628	5¢ Ericsson Memorial, May 29	10.00	5.00	110.00	(6)	22.50	20,280,500
629	2¢ Battle of White Plains,						
	Oct. 18	2.50	2.25	50.00	(6)	6.25	40,639,485

Benjamin Harrison

Benjamin Harrison (#622), the 23rd president of the United States, was part of an American political dynasty that began with his great-grandfather, who signed the Declaration of Independence. His grandfather, William Henry Harrison, was our ninth president. Nonetheless, when Benjamin became interested in public service, his congressman father warned him that "only knaves enter politics."

Harrison took office in 1889 and was dubbed the "centennial president" because he served 100 years after George Washington. He made notable contributions in several areas, including civil service reform. He also sought a more active role for the United States in foreign affairs, and it was under Harrison that the first legislation regulating business— the Sherman Antitrust Act—was passed.

614

615

616

617

618

619

620

621

622

623

627

628

629

83

631 633 643

644 645 646 647 648

649 650

651 654

	1926 continued	Un	U	PB/LP	#	FDC	Q
	International Philatelic Exhibition Issue, Oct. 18, Souvenir Sheet, Perf. 11						
630	2¢ car. rose, sheet of 25 with						
	selvage inscription (629)	500.00	425.00			1,500.00	107,398
	Imperf.						
631	1½¢ Harding, Aug. 27,						
	(18½-19x22½mm)	2.25	2.10	70.00	(4)	35.00	
	Issues of 1926-27, Perf. 11x10½						
632	1¢ green Franklin (552), 1927	.15	.05	2.00	(4)	55.00	
632a	Booklet pane of 6	2.50	.25				
633	1½¢ Harding, 1927	2.50	.08	90.00	(4)	55.00	
634	2¢ carmine Washington, type I						
	(554), 1926	.15	.05	1.20	(4)	57.50	
634d	Booklet pane of 6, 1927	1.00	.15				
634A	2¢ carmine Washington, type II						
	(554), 1926	350.00	25.00	2,100.00	(4)		
635	3¢ violet Lincoln (555), 1927	.50	.05	4.00	(4)	47.50	
636	4¢ yellow brown						
	M. Washington (556), 1927	3.50	.08	100.00	(4)	55.00	
637	5¢ dk. bl. T. Roosevelt (557), 1927	3.00	.05	21.00	(4)	55.00	
638	6¢ red Garfield (558), 1927	3.00	.05	21.00	(4)	65.00	
639	7¢ black McKinley (559), 1927	3.00	.08	21.00	(4)	67.50	
640	8¢ olive green Grant (560), 1927	3.00	.05	21.00	(4)	70.00	
641	9¢ or. red Jefferson (561), 1927	3.00	.05	21.00	(4)	85.00	
642	10¢ orange Monroe (562), 1927	5.50	.05	35.00	(4)	90.00	
	Issues of 1927, Perf. 11						
643	2¢ Vermont 150th Anniv., Aug. 3	1.50	1.65	40.00	(6)	6.00	39,974,900
644	2¢ Burgoyne Campaign, Aug. 3	5.00	3.75	65.00	(6)	16.50	25,628,450
	Issues of 1928						
645	2¢ Valley Forge, May 26	1.10	.65	40.00	(6)	5.00	101,330,328
	Perf. 11x10½						
646	2¢ Battle of Monmouth, Oct. 20	1.50	1.50	40.00	(4)	17.50	9,779,896
647	2¢ carmine, Aug. 13	7.00	6.00	150.00	(4)	17.50	5,519,897
648	5¢ Hawaii 150th Anniv., Aug. 13	20.00	17.50	300.00	(4)	32.50	1,459,897
	Aeronautics Conference Issue, Dec. 12, Perf. 11						
649	2¢ Wright Airplane	1.50	1.40	17.50	(6)	10.00	51,342,273
650	5¢ Globe and Airplane	8.50	5.00	90.00	(6)	15.00	10,319,700
	Issues of 1929						
651	2¢ George Rogers Clark, Feb. 25	.85	.80	16.00	(6)	7.50	16,684,674
652 not assigned.							
	Perf. 11x10½						
653	½¢ olive brown Nathan Hale						
	(551), May 25	.05	.05	1.00	(4)	30.00	
	Electric Light Jubilee, Perf. 11						
654	2¢ Edison's First Lamp, June 5	.90	1.00	35.00	(6)	13.00	31,679,200
	Perf. 11x10½						
655	2¢ carmine rose (654), June 11	.85	.25	55.00	(4)	90.00	210,119,474

	1929 continued, Coil Stamp, Perf. 10 Vertically	Un	U	PB/LP	#	FDC	Q
656	2¢ carmine rose (654), June 11	20.00	2.00	90.00		100.00	133,530,000
	Perf. 11						
657	2¢ Sullivan Expedition, June 17	1.00	.90	35.00	(6)	4.50	51,451,880
	Issues of 1929, 658-668 Overprinted Kans., May 1, Perf. 11x10½						
658	1¢ green Franklin	2.00	1.65	25.00	(4)	27.50	13,390,000
659	1½¢ brown Harding (553)	3.00	3.00	40.00	(4)	27.50	8,240,000
660	2¢ carmine Washington (554)	3.00	.65	40.00	(4)	27.50	87,410,000
661	3¢ violet Lincoln (555)	17.50	12.00	175.00	(4)	30.00	2,540,000
662	4¢ yellow brown						
	M. Washington (556)	17.50	7.50	175.00	(4)	32.50	2,290,000
663	5¢ deep blue T. Roosevelt						
	(557)	13.00	9.00	150.00	(4)	35.00	2,700,000
664	6¢ red orange Garfield (558)	27.50	17.50	400.00	(4)	42.50	1,450,000
665	7¢ black McKinley (559)	27.50	22.50	400.00	(4)	42.50	1,320,000
666	8¢ olive green Grant (560)	85.00	72.50	800.00	(4)	80.00	1,530,000
667	9¢ light rose Jefferson (561)	13.00	11.00	175.00	(4)	72.50	1,130,000
668	10¢ orange yel. Monroe (562)	21.00	11.00	325.00	(4)	85.00	2,860,000
	669-679 Overprinted Nebr., May 1						
669	1¢ green Franklin	2.00	2.00	25.00	(4)	27.50	8,220,000
670	1½¢ brown Harding (553)	3.00	2.25	40.00	(4)	25.00	8,990,000
671	2¢ carmine Washington (554)	2.00	.85	25.00	(4)	25.00	73,220,000
672	3¢ violet Lincoln (555)	12.00	8.75	150.00	(4)	32.50	2,110,000
673	4¢ yellow brown						
	M. Washington (556)	17.50	11.00	200.00	(4)	37.50	1,600,000
674	5¢ deep blue T. Roosevelt						
	(557)	16.00	13.50	210.00	(4)	37.50	1,860,000
675	6¢ red orange Garfield (558)	40.00	19.00	500.00	(4)	55.00	980,000
676	7¢ black McKinley (559)	21.00	15.00	275.00	(4)	57.50	850,000
677	8¢ olive green Grant (560)	30.00	22.50	375.00	(4)	60.00	1,480,000
678	9¢ light rose Jefferson (561)	35.00	25.00	400.00	(4)	62.50	530,000
679	10¢ orange yel. Monroe (562)	100.00	17.50	900.00	(4)	70.00	1,890,000
	Warning: Excellent forgeries of the Kansas and Nebraska overprints exist.						
	Perf. 11						
680	2¢ Battle of Fallen Timbers,						
	Sept. 14	1.00	1.00	40.00	(6)	5.00	29,338,274
681	2¢ Ohio River Canal, Oct. 19	.80	.80	32.50	(6)	4.50	32,680,900
	Issues of 1930						
682	2¢ Mass. Bay Colony, Apr. 8	.80	.60	40.00	(6)	5.25	74,000,774
683	2¢ Carolina-Charleston,						
	Apr. 10	1.65	1.60	65.00	(6)	5.50	25,215,574
	Perf. 11x10½						
684	1½¢ Warren G. Harding	.25	.05	1.50	(4)	6.25	
685	4¢ William H. Taft	.75	.06	10.00	(4)	10.00	

656 (Coil Pair) 657 658 669 680

681 682 683 684 685

688

689

690

702

703

704

705

706

707

708

709

710

711

712

713

714

715

716

717

	1930 continued, Coil Stamps, Perf. 10 Vertically	Un	U	PB/LP	#	FDC	Q
686	1½¢ brown Harding (684)	2.10	.07	7.00		7.50	
687	4¢ brown Taft (685)	4.00	.50	'12.50		30.00	
	Perf. 11						
688	2¢ Braddock's Field, July 9	1.40	1.40	55.00	(6)	6.00	25,609,470
689	2¢ von Steuben, Sept. 17	.80	.75	35.00	(6)	6.00	66,487,000
	Issues of 1931						
690	2¢ Pulaski, Jan. 16	.25	.18	17.50	(6)	5.00	96,559,400
691 not assigned							
	Perf. 11x10½						
692	11¢ light blue Hayes (563)	3.00	.10	19.00	(4)	80.00	
693	12¢ br. vio. Cleveland (564)	6.50	.06	35.00	(4)	80.00	
694	13¢ yellow gr. Harrison (622)	2.50	.10	18.00	(4)	85.00	
695	14¢ dark blue Indian (565)	4.00	.30	25.00	(4)	85.00	
696	15¢ gray Statue of Liberty						
	(566)	10.00	.06	60.00	(4)	100.00	
	Perf. 10½x11						
697	17¢ black Wilson (623)	5.00	.25	30.00	(4)	325.00	
698	20¢ car. rose Golden Gate						
	(567)	12.00	.05	65.00	(4)	185.00	
699	25¢ blue green Niagara						
	Falls (568)	11.00	.08	62.50	(4)	350.00	
700	30¢ brown Buffalo (569)	18.50	.07	100.00	(4)	275.00	
701	50¢ lilac Amphitheater (570)	55.00	.07	300.00	(4)	425.00	
	Perf. 11						
702	2¢ Red Cross, May 21	.15	.12	2.25	(4)	4.00	99,074,600
703	2¢ Yorktown, Oct. 12	.40	.35	3.50	(4)	5.00	25,006,400
	Issues of 1932, Washington Bicentennial Issue, Jan., 1, Perf. 11x10½						
704	½¢ Portrait by Charles W. Peale	.08	.05	4.00	(4)	5.00	87,969,700
705	1¢ Bust by Jean Antoine Houdon	.13	.05	5.00	(4)	5.50	1,265,555,100
706	1½¢ Portrait by Charles W. Peale	.55	.08	22.50	(4)	5.50	304,926,800
707	2¢ Portrait by Gilbert Stuart	.10	.05	1.50	(4)	5.50	4,222,198,300
708	3¢ Portrait by Charles W. Peale	.60	.06	16.00	(4)	5.75	456,198,500
709	4¢ Portrait by Charles P. Polk	.25	.06	5.00	(4)	5.75	151,201,300
710	5¢ Portrait by Charles W. Peale	2.25	.10	24.00	(4)	6.00	170,565,100
711	6¢ Portrait by John Trumbull	5.00	.06	75.00	(4)	6.75	111,739,400
712	7¢ Portrait by John Trumbull	.30	.20	6.00	(4)	6.75	83,257,400
713	8¢ Portrait by Charles B.J.F.						
	Saint Memin	4.50	.90	70.00	(4)	6.75	96,506,100
714	9¢ Portrait by W. Williams	4.00	.25	45.00	(4)	7.75	75,709,200
715	10¢ Portrait by Gilbert Stuart	15.00	.10	150.00	(4)	10.00	147,216,000
	Olympic Winter Games Issue, Jan. 25, Perf. 11						
716	2¢ Ski Jumper	.50	.25	17.50	(6)	7.50	51,102,800
	Perf. 11x10½						
717	2¢ Arbor Day, Apr. 22	.18	.08	12.50	(4)	5.00	100,869,300

	1932 continued	Un	U	PB/LP	#	FDC	Q
	Olympic Games Issue, June 15, Perf. 11x10½						
718	3¢ Runner at Starting Mark	2.00	.06	25.00	(4)	7.50	168,885,300
719	5¢ Myron's Discobolus	3.25	.30	40.00	(4)	9.50	52,376,100
720	3¢ Washington, June 16	.15	.05	1.50	(4)	10.00	
720b	Booklet pane of 6, July 25	22.50	5.00				
	Coil Stamps, Perf. 10 Vertically						
721	3¢ deep violet (720), June 24	3.00	.08	14.00		.20.00	
	Perf. 10 Horizontally						
722	3¢ deep violet (720), Oct. 12	1.85	.45	10.00		20.00	
	Perf. 10 Vertically						
723	6¢ red orange Garfield						
	(558), Aug. 18	12.50	.25	75.00		20.00	
	Perf. 11						
724	3¢ William Penn, Oct. 24	.35	.25	18.50	(6)	3.00	49,949,000
725	3¢ Daniel Webster, Oct. 24	.50	.40	30.00	(6)	3.00	49,538,500
	Issues of 1933						
726	3¢ Georgia Bicentennial,						
	Feb. 12	.35	.25	20.00	(6)	3.00	61,719,200
	Perf. 10½x11						
727	3¢ Peace of 1783, Apr. 19	.15	.10	6.50	(4)	3.50	73,382,400
	Century of Progress Issue, May 25						
728	1¢ Restoration of Ft. Dearborn	.12	.06	2.50	(4)	3.00	348,266,800
729	3¢ Fed. Building at Chicago	.18	.05	3.50	(4)	3.00	480,239,300
	American Philatelic Society Issue, Souvenir Sheets, Aug. 25, Without Gum, Imperf.						
730	1¢ deep yellow green						
	sheet of 25 (728)	35.00	35.00			120.00	456,704
730a	Single stamp	1.00	.50			3.25	11,417,600

William Penn

Pennsylvania claims to be the seat of American freedom: The Declaration of Independence was signed in Philadelphia, and the Continental Congress (America's first legislature) met there. But Pennsylvania's tradition of freedom dates back even farther, to its founder, William Penn (1644-1718).

Penn was a devout Quaker and political activist. (He was jailed several times for his "radical" religious and political views.) The Pennsylvania colony, which he inherited from his father, gave him an opportunity to try out his ideas. The colony's charter included rights we now take for granted—elective government, jury trials and religious freedom. Penn also was unique among colonial governors in advocating fair treatment for Indians.

The stamp commemorating Penn's arrival in his new colony (#724) represents freedom of a different kind. It shows only Penn's portrait with no frame or background, such as had been used in earlier stamps.

718

719

720

723

724

725

726

727

728

729

730

731

732

733

734

736

737

739

741

740

	1933 continued, Imperf.	Un	U	PB/LP	#	FDC	Q
731	3¢ deep violet, sheet of 25 (729)	30.00	30.00			120.00	441,172
731a	Single stamp	.85	.50			3.25	11,029,300
	Perf. 10½x11						
732	3¢ NRA, Aug. 15	.14	.05	1.75	(4)	3.25	1,978,707,300
	Perf. 11						
733	3¢ Byrd Antarctic Expedition,						
	Oct. 9	.85	.85	25.00	(6)	6.00	5,735,944
734	5¢ Tadeusz Kosciuszko, Oct. 13	.85	.40	45.00	(6)	5.50	45,137,700
	Issues of 1934						
	National Stamp Exhibition Issue, Souvenir Sheet, Feb. 10, Without Gum, Imperf.						
735	3¢ dk. blue sheet of 6 (733)	22.50	20.00			55.00	811,404
735a	Single Stamp	2.50	2.50			6.00	4,868,424
	Perf. 11						
736	3¢ Maryland 300th Anniversary,						
	Mar. 23	.20	.20	13.50	(6)	1.60	46,258,300
	Mothers of America Issue, May 2, Perf. 11x10½						
737	3¢ Whistler's Mother	.15	.06	1.75	(4)	1.60	193,239,100
	Perf. 11						
738	3¢ deep violet (737)	.20	.20	7.25	(6)	1.60	15,432,200
739	3¢ Wisconsin 300th Anniversary,						
	July 7	.20	.12	7.00	(6)	1.60	64,525,400
	National Parks Issue						
740	1¢ El Capitan, Yosemite, Calif.,						
	July 16	.10	.06	1.50	(6)	2.25	84,896,350
741	2¢ Grand Canyon, Arizona, July 24	.15	.06	2.00	(6)	2.25	74,400,200

Maryland

*On Saint Cecilia's Day (November 22) in 1633, some 200 travelers set forth for the New World. They sailed from the Isle of Wight in England aboard two ships, the **Arc** and the **Dove** (#736). The ships' names had religious associations with Noah's trek after the flood; the voyagers had religious associations, too. They were, however, out of the mainstream—a group of Catholics, including a Jesuit priest, intending to settle in the American colonies, a haven for Protestant dissenters.*

The journey took four months, and in March of 1634 the first settlement in Maryland was founded. Although it had strong religious affiliations, the colony was one of the first to grant religious freedom to its populace. In fact, the Act of Religious Toleration (1649) became a model, ultimately, for the religious guarantees in the U.S. Constitution.

	1934 continued, Perf. 11	Un	U	PB/LP	#	FDC	Q
742	3¢ Mt. Rainier and Mirror Lake,						
	Washington, Aug. 3	.20	.06	3.00	(6)	2.50	95,089,000
743	4¢ Mesa Verde, Colorado, Sept. 25	.55	.50	11.00	(6)	3.25	19,178,650
744	5¢ Old Faithful, Yellowstone						
	Wyoming, July 30	1.10	.90	16.00	(6)	3.25	30,980,100
745	6¢ Crater Lake, Oregon, Sept. 5	2.00	1.25	30.00	(6)	4.00	16,923,350
746	7¢ Great Head, Acadia Park,						
	Maine, Oct. 2	1.00	1.00	20.00	(6)	4.00	15,988,250
747	8¢ Great White Throne,						
	Zion Park, Utah, Sept. 18	2.85	2.50	30.00	(6)	*4.25*	15,288,700
748	9¢ Mt. Rockwell and Two Medicine						
	Lake, Glacier National Park,						
	Montana, Aug. 27	3.00	.90	30.00	(6)	4.50	17,472,600
749	10¢ Great Smoky Mountains,						
	North Carolina, Oct. 8	5.00	1.35	50.00	(6)	10.00	18,874,300
	American Philatelic Society Issue, Souvenir Sheet, Imperf.						
750	3¢ deep violet sheet of six						
	(742), Aug. 28	40.00	35.00			55.00	511,391
750a	Single stamp	4.50	4.50			6.25	3,068,346
	Trans-Mississippi Philatelic Exposition Issue, Souvenir Sheet, Imperf.						
751	1¢ green sheet of six						
	(740), Oct. 10	15.00	15.00			40.00	793,551
751a	Single stamp	1.75	1.75			4.50	4,761,306
	Issues of 1935, Special Printing (#752 to 771 inclusive), Issued March 15,						
	Without Gum, Perf. 10½x11						
752	3¢ violet Peace of 1783 (727)						
	Mar. 15	.20	.15	16.00	(4)	10.00	3,274,556
	Perf. 11						
753	3¢ blue Byrd Antarctic						
	Expedition (733)	.60	.60	25.00	(6)	12.00	2,040,760
	Imperf.						
754	3¢ dp. vio. Whistler's Mother						
	(737)	1.00	.60	35.00	(6)	12.00	2,389,288
755	3¢ deep violet Wisconsin						
	300th Anniversary (739)	1.00	.60	35.00	(6)	12.00	2,294,948
756	1¢ green Yosemite (740)	.30	.20	5.50	(6)	12.00	3,217,636
757	2¢ red Grand Canyon (741)	.40	.35	6.50	(6)	12.00	2,746,640
758	3¢ dp. vio. Mt. Rainier (742)	.75	.70	20.00	(6)	13.00	2,168,088
759	4¢ brown Mesa Verde (743)	2.00	2.00	27.50	(6)	13.00	1,822,684
760	5¢ blue Yellowstone (744)	2.75	2.25	35.00	(6)	13.00	1,724,576
761	6¢ dk. blue Crater Lake (745)	4.00	2.75	47.50	(6)	13.00	1,647,696
762	7¢ black Acadia (746)	3.00	2.50	42.50	(6)	13.00	1,682,948
763	8¢ sage green Zion (747)	3.50	2.75	55.00	(6)	15.00	1,638,644
764	9¢ red orange Glacier Nat'l Park						
	(748)	3.75	2.75	60.00	(6)	15.00	1,625,224
765	10¢ gray blk. Smoky Mts. (749)	6.25	5.50	72.50	(6)	15.00	1,644,900

742

743

744

745

746

747

748

749

772

773

774

775

776

777

778

782

783

784

	1935 continued, Imperf.	Un	U	PB/LP	#	FDC	Q
766	1¢ yellow green (728)						
	Pane of 25	35.00	35.00				98,712
766a	Single stamp	1.00	.50			11.00	2,467,800
767	3¢ violet (729)						
	Pane of 25	30.00	30.00				85,914
767a	Single stamp	.85	.50			11.00	2,147,850
768	3¢ dark blue (733)						
	Pane of 6	22.50	20.00				
768a	Single stamp	2.50	2.50			13.00	1,603,200
769	1¢ green (740)						
	Pane of 6	15.00	12.00				279,960
769a	Single stamp	1.75	1.75			8.00	1,679,760
770	3¢ deep violet (742)						
	Pane of 6	35.00	25.00				215,920
770a	Single stamp	3.75	3.75			10.00	1,295,520
771	16¢ dark blue Seal of U.S.	3.00	3.00	65.00	(6)	25.00	1,370,560
	Perf. 11x10½						
772	3¢ Connecticut 300th Anniv.,						
	Apr. 26	.15	.06	2.00	(4)	8.00	70,726,800
773	3¢ California-Pacific Exposition,						
	May 29	.12	.06	2.00	(4)	8.00	100,839,600
	Perf. 11						
774	3¢ Boulder Dam, Sept. 30	.12	.06	2.75	(6)	10.00	73,610,650
	Perf. 11x10½						
775	3¢ Michigan 100th Anniv., Nov. 1	.12	.06	2.00	(4)	8.00	75,823,900
	Issues of 1936						
776	3¢ Texas 100th Anniv., Mar. 2	.12	.06	2.00	(4)	12.50	124,324,500
	Perf. 10½x11						
777	3¢ Rhode Island 300th Anniv.,						
	May 4	.15	.06	2.00	(4)	8.00	67,127,650
	Third International Philatelic Exhibition Issue, Souvenir Sheet, Imperf.						
778	Violet, sheet of 4 different stamps						
	(772, 773, 775 and 776), May 9	3.50	3.50			13.00	2,809,039
779-81 not assigned							
	Perf. 11x10½						
782	3¢ Arkansas 100th Anniv.,						
	June 15	.12	.06	2.00	(4)	8.00	72,992,650
783	3¢ Oregon Territory, July 14	.12	.06	2.00	(4)	8.50	74,407,450
784	3¢ Susan B. Anthony, Aug. 26	.10	.05	.75	(4)	15.00	269,522,200

	Issues of 1936-37	Un	U	PB/LP	#	FDC	Q
	Army Issue, Perf. 11x10½						
785	1¢ George Washington and						
	Nathanael Green, Dec. 15, 1936	.10	.06	1.00	(4)	5.00	105,196,150
786	2¢ Andrew Jackson and						
	Winfield Scott, Jan. 15, 1937	.15	.06	1.10	(4)	5.00	93,848,500
787	3¢ Generals Sherman, Grant						
	and Sheridan, Feb. 18, 1937	.20	.08	1.50	(4)	5.00	87,741,150
788	4¢ Generals Robert E. Lee						
	and "Stonewall" Jackson,						
	Mar. 23, 1937	.65	.15	13.00	(4)	5.50	35,794,150
789	5¢ U.S. Military Academy						
	West Point, May 26, 1937	1.00	.15	15.00	(4)	5.50	36,839,250
	Navy Issue						
790	1¢ John Paul Jones and						
	John Barry, Dec. 15, 1936	.10	.06	1.00	(4)	5.00	104,773,450
791	2¢ Stephen Decatur and						
	Thomas Macdonough,						
	Jan. 15, 1937	.15	.06	1.10	(4)	5.00	92,054,550
792	3¢ Admirals David G. Farragut						
	and David D. Porter,						
	Feb. 18, 1937	.20	.08	1.50	(4)	5.00	93,291,650
793	4¢ Admirals William T. Sampson,						
	George Dewey and Winfield						
	S. Schley, Mar. 23, 1937	.65	.15	13.00	(4)	5.50	34,552,950
794	5¢ Seal of U.S. Naval Academy						
	and Naval Cadets, May 26, 1937	1.00	.15	15.00	(4)	5.50	36,819,050
	Issues of 1937						
795	3¢ Northwest Ordinance						
	150th Anniversary, July 13	.12	.06	2.00	(4)	6.00	84,825,250
	Perf. 11						
796	5¢ Virginia Dare, Aug. 18	.35	.25	10.00	(6)	7.00	25,040,400
	Society of Philatelic Americans, Souvenir Sheet, Imperf.						
797	10¢ blue green (749), Aug. 26	1.25	.85			6.00	5,277,445
	Perf. 11x10½						
798	3¢ Constitution 150th Anniv.,						
	Sept. 17	.15	.07	1.65	(4)	6.50	99,882,300
	Territorial Issue, Perf. 10½x11						
799	3¢ Hawaii, Oct. 18	.15	.07	2.00	(4)	7.00	78,454,450
	Perf. 11x10½						
800	3¢ Alaska, Nov. 12	.15	.07	2.00	(4)	7.00	77,004,200
801	3¢ Puerto Rico, Nov. 25	.15	.07	2.00	(4)	7.00	81,292,450
802	3¢ Virgin Islands, Dec. 15	.15	.07	2.00	(4)	7.00	76,474,550

785

786

787

788

789

790

791

792

793

794

795

796

798

799

800

801

802

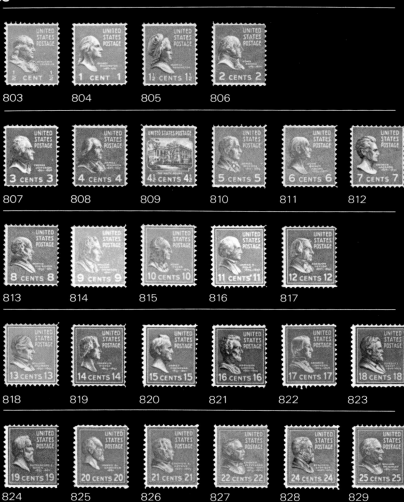

803 804 805 806

807 808 809 810 811 812

813 814 815 816 817

818 819 820 821 822 823

824 825 826 827 828 829

830 831 832 833 834

Issues of 1938-51	Un	U	PB/LP	#	FDC	Q
Presidential Issue, Perf. 11x10½ (#832b issued in 1951)						
803 ½¢ Benjamin Franklin, May 19	.05	.05	.40	(4)	1.25	
804 1¢ George Washington, Apr. 25	.06	.05	.25	(4)	2.00	
804b Booklet pane of 6	1.75	.20				
805 1½¢ Martha Washington, May 5	.06	.05	.30	(4)	2.00	
806 2¢ John Adams, June 3	.06	.05	.35	(4)	2.00	
806b Booklet pane of 6	4.25	.50				
807 3¢ Thomas Jefferson, June 16	.10	.05	.50	(4)	2.00	
807a Booklet pane of 6	8.50	.50				
808 4¢ James Madison, July 1	.45	.05	2.00	(4)	2.00	
809 4½¢ White House, July 11	.20	.06	1.60	(4)	2.50	
810 5¢ James Monroe, July 21	.40	.05	1.80	(4)	2.25	
811 6¢ John Q. Adams, July 28	.45	.05	2.00	(4)	2.25	
812 7¢ Andrew Jackson, Aug. 4	.50	.05	2.20	(4)	2.50	
813 8¢ Martin Van Buren, Aug. 11	.65	.05	2.75	(4)	2.50	
814 9¢ William H. Harrison, Aug 18	.70	.05	3.00	(4)	2.65	
815 10¢ John Tyler, Sept. 2	.50	.05	2.20	(4)	2.75	
816 11¢ James K. Polk, Sept. 8	1.00	.08	4.50	(4)	2.75	
817 12¢ Zachary Taylor, Sept. 14	1.90	.06	8.00	(4)	3.00	
818 13¢ Millard Fillmore, Sept. 22	2.00	.08	8.50	(4)	3.00	
819 14¢ Franklin Pierce, Oct. 6	1.75	.10	7.50	(4)	3.25	
820 15¢ James Buchanan, Oct. 13	.75	.05	3.25	(4)	3.25	
821 16¢ Abraham Lincoln, Oct. 20	1.75	.35	7.50	(4)	3.50	
822 17¢ Andrew Johnson, Oct. 27	1.50	.12	7.00	(4)	3.75	
823 18¢ Ulysses S. Grant, Nov. 3	3.25	.08	14.00	(4)	4.25	
824 19¢ Rutherford B. Hayes, Nov. 10	2.00	.50	9.00	(4)	4.25	
825 20¢ James A. Garfield, Nov. 10	1.20	.05	5.75	(4)	4.50	
826 21¢ Chester A. Arthur, Nov. 22	2.25	.10	10.50	(4)	5.00	
827 22¢ Grover Cleveland, Nov. 22	2.25	.50	11.50	(4)	5.25	
828 24¢ Benjamin Harrison, Dec. 2	7.00	.25	30.00	(4)	5.25	
829 25¢ William McKinley, Dec. 2	1.40	.05	6.00	(4)	6.50	
830 30¢ Theodore Roosevelt, Dec. 8	9.00	.05	37.50	(4)	10.00	
831 50¢ William Howard Taft, Dec. 8	13.50	.06	57.50	(4)	20.00	
Perf. 11						
832 $1 Woodrow Wilson, Aug. 29	12.50	.10	55.00	(4)	55.00	
Wmkd. USIR						
832b Purple and black, 1951	350.00	90.00				
Unwmkd.						
833 $2 Warren G. Harding, Sept. 29	32.50	6.00	165.00	(4)	110.00	
834 $5 Calvin Coolidge, Nov. 17	125.00	5.50	575.00	(4)	175.00	

This series was in use for approximately 16 years when the Liberty Series began replacing it. Various shades of these stamps are in existence due to the numerous reprintings.

	1938 continued, Perf. 11x10½	Un	U	PB/LP	#	FDC	Q
835	3¢ Constitution Ratification,						
	June 21	.25	.08	5.50	(4)	6.50	73,043,650
	Perf. 11						
836	3¢ Swedish-Finnish 300th Anniv.,						
	June 27	.25	.10	6.00	(6)	6.00	58,564,368
	Perf. 11x10½						
837	3¢ Northwest Territory,						
	July 15	.25	.08	15.00	(4)	6.00	65,939,500
838	3¢ Iowa Territory 100th Anniv.						
	Aug. 24	.25	.08	9.00	(4)	6.00	47,064,300
	Issues of 1939, Coil Stamps, Jan. 20, Perf. 10 Vertically						
839	1¢ green Washington (804)	.25	.06	1.50		7.00	
840	1½¢ bistre brown						
	M. Washington (805)	.30	.06	1.50		7.00	
841	2¢ rose car. Adams (806)	.30	.05	1.75		7.00	
842	3¢ deep violet Jefferson (807)	.75	.05	3.00		8.00	
843	4¢ red violet Madison (808)	9.00	.35	35.00		10.00	
844	4½¢ dk. gray White House (809)	.60	.45	4.00		10.00	
845	5¢ bright blue Monroe (810)	6.50	.35	30.00		11.00	
846	6¢ red or. J.Q. Adams (811)	1.40	.20	8.75		16.00	
847	10¢ brown red Tyler (815)	15.00	.40	60.00		22.00	
	Jan. 27, Perf. 10 Horizontally						
848	1¢ green Washington (804)	1.00	.12	3.75		7.00	
849	1½¢ bistre brown						
	M. Washington (805)	1.50	.40	4.75		9.00	
850	2¢ rose car. Adams (806)	3.50	.50	9.00		11.00	
851	3¢ deep violet Jefferson (807)	2.75	.45	7.50		13.50	
	Perf. 10½x11						
852	3¢ Golden Gate Exposition. Feb. 18	.12	.06	1.75	(4)	5.00	114,439,600
853	3¢ New York World's Fair, Apr. 1	.15	.06	2.00	(4)	8.00	101,699,550
	Perf. 11						
854	3¢ Washington's Inauguration,						
	Apr. 30	.35	.10	4.25	(6)	5.00	72,764,550
	Perf. 11x10½						
855	3¢ Baseball 100th Anniversary,						
	June 12	.35	.08	4.00	(4)	18.00	81,269,600
	Perf. 11						
856	3¢ Panama Canal, Aug. 15	.30	.08	6.00	(6)	5.00	67,813,350
	Perf. 10½x11						
857	3¢ 300th Anniv. of Printing,						
	Sept. 25	.15	.08	1.65	(4)	5.00	71,394,750
	Perf. 11x10½						
858	3¢ 50th Anniv. of Statehood						
	Nov. 2	.15	.08	· 1.65	(4)	5.00	66,835,000

835

836

837

838

852

853

854

855

856

857

858

859

860

861

862

863

864

865

866

867

868

869

870

871

872

873

874

875

876

877

878

879

880

881

882

883

	Issues of 1940	Un	U	PB/LP	#	FDC	Q
	Famous Americans Issue, Perf. 10½x11						
	Authors						
859	1¢ Washington Irving, Jan. 29	.08	.06	1.10	(4)	1.75	56,348,320
860	2¢ James Fenimore Cooper,						
	Jan. 29	.10	.08	1.25	(4)	1.75	53,177,110
861	3¢ Ralph Waldo Emerson, Feb. 5	.12	.06	2.00	(4)	1.75	53,260,270
862	5¢ Louisa May Alcott, Feb. 5	.35	.30	11.00	(4)	4.50	22,104,950
863	10¢ Samuel L. Clemens						
	(Mark Twain), Feb. 13	2.50	2.35	50.00	(4)	7.50	13,201,270
	Poets						
864	1¢ Henry W. Longfellow, Feb. 16	.12	.08	1.75	(4)	1.75	51,603,580
865	2¢ John Greenleaf Whittier,						
	Feb. 16	.10	.08	1.75	(4)	1.75	52,100,510
866	3¢ James Russell Lowell, Feb. 20	.18	.06	3.50	(4)	1.75	51,666,580
867	5¢ Walt Whitman, Feb. 20	.35	.25	11.00	(4)	4.00	22,207,780
868	10¢ James Whitcomb Riley,						
	Feb. 24	3.25	3.00	45.00	(4)	7.50	11,835,530
	Educators						
869	1¢ Horace Mann, Mar. 14	.09	.08	1.75	(4)	1.75	52,471,160
870	2¢ Mark Hopkins, Mar. 14	.10	.06	1.40	(4)	1.75	52,366,440
871	3¢ Charles W. Eliot, Mar. 28	.30	.06	3.25	(4)	1.75	51,636,270
872	5¢ Frances E. Willard, Mar. 28	.50	.35	12.00	(4)	4.00	20,729,030
873	10¢ Booker T. Washington, Apr. 7	2.25	2.25	32.50	(4)	7.50	14,125,580
	Scientists						
874	1¢ John James Audubon, Apr. 8	.08	.06	1.00	(4)	1.75	59,409,000
875	2¢ Dr. Crawford W. Long, Apr. 8	.10	.06	1.20	(4)	1.75	57,888,600
876	3¢ Luther Burbank, Apr. 17	.10	.06	1.75	(4)	2.75	58,273,180
877	5¢ Dr. Walter Reed, Apr. 17	.30	.25	9.00	(4)	4.00	23,779,000
878	10¢ Jane Addams, Apr. 26	2.00	2.00	32.50	(4)	7.50	15,112,580
	Composers						
879	1¢ Stephen Collins Foster, May 3	.08	.06	1.25	(4)	1.75	57,322,790
880	2¢ John Philip Sousa, May 3	.10	.06	1.25	(4)	1.75	58,281,580
881	3¢ Victor Herbert, May 13	.15	.06	1.75	(4)	1.75	56,398,790
882	5¢ Edward MacDowell, May 13	.60	.30	12.50	(4)	4.00	21,147,000
883	10¢ Ethelbert Nevin, June 10	5.00	2.25	50.00	(4)	7.00	13,328,000

	1940 continued, Perf. 10½x11	Un	U	PB/LP	#	FDC	Q
	Artists						
884	1¢ Gilbert Charles Stuart, Sept. 5	.08	.06	1.10	(4)	1.75	54,389,510
885	2¢ James A. McNeill Whistler,						
	Sept. 5	.10	.06	1.10	(4)	1.75	53,636,580
886	3¢ Augustus Saint-Gaudens,						
	Sept. 16	.10	.06	1.25	(4)	1.75	55,313,230
887	5¢ Daniel Chester French,						
	Sept. 16	.40	.22	11.50	(4)	3.50	21,720,580
888	10¢ Frederic Remington,						
	Sept. 30	2.50	2.25	35.00	(4)	7.00	13,600,580
	Inventors						
889	1¢ Eli Whitney, Oct. 7	.12	.08	2.50	(4)	1.75	47,599,580
890	2¢ Samuel F.B. Morse, Oct. 7	.10	.06	1.30	(4)	1.75	53,766,510
891	3¢ Cyrus Hall McCormick, Oct. 14	.20	.06	2.50	(4)	1.75	54,193,580
892	5¢ Elias Howe, Oct. 14	1.25	.40	20.00	(4)	4.50	20,264,580
893	10¢ Alexander Graham Bell,						
	Oct. 28	14.50	3.25	100.00	(4)	12.50	13,726,580
	Perf. 11x10½						
894	3¢ Pony Express, Apr. 3	.50	.15	6.50	(4)	6.00	46,497,400
	Perf. 10½x11						
895	3¢ Pan American Union, Apr. 14	.40	.12	5.50	(4)	4.50	47,700,000
	Perf. 11x10½						
896	3¢ Idaho Statehood,						
	50th Anniversary, July 3	.20	.08	3.50	(4)	4.50	50,618,150
	Perf. 10½x11						
897	3¢ Wyoming Statehood,						
	50th Anniversary, July 10	.20	.08	2.75	(4)	4.50	50,034,400
	Perf. 11x10½						
898	3¢ Coronado Expedition, Sept. 7	.20	.08	2.75	(4)	4.50	60,943,700
	National Defense Issue, Oct. 16						
899	1¢ Statue of Liberty	.05	.05	.70	(4)	4.25	
900	2¢ Anti-aircraft Gun	.06	.05	.70	(4)	4.25	
901	3¢ Torch of Enlightenment	.12	.05	1.40	(4)	4.25	
	Perf. 10½x11						
902	3¢ Thirteenth Amendment,						
	Oct. 20	.25	.15	6.00	(4)	5.00	44,389,550
	Issue of 1941, Perf. 11x10½						
903	3¢ Vermont Statehood, Mar. 4	.22	.10	2.50	(4)	4.50	54,574,550
	Issues of 1942						
904	3¢ Kentucky Statehood, June 1	.15	.12	2.25	(4)	4.00	63,558,400
905	3¢ Win the War, July 4	.10	.05	.60	(4)	3.75	

884

 885

 886

 887

 888

 889

 890

 891

 892

 893

 894

 895

 896

 897

 898

 899

 900

 901

902

 903

 904

 905

 902

906   907   908

909   910   911

912   913   914

915   916   917

918   919   920

921   922   923

	1942 continued, Perf. 11x10½	Un	U	PB/LP	#	FDC	Q
906	5¢ Chinese Resistance, July 7	.40	.30	18.50	(4)	5.75	21,272,800
	Issues of 1943						
907	2¢ Allied Nations, Jan. 14	.08	.05	.50	(4)	3.50	1,671,564,200
908	1¢ Four Freedoms, Feb. 12	.06	.05	1.00	(4)	3.50	1,227,334,200
	Issue of 1943-44, Overrun Countries Issue, Perf. 12						
909	5¢ Poland, June 22	.35	.20			6.00	19,999,646
910	5¢ Czechoslovakia, July 12	.30	.15			5.00	19,999,646
911	5¢ Norway, July 27	.25	.12			4.00	19,999,646
912	5¢ Luxembourg, Aug. 10	.25	.12			4.00	19,999,646
913	5¢ Netherlands, Aug. 24	.25	.12			4.00	19,999,646
914	5¢ Belgium, Sept. 14	.25	.12			4.00	19,999,646
915	5¢ France, Sept. 28	.25	.10			4.00	19,999,646
916	5¢ Greece, Oct. 12	.85	.60			4.00	14,999,646
917	5¢ Yugoslavia, Oct. 26	.50	.40			4.00	14,999,646
918	5¢ Albania, Nov. 9	.50	.40			4.00	14,999,646
919	5¢ Austria, Nov. 23	.30	.25			4.00	14,999,646
920	5¢ Denmark, Dec. 7	.50	.50			4.00	14,999,646
921	5¢ Korea, Nov. 2, 1944	.28	.25			5.00	14,999,646
	Issues of 1944, Perf. 11x10½						
922	3¢ Transcontinental Railroad,						
	May 10	.20	.15	2.50	(4)	6.00	61,303,000
923	3¢ Steamship, May 22	.15	.15	2.50	(4)	4.00	61,001,450

Four Freedoms

When the United States entered World War II in December 1941, the fate of the allied forces seemed bleak, indeed. Twelve European countries, including France, a major ally, had fallen under Nazi control. England suffered a protracted series of air strikes during the "Battle of Britain," and Nazi forces were working their way into Russia. The United States, still not fully recovered from the Great Depression, turned its attention to an even greater threat.

"Liberty holding the torch of freedom and enlightenment" (as seen on #908) is one symbol of the struggle, a statement of the basic four freedoms — "of speech and religion, from want and fear" — that the war was all about. The stamp was issued on February 12, 1943, a pivotal time for the allied forces. A month earlier President Franklin D. Roosevelt had called for "unconditional surrender" by the enemy. Russian forces were slowly repulsing the Nazi onslaught. (On the day the stamp was issued, Soviet troops had regained control of vital rail links to the West.) And Britain had begun retaliatory air strikes against key German installations in Dresden and Hamburg. Nonetheless, the war was hard fought and hard won: It was another two years before those basic four freedoms were reestablished.

	1944 continued, Perf. 11x10½	Un	U	PB/LP	#	FDC	Q
924	3¢ Telegraph, May 24	.12	.10	1.60	(4)	3.50	60,605,000
925	3¢ Philippines, Sept. 27	.12	.12	3.00	(4)	3.50	50,129,350
926	3¢ 50th Anniversary of						
	Motion Picture, Oct. 31	.12	.10	2.00	(4)	3.50	53,479,400
	Issues of 1945						
927	3¢ Florida Statehood, Mar. 3	.10	.08	1.00	(4)	3.50	61,617,350
928	5¢ United Nations Conference,						
	Apr. 25	.12	.08	.70	(4)	3.50	75,500,000
	Perf. 10½x11						
929	3¢ Iwo Jima (Marines), July 11	.10	.05	.50	(4)	5.25	137,321,000
	Issues of 1945-46, Franklin D. Roosevelt Issue, Perf. 11x10½						
930	1¢ F.D.R. and home at						
	Hyde Park, July 26, 1945	.05	.05	.30	(4)	2.50	128,140,000
931	2¢ Roosevelt and "Little						
	White House," Ga.,						
	Aug. 24, 1945	.08	.08	.40	(4)	2.50	67,255,000
932	3¢ Roosevelt and White House,						
	June 27, 1945	.10	.08	.65	(4)	2.50	133,870,000
933	5¢ F.D.R. Globe and						
	Four Freedoms, Jan. 30, 1946	.12	.08	.75	(4)	3.00	76,455,400
934	3¢ U.S. Army in Paris, Sept. 28	.10	.05	.60	(4)	3.50	128,357,750
935	3¢ U.S. Navy, Oct. 27	.10	.05	.60	(4)	3.50	135,863,000
936	3¢ U.S. Coast Guard, Nov. 10	.10	.05	.60	(4)	3.50	111,616,700
937	3¢ Alfred E. Smith, Nov. 26	.10	.05	.50	(4)	2.50	308,587,700
938	3¢ Texas Statehood, Dec. 29	.10	.05	.50	(4)	3.50	170,640,000
	Issues of 1946						
939	3¢ Merchant Marine, Feb. 26	.10	.05	.50	(4)	2.50	135,927,000

U.S. Coast Guard

During the first six months of U.S. involvement in WW II, three million tons of needed supplies and munitions destined for the European front were lost off American coastal waters. As many as 40 German submarines (U-boats) blocked shipping lanes off the Eastern seaboard, sinking as many ships as possible.

The Coast Guard (#936) cleared the lanes by dropping depth charges onto the subs. According to one eyewitness the U-boats sometimes were so close that a man could have jumped from a Guard cutter onto a U-boat's deck. Nonetheless, the Coast Guard persevered in its perilous job, clearing the way for the last great campaign in the European theater — the invasion of Normandy Beach (June 1944) — and allied victory.

924

925

926

927

928

929

930

931

932

933

934

935

936

937

938

939

940

941

942

943

944

945

946

947

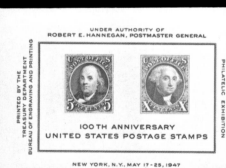

948

949

950

951

	1946 continued, Perf. 11x10½	Un	U	PB/LP	#	FDC	Q
940	3¢ Veterans of World War II, May 9	.10	.05	.55	(4)	2.50	260,339,100
941	3¢ Tennesse Statehood, June 1	.10	.05	.50	(4)	2.50	132,274,500
942	3¢ Iowa Statehood, Aug. 3	.10	.05	.50	(4)	2.50	132,430,000
943	3¢ Smithsonian Institution, Aug. 10	.10	.05	.50	(4)	2.50	139,209,500
944	3¢ Kearny Expedition, Oct. 16	.10	.05	.50	(4)	2.50	114,684,450
	Issues of 1947, Perf. 10½x11						
945	3¢ Thomas A. Edison, Feb. 11	.10	.05	.50	(4)	2.50	156,540,510
	Perf. 11x10½						
946	3¢ Joseph Pulitzer, Apr. 10	.10	.05	.50	(4)	2.50	120,452,600
947	3¢ 100th Anniv. of First. U.S.						
	Postage Stamps, May 17	.10	.05	.50	(4)	2.50	127,104,300
	Centenary International Philatelic Exhibition Issue, Souvenir Sheet, Imperf.						
948	Souvenir sheet of two, May 19	1.50	1.00			3.00	10,299,600
948a	5¢ blue, single stamp	.35	.30				
948b	10¢ brn. org., single stamp	.50	.30				
	Perf. 11x10½						
949	3¢ Doctors, June 9	.10	.05	.50	(4)	1.50	132,902,000
950	3¢ Utah, July 24	.10	.05	.50	(4)	1.50	131,968,000
951	3¢ U.S. Frigate Constitution,						
	Oct. 21	.10	.05	.50	(4)	1.50	131,488,000
	Perf. 10½x11						
952	3¢ Everglades Nat'l. Park, Dec. 5	.10	.05	.50	(4)	1.50	122,362,000

Stamps

George Washington, our first president, and Benjamin Franklin, the first Postmaster General, are the two most popular U.S. stamp subjects. They are depicted on the U.S. postage stamp centennial issue (#947), as they were on the first U.S. postage stamps issued in 1847.

These "first" stamps are a matter of definition. Before the federal government began issuing stamps, private postal services were on the scene. Alexander Greig, who ran such a service in New York City, actually issued the first American adhesive postage stamp in 1842. It was not until 1861 that the federal government took sole control of postage stamps.

Letter writers had to wait until 1857 before they could pull their stamps apart. Stamps originally were issued in sheets that had to be cut. Perforations were invented by Henry Archer, an Irishman, who supposedly lost his scissors and decided there must be a better way.

Today some of those early stamps are quite valuable, but at the time they were worth no more than face value. There was a shortage of the 1847 stamps, issued in 5¢ and 10¢ denominations, so people cut 10¢ stamps in half for five cents' worth of postage. During the Civil War, stamps were used as currency because there was a shortage of coins.

	Issues of 1948, Perf. 10½x11	Un	U	PB/LP	#	FDC	Q
953	3¢ Dr. George Washington Carver,						
	Jan. 5	.10	.05	.50	(4)	1.50	121,548,000
	Perf. 11x10½						
954	3¢ Calif. Gold 100th Anniversary,						
	Jan. 24	.10	.05	.50	(4)	1.50	131,109,500
955	3¢ Mississippi Territory, Apr. 7	.10	.05	.50	(4)	1.50	122,650,500
956	3¢ Four Chaplains, May 28	.10	.05	.50	(4)	1.50	121,953,500
957	3¢ Wisconsin Statehood, May 29	.10	.05	.50	(4)	1.50	115,250,000
958	5¢ Swedish Pioneer, June 4	.15	.10	1.00	(4)	1.50	64,198,500
959	3¢ Progress of Women, July 19	.10	.05	.50	(4)	1.50	117,642,500
	Perf. 10½x11						
960	3¢ William Allen White, July 31	.10	.06	.60	(4)	1.50	77,649,600
	Perf. 11x10½						
961	3¢ U.S.-Canada Friendship,						
	Aug. 2	.10	.05	.50	(4)	1.50	113,474,500
962	3¢ Francis Scott Key, Aug. 9	.10	.05	.50	(4)	1.50	120,868,500
963	3¢ Salute to Youth, Aug. 11	.10	.06	.50	(4)	1.50	77,800,500
964	3¢ Oregon Territory, Aug. 14	.10	.10	.90	(4)	1.50	52,214,000
	Perf. 10½x11						
965	3¢ Harlan Fiske Stone, Aug. 25	.10	.08	1.70	(4)	1.50	53,958,100
966	3¢ Palomar Mtn. Obs., Aug. 30	.12	.10	2.50	(4)	1.50	61,120,010
	Perf. 11x10½						
967	3¢ Clara Barton, Sept. 7	.10	.08	.60	(4)	1.25	57,823,000
968	3¢ Poultry Industry, Sept. 9	.12	.08	.80	(4)	1.25	52,975,000
	Perf. 10½x11						
969	3¢ Gold Star Mothers, Sept. 21	.12	.08	.65	(4)	1.50	77,149,000
970	3¢ Fort Kearny, Sept. 22	.12	.08	.65	(4)	1.50	58,332,000
971	3¢ Volunteer Firemen, Oct. 4	.12	.08	.75	(4)	1.50	56,228,000

Women's Progress

Lucretia Mott and Elizabeth Stanton first met in London in 1840 as delegates to an international convention against slavery. Both women were denied seats because of their sex. The unfair irony of the situation became the germ of an idea. It took eight years, but in July 1848 Mott and Stanton convened the first Women's Rights convention in Seneca Falls, New York. At the time, women had few rights. Not only were they denied the vote but, especially if married, they could not own property or conduct business independently. The black slaves for whom Mott and Stanton worked so hard were given the right to vote 50 years before women.

Carrie C. Catt, the third woman depicted on the Progress of Women stamp (#959, in the middle), was a leading lecturer and organizer in the campaign for women's suffrage. Catt served as president of the National American Woman Suffrage Association from 1900 to 1904 and from 1915 to 1920. In 1920 (the year suffrage finally was granted to women), she founded the National League of Women Voters.

953   954   955   956

957   958   959   960

961   962   963

964   965   966   967

968   969   970   971

972

973

974

975

976

977

978

981

982

979

980

983

984

985

986

987

988

989

990

	1948 continued, Perf. 11x10½	Un	U	PB/LP	#	FDC	Q
972	3¢ Five Indian Tribes, Oct. 15	.12	.08	.75	(4)	1.25	57,832,000
973	3¢ Rough Riders, Oct. 27	.12	.10	1.20	(4)	1.25	53,875,000
974	3¢ Juliette Low, Oct. 29	.12	.08	.65	(4)	1.25	63,834,000
	Perf. 10½x11						
975	3¢ Will Rogers, Nov. 4	.12	.08	1.00	(4)	1.25	67,162,200
976	3¢ Fort Bliss 100th Anniv., Nov. 5	.15	.08	1.50	(4)	1.25	64,561,000
	Perf. 11x10½						
977	3¢ Moina Michael, Nov. 9	.12	.08	.65	(4)	1.25	64,079,500
978	3¢ Gettysburg Address, Nov. 19	.12	.08	.70	(4)	1.25	63,388,00
	Perf. 10½x11						
979	3¢ American Turners, Nov. 20	.12	.08	.55	(4)	1.25	62,285,000
980	3¢ Joel Chandler Harris, Dec. 9	.12	.08	.85	(4)	1.25	57,492,610
	Issues of 1949, Perf. 11x10½						
981	3¢ Minnesota Territory, Mar. 3	.10	.08	.50	(4)	1.25	99,190,000
982	3¢ Washington & Lee University,						
	Apr. 12	.10	.05	.50	(4)	1.25	104,790,000
983	3¢ Puerto Rico Election, Apr. 27	.10	.05	.50	(4)	1.25	108,805,000
984	3¢ Annapolis 300th Anniv.,						
	May 23	.10	.05	.50	(4)	1.25	107,340,000
985	3¢ Grand Army of the Republic,						
	Aug. 29	.10	.05	.50	(4)·	1.25	117,020,000
	Perf. 10½x11						
986	3¢ Edgar Allen Poe, Oct. 7	.10	.05	.60	(4)	1.25	122,633,000
	Issues of 1950, Perf. 11x10½						
987	3¢ American Bankers Association,						
	Jan. 3	.10	.05	.50	(4)	1.25	130,960,000
	Perf. 10½x11						
988	3¢ Samuel Gompers, Jan. 27	.10	.05	.65	(4)	1.25	128,478,000
	National Capital 150th Anniversary Issue, Perf. 10½x11, 11x10½ (See also #991-992)						
989	3¢ Statue of Freedom, Apr. 27	.10	.05	.50	(4)	1.25	132,090,000
990	3¢ Executive Mansion, June 12	.10	.05	.50	(4)	1.25	130,050,000

1950 continued	Un	U	PB/LP	#	FDC	Q
National Capital 150th Anniversary Issue, Perf. 10½x11, 11x10½ (See also #989-990)						
991	3¢ Supreme Court Building, Aug. 2	.10	.05	.50	(4)	1.25	131,350,000
992	3¢ U.S. Capitol Building, Nov. 22	.10	.05	.50	(4)	1.25	129,980,000
Perf. 11x10½						
993	3¢ Railroad Engineers, Apr. 29	.10	.05	.50	(4)	1.25	122,315,000
994	3¢ Kansas City, Mo., June 3	.10	.05	.50	(4)	1.25	122,170,000
995	3¢ Boy Scouts, June 30	.10	.06	.55	(4)	2.00	131,635,000
996	3¢ Indiana Territory, July 4	.10	.05	.50	(4)	1.25	121,860,000
997	3¢ California Statehood, Sept. 9	.10	.05	.50	(4)	1.25	121,120,000
Issues of 1951						
998	3¢ Confederate Veterans, May 30	.10	.05	.50	(4)	1.25	119,120,000
999	3¢ Nevada 100th Anniv., July 14	.10	.05	.50	(4)	1.25	112,125,000
1000	3¢ Landing of Cadillac, July 24	.10	.05	.50	(4)	1.25	114,140,000
1001	3¢ Colorado Statehood, Aug. 1	.10	.05	.50	(4)	1.25	114,490,000
1002	3¢ American Chemical Society, Sept. 4	.10	.05	.50	(4)	1.25	117,200,000
1003	3¢ Battle of Brooklyn, Dec. 10	.10	.05	.50	(4)	1.25	116,130,000
Issues of 1952						
1004	3¢ Betsy Ross, Jan. 2	.10	.05	.50	(4)	1.25	116,175,000
1005	3¢ 4-H Club, Jan. 15	.10	.05	.60	(4)	1.25	115,945,000
1006	3¢ B&O Railroad, Feb. 28	.10	.05	.50	(4)	1.50	112,540,000
1007	3¢ American Auto Assn., Mar. 4	.10	.05	.60	(4)	.85	117,415,000
1008	3¢ NATO, Apr. 4	.10	.05	.55	(4)	.85	2,899,580,000
1009	3¢ Grand Coulee Dam, May 15	.10	.05	.50	(4)	.85	114,540,000

Supreme Court Building and the National Capital

Three buildings are shown on the issues commemorating the 150th birthday of our nation's capital (#989-992) in 1950. One of them, the Supreme Court Building (#991), was only 15 years old when the stamp was issued. Designed by Cass Gilbert, the building followed the style of a Greek temple, and it was completed a year after the American architect's death. Gilbert was no stranger to monumental architecture: He also designed the state capitols of Minnesota, Arkansas and West Virginia, as well as skyscrapers such as New York City's Woolworth Building (1913).

Washington, D.C. was designed and laid out by Pierre Charles L'Enfant, a French military engineer and veteran of the American Revolution. He was chosen for the work by George Washington. The cornerstone for the new city was laid in 1793, but it was seven years before President John Adams and the Congress could move in; 1800 is the capital's official "birth date."

Washington was, and remains, one of America's few planned cities. Its radial design later was copied for Indianapolis, Indiana by Alexander Ralston, who had worked with L'Enfant in laying out the District of Columbia. The United States Postal Service is headquartered in a building at L'Enfant Plaza in Washington.

991

992

993

994

995

996

997

998

999

1000

1001

1002

1003

1004

1005

1006

1007

1008

1009

1010

1011

1012

1013

1014

1015

1016

1017

1018

1019

1020

1021

1022

1023

1024

1025

1026

1027

1952 continued, Perf. 11x10½	Un	U	PB/LP	#	FDC	Q
1010	3¢ Maj. Gen. Lafayette, June 13	.10	.05	.50	(4)	.85	113,135,000
Perf. 10½x11						
1011	3¢ Mt. Rushmore Mem., Aug. 11	.10	.05	.60	(4)	.85	116,255,000
Perf. 11x10½						
1012	3¢ Engineering, Sept. 6	.10	.05	.50	(4)	.85	113,860,000
1013	3¢ Service Women, Sept. 11	.10	.05	.50	(4)	.85	124,260,000
1014	3¢ Gutenberg Bible, Sept. 30	.10	.05	.50	(4)	.85	115,735,000
1015	3¢ Newspaper Boys, Oct. 4	.10	.05	.50	(4)	.85	115,430,000
1016	3¢ Red Cross, Nov. 21	.10	.05	.50	(4)	.85	136,220,000
Issues of 1953						
1017	3¢ National Guard, Feb. 23	.10	.05	.50	(4)	.85	114,894,000
1018	3¢ Ohio Statehood, Mar. 2	.10	.05	.80	(4)	.85	118,706,000
1019	3¢ Washington Territory, Mar. 2	.10	.05	.50	(4)	.85	114,190,000
1020	3¢ Louisiana Purchase, Apr. 30	.10	.05	.50	(4)	.85	113,990,000
1021	5¢ Opening of Japan 100th Anniv., July 14	.15	.10	1.40	(4)	.85	89,289,600
1022	3¢ American Bar Assn., Aug. 24	.10	.05	.50	(4)	.85	114,865,000
1023	3¢ Sagamore Hill, Sept. 14	.10	.05	.50	(4)	1.00	115,780,000
1024	3¢ Future Farmers, Oct. 13	.10	.05	.50	(4)	.85	115,244,600
1025	3¢ Trucking Industry, Oct. 27	.10	.05	.50	(4)	.85	123,709,600
1026	3¢ General Patton, Nov. 11	.10	.05	.60	(4)	.85	114,798,600
1027	3¢ New York City 300th Anniversary, Nov. 20	.10	.05	.60	(4)	.85	115,759,600

George S. Patton

By World War II, armored divisions had, for the most part, replaced the mounted cavalry. But one of the military's most brilliant armored tacticians got his start on horseback. General George S. Patton, Jr. originally was assigned to the cavalry. Commissioned in 1909, he trained at the French military riding school in Samur and the U.S. school at Fort Riley, Kansas.

It was not until World War I that Patton received his first training on tanks, which were new weapons at the time. His association with armored warfare continued into World War II, when his tactical maneuvers helped the allies to victory in Italy and France, particularly during the Battle of the Bulge. Yet much of Patton's success was due to his study of mounted cavalry tactics, which he applied to armored weapons. Ironically, "Old Blood and Guts" (a nickname the general earned based on his toughness) died of injuries from an automobile accident—not from battle. He was commemorated on a stamp (#1026) and by a medium-weight tank named after him.

121

	1953 continued, Perf. 11x10½	Un	U	PB/LP	#	FDC	Q
1028	3¢ Gadsden Purchase, Dec. 30	.10	.05	.50	(4)	.85	116,134,600
	Issues of 1954						
1029	3¢ Columbia University 200th						
	Anniv., Jan. 4	.10	.05	.50	(4)	.85	118,540,000
	Liberty Issue, 1954-61, Perf. 11x10½x 10½x11						
1030	½¢ Benjamin Franklin, 1955	.05	.05	.30	(4)	.85	Unlimited
1031	1¢ George Washington, 1954	.05	.05	.25	(4)	.85	Unlimited
1031A	1¼¢ Palace of the Governors,						
	Santa Fe, 1960	.05	.05	1.75	(4)	.85	Unlimited
1032	1½¢ Mount Vernon, 1956	.08	.05	7.50	(4)	.60	Unlimited
1033	2¢ Thomas Jefferson, 1954	.05	.05	.25	(4)	.60	Unlimited
1034	2½¢ Bunker Hill Monument						
	and Massachusetts Flag, 1959	.08	.05	2.00	(4)	.60	Unlimited
1035	3¢ Statue of Liberty, 1954	.08	.05	.40	(4)	.60	Unlimited
1035a	Booklet pane of 6	3.00	.50				
1036	4¢ Abraham Lincoln, 1954	.10	.05	.50	(4)	.60	Unlimited
1036a	Booklet pane of 6	2.00	.50				
1037	4½¢ The Hermitage, 1959	.15	.08	1.75	(4)	.60	Unlimited
1038	5¢ James Monroe, 1954	.17	.05	.75	(4)	.60	Unlimited
1039	6¢ Theodore Roosevelt, 1955	.40	.05	2.00	(4)	.65	Unlimited
1040	7¢ Woodrow Wilson, 1956	.25	.05	1.50	(4)	.70	Unlimited
	Perf. 11						
1041	8¢ Statue of Liberty, 1954	.30	.06	5.00	(4)	.80	Unlimited
1042	8¢ Statue of Liberty,						
	redrawn, 1958	.30	.05	1.75	(4)	.60	Unlimited
	Perf. 11x10½, 10½x11						
1042A	8¢ John J. Pershing, 1961	.25	.05	1.50	(4)	.60	Unlimited
1043	9¢ The Alamo, 1956	.30	.05	1.50	(4)	1.50	Unlimited
1044	10¢ Independence Hall, 1956	.35	.05	1.65	(4)	.90	Unlimited
	Perf. 11						
1044A	11¢ Statue of Liberty, 1961	.30	.06	1.50	(4)	.90	Unlimited
	Perf. 11x10½, 10½x11						
1045	12¢ Benjamin Harrison, 1959	.55	.05	2.75	(4)	.90	Unlimited
1046	15¢ John Jay, 1958	.85	.05	3.75	(4)	1.00	Unlimited
1047	20¢ Monticello, 1956	.90	.05	4.50	(4)	1.20	Unlimited
1048	25¢ Paul Revere, 1958	2.75	.05	12.00	(4)	1.30	Unlimited
1049	30¢ Robert E. Lee, 1955	2.00	.08	8.50	(4)	1.50	Unlimited
1050	40¢ John Marshall, 1955	3.00	.10	13.00	(4)	1.75	Unlimited
1051	50¢ Susan B. Anthony, 1955	3.25	.05	14.00	(4)	6.00	Unlimited
1052	$1 Patrick Henry, 1955	10.00	.06	42.50	(4)	13.00	Unlimited
	Perf. 11						
1053	$5 Alexander Hamilton, 1956	100.00	8.00	425.00	(4)	75.00	Unlimited
	Coil Stamps, Perf. 10 Vertically						
1054	1¢ dark green Washington						
	(1031), 1954	.35	.12	2.00		.75	Unlimited

1028   1029   1030   1031

1031A   1032   1033   1034   1035

1036   1037   1038   1039   1040

1041   1042   1042A   1043   1044   1044A

1045   1046   1047   1048   1049

1060

1061

1062

1063

1064

1065

1066

1067

1068

1069

1070

1071

1072

1074

	1954-65 continued, Coil Stamps, Perf. 10 Horizontally	Un	U	PB/LP	#	FDC	Q
1054A	1¼¢ turquoise, Palace of the						
	Governors, Sante Fe (1031A), 1960	.25	.20	3.00		1.00	Unlimited
	Perf. 10 Vertically						
1055	2¢ rose carmine						
	Jefferson (1033), 1954	.10	.05	.75		.75	Unlimited
1056	2½¢ gray blue, Bunker Hill Monument						
	& Massachusetts Flag (1034), 1959	.55	.35	7.50		1.20	Unlimited
1057	3¢ deep violet Statue of Liberty						
	(1035), 1954	.15	.05	1.00		.75	Unlimited
1058	4¢ red violet Lincoln (1036), 1958	.15	.05	1.20		.75	Unlimited
	Perf. 10 Horizontally						
1059	4½¢ bl. grn. Hermitage (1037), 1959	3.25	1.20	20.00		1.75	Unlimited
	Perf. 10 Vertically						
1059A	25¢ green P. Revere (1048), 1965	.70	.30	3.25		1.20	Unlimited
	Issues of 1954, Perf. 11x10½						
1060	3¢ Nebraska Territory, May 7	.10	.05	.50	(4)	.75	115,810,000
1061	3¢ Kansas Territory, May 31	.10	.05	.50	(4)	.45	113,603,700
	Perf. 10½x11						
1062	3¢ George Eastman, July 12	.10	.05	.60	(4)	.75	128,002,000
	Perf. 11x10½						
1063	3¢ Lewis and Clark Expedition,						
	July 28	.10	.05	.50	(4)	.75	116,078,150
	Issues of 1955, Perf. 10½x11						
1064	3¢ Pennsylvania Academy of						
	Fine Arts, Jan. 15	.10	.05	.50	(4)	.75	116,139,800
	Perf. 11x10½						
1065	3¢ Land Grant Colleges, Feb. 12	.10	.05	.50	(4)	.75	120,484,800
1066	8¢ Rotary International, Feb. 23	.20	.12	1.50	(4)	.90	53,854,750
1067	3¢ Armed Forces Reserve, May 21	.10	.05	.50	(4)	.75	175,075,000
	Perf. 10½x11						
1068	3¢ New Hampshire, June 21	.10	.05	.50	(4)	.75	125,944,400
	Perf. 11x10½						
1069	3¢ Soo Locks, June 28	.10	.05	.50	(4)	.75	122,284,600
1070	3¢ Atoms for Peace, July 28	.12	.05	.70	(4)	.75	133,638,850
1071	3¢ Fort Ticonderoga, Sept. 18	.10	.05	.50	(4)	.75	118,664,600
	Perf. 10½x11						
1072	3¢ Andrew W. Mellon, Dec. 20	.10	.05	.60	(4)	.75	112,434,000
	Issues of 1956						
1073	3¢ Benjamin Franklin, Jan. 17	.10	.05	.50	(4)	.75	129,384,550
	Perf. 11x10½						
1074	3¢ Booker T. Washington, Apr. 5	.10	.05	.50	(4)	.75	121,184,600
	Fifth International Philatelic Exhibition, Souvenir Sheet, Imperf.						
1075	Sheet of 2 stamps, Apr. 28	4.00	.350			7.50	2,900,731
1075a	3¢ deep violet (1035)	1.35	1.10				

	1956 continued, Imperf.	Un	U	PB/LP	#	FDC	Q
1075b	8¢ dk. vio., bl. and car. (1041)	1.75	1.50				
	Perf. 11x10½						
1076	3¢ New York Coliseum and						
	Columbus Monument, Apr. 30	.10	.05	.50	(4)	.75	119,784,200
	Wildlife Conservation Issue						
1077	3¢ Wild Turkey, May 5	.12	.05	.65	(4)	1.10	123,159,400
1078	3¢ Pronghorn Antelope, June 22	.12	.05	.65	(4)	1.10	123,138,800
1079	3¢ King Salmon, Nov. 9	.12	.05	.65	(4)	1.10	109,275,000
	Perf. 10½x11						
1080	3¢ Pure Food and Drug Laws,						
	June 27	.10	.05	.50	(4)	.80	112,932,200
	Perf. 11x10½						
1081	3¢ Wheatland, Aug. 5	.10	.05	.50	(4)	.80	125,475,000
	Perf. 10½x11						
1082	3¢ Labor Day, Sept. 3	.10	.05	.50	(4)	.80	117,855,000
	Perf. 11x10½						
1083	3¢ Nassau Hall, Sept. 22	.10	.05	.50	(4)	.80	122,100,000
	Perf. 10½x11						
1084	3¢ Devils Tower, Sept. 24	.10	.05	.50	(4)	.80	118,180,000
	Perf. 11x10½						
1085	3¢ Children's Issue, Dec. 15	.10	.05	.50	(4)	.80	100,975,000
	Issues of 1957						
1086	3¢ Alexander Hamilton, Jan. 11	.10	.05	.50	(4)	.80	115,299,450
	Perf. 10½x11						
1087	3¢ Polio, Jan. 15	.10	.05	.50	(4)	.80	186,949,627
	Perf. 11x10½						
1088	3¢ Coast and Geodetic Survey,						
	Feb. 11	.10	.05	.50	(4)	.80	115,235,000
1089	3¢ Architects, Feb. 23	.10	.05	.50	(4)	.80	106,647,500
	Perf. 10½x11						
1090	3¢ Steel Industry, May 22	.10	.05	.50	(4)	.80	112,010,000
	Perf. 11x10½						
1091	3¢ Int'l. Naval Review, June 10	.10	.05	.50	(4)	.80	118,470,000
1092	3¢ Oklahoma Statehood, June 14	.10	.05	.60	(4)	.80	102,230,000
1093	3¢ School Teachers, July 1	.10	.05	.50	(4)	.80	102,410,000

1076

1077

1078

1079

1080

1081

1082

1083

1084

1085

1086

1087

1088

1089

1090

1091

1092

1093

1094

1095

1096

1097

1098

1099

1100

1104

1105

1106

1107

1108

1109

1110

1111

1112

	1957 continued, Perf. 11	Un	U	PB/LP	#	FDC	Q
1094	4¢ Flag Issue, July 4	.10	.05	.60	(4)	.80	84,054,400
	Perf. 10½x11						
1095	3¢ Shipbuilding, Aug. 15	.10	.05	.70	(4)	.80	126,266,000
	Perf. 11						
1096	8¢ Champion of Liberty,						
	Ramon Magsaysay, Aug. 31	.22	.15	1.75	(4)	.80	39,489,600
	Perf. 10½x11						
1097	3¢ Lafayette, Sept. 6	.10	.05	.50	(4)	.80	122,990,000
	Perf. 11						
1098	3¢ Wildlife Conservation, Nov. 22	.10	.05	.65	(4)	1.00	174,372,800
	Perf. 10½x11						
1099	3¢ Religious Freedom, Dec. 27	.10	.05	.50	(4)	.80	114,365,000
	Issues of 1958						
1100	3¢ Gardening-Horticulture, Mar. 15	.10	.05	.50	(4)	.80	122,765,200
1101-03 not assigned							
	Perf. 11x10½						
1104	3¢ Brussels Fair, Apr. 17	.10	.05	.50	(4)	.80	113,660,200
1105	3¢ James Monroe, Apr. 28	.10	.05	.60	(4)	.80	120,196,580
1106	3¢ Minnesota Statehood, May 11	.10	.05	.50	(4)	.80	120,805,200
	Perf. 11						
1107	3¢ Geophysical Year, May 31	.10	.05	.75	(4)	.80	125,815,200
	Perf. 11x10½						
1108	3¢ Gunston Hall, June 12	.10	.05	.50	(4)	.80	108,415,200
	Perf. 10½x11						
1109	3¢ Mackinac Bridge, June 25	.10	.05	.50	(4)	.80	107,195,200
1110	4¢ Champion of Liberty,						
	Simon Bolivar, July 24	.10	.05	.60	(4)	.80	115,745,280
	Perf. 11						
1111	8¢ Champion of Liberty,						
	Simon Bolivar, July 24	.25	.15	5.00	(4)	.80	39,743,640
	Perf. 11x10½						
1112	4¢ Atlantic Cable 100th Anniversary,						
	Aug. 15	.10	.05	.50	(4)	.80	114,570,200

	1958 continued	Un	U	PB/LP	#	FDC	Q
	Lincoln 150th Anniversary Issue, 1958-59, Perf. 10½x11, 11x10½						
1113	1¢ Portrait by George Healy,						
	Feb. 12, 1959	.05	.05	.40	(4)	.80	120,400,200
1114	3¢ Sculptured Head,						
	by Gutzon Borglum, Feb. 27, 1959	.10	.06	.60	(4)	.80	91,160,200
1115	4¢ Lincoln and Stephen Douglas						
	Debating, Aug. 27, 1958	.10	.05	.55	(4)	.80	114,860,200
1116	4¢ Statue in Lincoln Memorial						
	by Daniel Chester French,						
	May 30, 1959	.10	.05	.65	(4)	.80	126,500,000
	Issues of 1958, Perf. 10½x11						
1117	4¢ Champion of Liberty,						
	Lajos Kossuth, Sept. 19	.10	.05	.60	(4)	.80	120,561,280
	Perf. 11						
1118	8¢ Champion of Liberty,						
	Lajos Kossuth, Sept. 19	.22	.12	3.50	(4)	.80	44,064,576
	Perf. 10½x11						
1119	4¢ Freedom of Press, Sept. 22	.10	.05	.50	(4)	.80	118,390,200
	Perf. 11x10½						
1120	4¢ Overland Mail, Oct. 10	.10	.05	.50	(4)	.80	125,770,200
	Perf. 10½x11						
1121	4¢ Noah Webster, Oct. 16	.10	.05	.50	(4)	.80	114,114,280
	Perf. 11						
1122	4¢ Forest Conservation, Oct. 27	.10	.05	.60	(4)	.80	156,600,200
	Perf. 11x10½						
1123	4¢ Fort Duquesne, Nov. 25	.10	.05	.50	(4)	.80	124,200,200
	Issues of 1959						
1124	4¢ Oregon Statehood, Feb. 14	.10	.05	.50	(4)	.80	120,740,200
	Perf. 10½x11						
1125	4¢ Champion of Liberty,						
	José de San Martin, Feb. 25	.10	.05	.55	(4)	.80	133,623,280
	Perf. 11						
1126	8¢ Champion of Liberty,						
	José de San Martin, Feb. 25	.20	.12	1.75	(4)	.80	45,569,088
	Perf. 10½x11						
1127	4¢ NATO, Apr. 1	.10	.05	.50	(4)	.80	122,493,280
	Perf. 11x10½						
1128	4¢ Arctic Explorations, Apr. 6	.13	.05	.85	(4)	.80	131,260,200
1129	8¢ World Peace through World						
	Trade, Apr. 20	.20	.12	1.50	(4)	.80	47,125,200
1130	4¢ Silver Centennial, June 8	.10	.05	.50	(4)	.80	123,105,000
	Perf. 11						
1131	4¢ St. Lawrence Seaway, June 26	.10	.05	.50	(4)	.80	126,105,050

1113

1114

1115

1116

1117

1118

1119

1120

1121

1122

1123

1124

1125

1126

1127

1128

1129

1130

1131

1132

1133

1134

1135

1136

1137

1138

1139

1140

1141

1142

1143

1144

1145

1146

1147

1148

	1959 continued, Perf. 11	Un	U	PB/LP	#	FDC	Q
1132	4¢ 49-Star Flag, July 4	.10	.05	.50	(4)	.80	209,170,000
1133	4¢ Soil Conservation, Aug. 26	.10	.05	.65	(4)	.80	120,835,000
	Perf. 10½x11						
1134	4¢ Petroleum Industry, Aug. 27	.10	.05	.50	(4)	.80	115,715,000
	Perf. 11x10½						
1135	4¢ Dental Health, Sept. 14	.10	.05	.50	(4)	.80	118,445,000
	Perf. 10½x11						
1136	4¢ Champion of Liberty,						
	Ersnt Reuter, Sept. 29	.10	.05	.60	(4)	.80	111,685,000
	Perf. 11						
1137	8¢ Champion of Liberty,						
	Ernst Reuter, Sept. 29	.20	.12	1.75	(4)	.80	43,099,200
	Perf. 10½x11						
1138	4¢ Dr. Ephraim McDowell, Dec. 3	.10	.05	.50	(4)	.80	115,444,000
	Issues of 1960-61, American Credo Issue, Perf. 11						
1139	4¢ Quotation from Washington's						
	Farewell Address, Jan. 20, 1960	.18	.05	1.00	(4)	1.25	126,470,000
1140	4¢ B. Franklin Quotation,						
	Mar. 31, 1960	.18	.05	1.00	(4)	1.00	124,560,000
1141	4¢ T. Jefferson Quotation,						
	May 18, 1960	.18	.05	1.00	(4)	1.00	115,455,000
1142	4¢ Francis Scott Key Quotation,						
	Sept. 14, 1960	.18	.05	1.00	(4)	1.25	122,060,000
1143	4¢ Lincoln Quotation,						
	Nov. 19, 1960	.18	.05	1.00	(4)	1.25	120,540,000
1144	4¢ Patrick Henry Quotation,						
	Jan. 11, 1961	.18	.05	1.00	(4)	1.25	113,075,000
	Issues of 1960						
1145	4¢ Boy Scout Jubilee, Feb. 8	.10	.05	.50	(4)	1.25	139,325,000
	Olympic Winter Games Issue, Feb. 18, Perf. 10½x11						
1146	4¢ Olympic Rings and Snowflake	.10	.05	.50	(4)	.80	124,445,000
1147	4¢ Champion of Liberty,						
	Thomas G. Masaryk, Mar. 7	.10	.05	.60	(4)	.80	113,792,000
	Perf. 11						
1148	8¢ Champion of Liberty,						
	Thomas G. Masaryk, Mar. 7	.20	.12	1.75	(4)	.80	44,215,200

American Credo

The American Credo Series (#1139-1144) was meant to emphasize American ideals and the persons who shaped them. The quotations are from an eclectic group of patriots: Patrick Henry, George Washington, Benjamin Franklin and Thomas Jefferson were all revolutionary-era heroes; Abraham Lincoln was, of course, the president who freed the slaves; and Francis Scott Key wrote our national anthem, the "Star-Spangled Banner," during the War of 1812.

1960

	1960 continued, Perf. 11x10½	Un	U	PB/LP	#	FDC	Q
1149	4¢ World Refugee Year, Apr. 7	.10	.05	.50	(4)	.80	113,195,000
	Perf. 11						
1150	4¢ Water Conservation, Apr. 18	.10	.05	.65	(4)	.80	121,805,000
	Perf. 10½x11						
1151	4¢ SEATO, May 31	.10	.05	.50	(4)	.80	115,353,000
	Perf. 11x10½						
1152	4¢ American Woman, June 2	.10	.05	.50	(4)	.80	111,080,000
	Perf. 11						
1153	4¢ 50-Star Flag, July 4	.10	.05	.50	(4)	.80	153,025,000
	Perf. 11x10½						
1154	4¢ Pony Express 100th Anniv., July 19	.10	.05	.50	(4)	.80	119,665,000
	Perf. 10½x11						
1155	4¢ Employ the Handicapped, Aug. 28	.10	.05	.50	(4)	.80	117,855,000
1156	4¢ World Forestry Congress, Aug. 29	.10	.05	.50	(4)	.80	118,185,000
	Perf. 11						
1157	4¢ Mexican Independence, Sept. 16	.10	.05	.50	(4)	.80	112,260,000
1158	4¢ U.S.-Japan Treaty, Sept. 28	.10	.05	.50	(4)	.80	125,010,000
	Perf. 10½x11						
1159	4¢ Champion of Liberty, Ignacy Jan Paderewski, Oct. 8	.10	.05	.55	(4)	.80	119,798,000
	Perf. 11						
1160	8¢ Champion of Liberty, Ignacy Jan Paderewski, Oct. 8	.20	.12	1.75	(4)	.80	42,696,000
	Perf. 10½x11						
1161	4¢ Sen. Taft Memorial, Oct. 10	.10	.05	.50	(4)	.80	106,610,000
	Perf. 11x10½						
1162	4¢ Wheels of Freedom, Oct. 15	.10	.05	.50	(4)	.80	109,695,000
	Perf. 11						
1163	4¢ Boy's Club of America, Oct. 18	.10	.05	.50	(4)	.80	123,690,000
1164	4¢ Automated P.O., Oct. 20	.10	.05	.50	(4)	.80	123,970,000
	Perf. 10½x11						
1165	4¢ Champion of Liberty, Baron Gustaf Mannerheim, Oct. 26	.10	.05	.55	(4)	.80	124,796,000
	Perf. 11						
1166	8¢ Champion of Liberty, Baron Gustaf Mannerheim, Oct. 26	.20	.12	1.75	(4)	.80	42,076,800

1149

1150

1151

1152

1153

1154

1155

1156

1157

1158

1159

1160

1161

1162

1163

1164

1165

1166

135

1167

1168

1169

1170

1171

1172

1173

1174

1175

1176

1177

1178

1179

1180

1181

1182

1183

1184

	1960 continued, Perf. 11	Un	U	PB/LP	#	FDC	Q
1167	4¢ Camp Fire Girls, Nov. 4	.10	.05	.50	(4)	.80	116,210,000
	Perf. 10½x11						
1168	4¢ Champion of Liberty,						
	Giuseppe Garibaldi, Nov. 2	.10	.05	.55	(4)	.80	126,252,000
	Perf. 11						
1169	8¢ Champion of Liberty,						
	Giuseppe Garibaldi, Nov. 2	.20	.12	1.75	(4)	.80	42,746,400
	Perf. 10½x11						
1170	4¢ Sen. George Memorial, Nov. 5	.10	.05	.50	(4)	.80	124,117,000
1171	4¢ Andrew Carnegie, Nov. 25	.10	.05	.50	(4)	.80	119,840,000
1172	4¢ John Foster Dulles Memorial,						
	Dec. 6	.10	.05	.55	(4)	.80	117,187,000
	Perf. 11x10½						
1173	4¢ Echo 1-Communications for						
	Peace, Dec. 15	.35	.12	2.25	(4)	1.75	124,390,000
	Issues of 1961, Perf. 10½x11						
1174	4¢ Champion of Liberty,						
	Mahatma Gandhi, Jan. 26	.10	.05	.55	(4)	.80	112,966,000
	Perf. 11						
1175	8¢ Champion of Liberty,						
	Mahatma Gandhi, Jan. 26	.20	.12	2.00	(4)	.80	41,644,200
1176	4¢ Range Conservation, Feb. 2	.10	.05	.65	(4)	.75	110,850,000
	Perf. 10½x11						
1177	4¢ Horace Greeley, Feb. 3	.10	.05	.55	(4)	.75	98,616,000
	Issues of 1961-65, Civil War Centennial Issue, Perf. 11x10½						
1178	4¢ Fort Sumter, Apr. 12, 1961	.18	.05	1.10	(4)	1.75	101,125,000
1179	4¢ Shiloh, Apr. 7, 1962	.15	.05	1.00	(4)	1.75	124,865,000
	Perf. 11						
1180	5¢ Gettysburg, July 1, 1963	.15	.05	1.00	(4)	1.75	79,905,000
1181	5¢ Wilderness, May 5, 1964	.15	.05	1.00	(4)	1.75	125,410,000
1182	5¢ Appomattox, Apr. 9, 1965	.15	.05	1.10	(4)	1.75	112,845,000
	Issues of 1961						
1183	4¢ Kansas Statehood, May 10	.10	.05	.55	(4)	.75	106,210,000
	Perf. 11x10½						
1184	4¢ Sen. George W. Norris, July 11	.10	.05	.55	(4)	.75	110,810,000

	1961 continued, Perf. 11x10½	Un	U	PB/LP	#	FDC	Q
1185	4¢ Naval Aviation, Aug. 20	.10	.05	.55	(4)	.90	116,995,000
	Perf. 10½x11						
1186	4¢ Workmen's Comp., Sept. 4	.10	.05	.55	(4)	.75	121,015,000
	Perf. 11						
1187	4¢ Frederic Remington, Oct. 4	.12	.05	1.00	(4)	.75	111,600,000
	Perf. 10½x11						
1188	4¢ Republic of China, Oct. 10	.10	.05	.55	(4)	.75	110,620,000
1189	4¢ Naismith-Basketball, Nov. 6	.10	.05	.55	(4)	1.50	109,110,000
	Perf. 11						
1190	4¢ Nursing, Dec. 28	.10	.05	.70	(4)	.75	145,350,000
	Issues of 1962						
1191	4¢ New Mexico Statehood, Jan. 6	.10	.05	.55	(4)	.75	112,870,000
1192	4¢ Arizona Statehood, Feb. 14	.10	.05	.65	(4)	.75	121,820,000
1193	4¢ Project Mercury, Feb. 20	.10	.10	.65	(4)	1.50	289,240,000
1194	4¢ Malaria Eradication, Mar. 30	.10	.05	.55	(4)	.75	120,155,000
	Perf. 10½x11						
1195	4¢ Charles Evans Hughes, Apr. 11	.10	.05	.55	(4)	.75	124,595,000
	Perf. 11						
1196	4¢ Seattle World's Fair, Apr. 25	.10	.05	.65	(4)	.75	147,310,000
1197	4¢ Louisiana Statehood, Apr. 30	.10	.05	.55	(4)	.75	118,690,000
	Perf. 11x10½						
1198	4¢ Homestead Act, May 20	.10	.05	.55	(4)	.75	122,730,000
1199	4¢ Girl Scout Jubilee, July 24	.10	.05	.55	(4)	1.00	126,515,000
1200	4¢ Sen. Brien McMahon, July 28	.10	.05	.65	(4)	.75	130,960,000
1201	4¢ Apprenticeship, Aug. 31	.10	.05	.55	(4)	.75	120,055,000

Louisiana Statehood

Louisiana was part of the biggest real estate deal in history, the Louisiana Purchase (#327). But the state that now shares the name of this huge land mass (covering 827,987 square miles and all or parts of 15 states) very nearly was not included as part of the bargain.

By the time the United States purchased the French territory called Louisiana in 1803, the area around New Orleans—at the mouth of the Mississippi River—had changed hands on seven occasions. Originally claimed by France in 1682, the territory was ceded to Spain, controlled by Britain and returned to France before once again becoming part of the Spanish colonies just three years before the purchase was made. In fact, when Spain returned the territory to France in 1800, it retained control of the state's current capital (Baton Rouge), which did not become part of the United States until 1810.

Even after Louisiana became a state in 1812 (#1197), its fate once again was in question. A war between the United States and England began the same year. American control of the Mississippi River, a valuable shipping route, was established during the Battle of New Orleans (January 1815), a skirmish that took place three weeks after the war had officially ended.

1185

1186

1187

1188

1189

1190

1191

1192

1193

1194

1195

1196

1197

1198

1199

1200

1201

1202

1203

1204

1205

1206

1207

1208

1209

1213

1230

1231

1232

1233

1234

1235

1236

1237

	1962 continued, Perf. 11	Un	U	PB/LP	#	FDC	Q
1202	4¢ Sam Rayburn, Sept. 16	.10	.05	.55	(4)	.75	120,715,000
1203	4¢ Dag Hammarskjold, Oct. 23	.10	.05	.70	(4)	.75	121,440,000
1204	4¢ Dag Hammarskjold, Special						
	Printing black, brown and yellow						
	(yellow inverted), Nov. 16	.12	.08	4.00	(4)	6.00	40,270,000
1205	4¢ Christmas Issue, Nov. 1	.10	.05	.50	(4)	.75	861,970,000
1206	4¢ Higher Education, Nov. 14	.10	.05	.55	(4)	.75	120,035,000
1207	4¢ Winslow Homer, Dec. 15	.15	.05	1.00	(4)	.75	117,870,000
	Issue of 1963						
1208	5¢ Flag over White House, Jan. 9	.12	.05	.55	(4)	.75	
	Regular Issues of 1962-66, Perf. 11x10½						
1209	1¢ Andrew Jackson, March 22	.05	.05	.25	(4)	.75	
1210-12 not assigned							
1213	5¢ George Washington, Nov. 23	.12	.05	.75	(4)	.75	
1213a	Booklet pane of 5 + label	2.00	.75				
1214-24 not assigned							
	Coil Stamps, Perf. 10 Vertically						
1225	1¢ green Jackson (1209), May 31	.20	.05	.85		.75	
1226-28 not assigned							
1229	5¢ dk. blue gray Washington						
	(1213), Nov. 23	1.75	.05	4.75		.75	
	Issues of 1963, Perf. 11						
1230	5¢ Carolina Charter, Apr. 6	.12	.05	.60	(4)	.75	129,945,000
1231	5¢ Food for Peace-Freedom from						
	Hunger, June 4	.12	.05	.60	(4)	.75	135,620,000
1232	5¢ West Virginia Statehood, June 20	.12	.05	.60	(4)	.75	137,540,000
1233	5¢ Emancipation Proclamation,						
	Aug. 16	.12	.05	.60	(4)	.75	132,435,000
1234	5¢ Alliance for Progress, Aug. 17	.12	.05	.60	(4)	.75	135,520,000
	Perf. 10½x11						
1235	5¢ Cordell Hull, Oct. 5	.12	.05	.60	(4)	.75	131,420,000
	Perf. 11x10½						
1236	5¢ Eleanor Roosevelt, Oct. 11	.12	.05	.60	(4)	.75	133,170,000
	Perf. 11						
1237	5¢ Science, Oct. 14	.12	.05	.60	(4)	.75	130,195,000

	1963 continued, Perf. 11	Un	U	PB/LP	#	FDC	Q
1238	5¢ City Mail Delivery, Oct. 26	.12	.05	.60	(4)	.75	128,450,000
1239	5¢ Red Cross 100th Anniv., Oct. 29	.12	.05	.60	(4)	.75	118,665,000
	Christmas Issue, Nov. 1						
1240	5¢ National Christmas Tree and						
	White House	.12	.05	.60	(4)	.75	1,291,250,000
1241	5¢ John James Audubon, Dec. 7,						
	(see also #C71)	.12	.05	.60	(4)	.75	175,175,000
	Issues of 1964, Perf. 10½x11						
1242	5¢ Sam Houston, Jan. 10	.12	.05	.60	(4)	.75	125,995,000
	Perf. 11						
1243	5¢ Charles M. Russell, Mar. 9	.15	.05	.75	(4)	.75	128,925,000
	Perf. 11x10½						
1244	5¢ New York World's Fair, Apr. 22	.12	.05	.60	(4)	.75	145,700,000
	Perf. 11						
1245	5¢ John Muir, Apr. 29	.12	.05	.60	(4)	.75	120,310,000
	Perf. 11x10½						
1246	5¢ Kennedy Memorial, May 29	.12	.05	.60	(4)	.75	511,750,000
	Perf. 10½x11						
1247	5¢ New Jersey 300th Anniv.,						
	June 15	.12	.05	.60	(4)	.75	123,845,000
	Perf. 11						
1248	5¢ Nevada Statehood, July 22	.12	.05	.60	(4)	.75	122,825,000
1249	5¢ Register and Vote, Aug. 1	.12	.05	.60	(4)	.75	453,090,000
	Perf. 10½x11						
1250	5¢ Shakespeare, Aug. 14	.12	.05	.60	(4)	.75	123,245,000
1251	5¢ Doctors Mayo, Sept. 11	.12	.05	.60	(4)	.75	123,355,000
	Perf. 11						
1252	5¢ American Music, Oct. 15	.12	.05	.60	(4)	.75	126,970,000
1253	5¢ Homemakers, Oct. 26, Perf. 11	.12	.05	.60	(4)	.75	121,250,000

Register and Vote

Stamps often convey important messages, such as Register and Vote (#1249 and 1344). This first stamp was issued in 1964, a milestone year in which the Civil Rights Act guaranteed all citizens the right to vote regardless of race. In February of that year, the Supreme Court handed down a decision that guaranteed all Americans equal representation by ensuring that the size of Congressional districts reflected the number of voters residing in them.

The 1964 presidential election was a resounding victory for incumbent Lyndon B. Johnson. He defeated Barry Goldwater in the electoral college by a margin of eight to one (486-52). However, "Register and Vote" did not meet with quite as much success. Voter turnout in the election was almost a full percentage point lower than in 1960.

1238

1239

1240

1241

1242

1243

1244

1245

1246

1247

1248

1249

1250

1251

1252

1253

1254   1255
1256   1257

1258

1259

1260

1261

1262

1263

1264

1265

1266

1267

1268

1269

1270

1271

1272

144

	1964 continued	Un	U	PB/LP	#	FDC	Q
	Christmas Issue, Nov. 9, Perf. 11						
1254	5¢ Holly	.50	.05	3.25	(4)	.75	351,940,000
1255	5¢ Mistletoe	.50	.05	3.25	(4)	.75	351,940,000
1256	5¢ Poinsettia	.50	.05	3.25	(4)	.75	351,940,000
1257	5¢ Sprig of Conifer	.50	.05	3.25	(4)	.75	351,940,000
1257a	Block of four, #1254-1257	2.75	1.25			3.00	
	Perf. 10½x11						
1258	5¢ Verrazano Narrows Bridge,						
	Nov. 21	.12	.05	.60	(4)	.75	120,005,000
	Perf. 11						
1259	5¢ Fine Arts, Dec. 2	.12	.05	.75	(4)	.75	125,800,000
	Perf. 10½x11						
1260	5¢ Amateur Radio, Dec. 15	.12	.05	.75	(4)	.75	122,230,000
	Issues of 1965, Perf. 11						
1261	5¢ Battle of New Orleans, Jan. 8	.12	.05	.75	(4)	.75	115,695,000
1262	5¢ Physical Fitness-Sokol, Feb. 15	.12	.05	.75	(4)	.75	115,095,000
1263	5¢ Crusade Against Cancer, Apr. 1	.12	.05	.75	(4)	.75	119,560,000
	Perf. 10½x11						
1264	5¢ Churchill Memorial, May 13	.12	.05	.75	(4)	.75	125,180,000
	Perf. 11						
1265	5¢ Magna Carta, June 15	.12	.05	.75	(4)	.75	120,135,000
1266	5¢ Intl. Cooperation Year, June 26	.12	.05	.75	(4)	.75	115,405,000
1267	5¢ Salvation Army, July 2	.12	.05	.75	(4)	.75	115,855,000
	Perf. 10½x11						
1268	5¢ Dante Alighieri, July 27	.12	.05	.75	(4)	.75	115,340,000
1269	5¢ Herbert Hoover, Aug. 10	.12	.05	.75	(4)	.75	114,840,000
	Perf. 11						
1270	5¢ Robert Fulton, Aug. 19	.12	.05	.75	(4)	.75	116,140,000
1271	5¢ Settlement of Florida, Aug. 28	.12	.05	1.00	(4)	.75	116,900,000
1272	5¢ Traffic Safety, Sept. 3	.12	.05	1.00	(4)	.75	114,085,000

Winston Churchill

It seems fitting that Sir Winston Churchill would be honored on a U.S. stamp (#1264). The charismatic Prime Minister of Britain was a staunch ally of the United States during the dark days of World War II. The postal memorial tribute was only one honor bestowed on Churchill by the United States: Congress had made him an honorary citizen in 1963.

	1965 continued, Perf. 11	Un	U	PB/LP	#	FDC	Q
1273	5¢ John Singleton Copley, Sept. 17	.15	.05	1.25	(4)	.75	114,880,000
1274	11¢ Intl. Telecom. Union, Oct. 6	.50	.25	9.00	(4)	.75	26,995,000
1275	5¢ Adlai E. Stevenson, Oct. 23	.12	.05	.75	(4)	.75	128,495,000
	Christmas Issue, Nov. 2						
1276	5¢ Angel with Trumpet	.12	.05	.60	(4)	.75	1,139,930,000
1277, 1296, 1300-02 not assigned							
	Issues of 1965-78, Prominent Americans Issue, Perf. 11x10½, 10½x11						
1278	1¢ Thomas Jefferson, 1968	.05	.05	.25	(4)	.60	
1278a	Booklet pane of 8, 1968	1.00	*.25*				
1278b	Booklet pane of 4, 1971	.75	*.20*				
1279	1¼¢ Albert Gallatin, 1967	.10	.05	25.00	(4)	.60	
1280	2¢ Frank Lloyd Wright, 1966	.05	.05	.30	(4)	.60	
1280a	Booklet pane of 5+ label, 1968	1.20	*.40*				
1280c	Booklet pane of 6, 1971	1.00	*.35*				
1281	3¢ Francis Parkman, 1967	.06	.05	.40	(4)	.60	
1282	4¢ Abraham Lincoln, 1965	.08	.05	.40	(4)	.60	
1283	5¢ George Washington, 1966	.10	.05	.50	(4)	.60	
1283B	5¢ Washington redrawn, 1967	.12	.05	1.00	(4)	.45	
1284	6¢ Franklin D. Roosevelt, 1966	.18	.05	.80	(4)	.45	
1284b	Booklet pane of 8, 1967	1.50	*.50*				
1284c	Booklet pane of 5+ label, 1968	1.25	*.50*				
1285	Albert Einstein, 1966	.25	.05	1.25	(4)	.50	
1286	10¢ Andrew Jackson, 1967	.25	.05	2.00	(4)	.60	
1286A	Henry Ford, 1968	.30	.05	1.50	(4)	.50	
1287	13¢ John F. Kennedy, 1967	.30	.05	1.65	(4)	.65	
1288	15¢ Oliver Wendell Holmes, 1968	.30	.06	1.50	(4)	.60	
	Perf. 10						
1288B	15¢ dk. rose claret Holmes (1288),						
	Single from booklet, 1978	.30	.05			.65	
1288Bc	Booklet pane of 8, 1978	2.40	*1.25*				
	Perf. 11x10½, 10½x11						
1289	20¢ George C. Marshall, 1967	.55	.06	2.50	(4)	.80	
1290	25¢ Frederick Douglass, 1967	.60	.05	2.75	(4)	1.00	
1291	30¢ John Dewey, 1968	.75	.08	3.50	(4)	1.20	
1292	40¢ Thomas Paine, 1968	.95	.10	4.25	(4)	1.60	
1293	50¢ Lucy Stone, 1968	1.00	.05	4.50	(4)	3.25	
1294	$1 Eugene O'Neill, 1967	2.40	.08	10.50	(4)	7.50	
1295	$5 John Bassett Moore, 1966	12.50	2.00	50.00	(4)	60.00	
	Issues of 1966-78, Coil Stamps, Perf. 10 Horizontally						
1297	3¢ violet Parkman, (1281), 1975	.12	.05	.60		.75	
1298	6¢ gray brown F.D.R. (1284), 1967	.30	.05	3.00		.75	
	Perf. 10 Vertically						
1299	1¢ green Jefferson (1278), 1968	.06	.05	.35		.75	
1303	4¢ black Lincoln (1282), 1966	.15	.05	2.25		.75	
1304	5¢ blue Washington (1283), 1966	.15	.05	.90		.75	
1305	6¢ gray brown F.D.R. (1284), 1968	.20	.05	1.25		.75	

1273

1274

1275

1276

1278

1279

1280

1281

1282

1283

1283B

1284

1285

1286

1286A

1287

1288

1289

1290

1291

1292

1293

1294

1295

1306

1307

1308

1309

1310

1312

1313

1314

1311

1315

1316

1317

1318

1319

	1966-78 continued, Coil Stamps, Perf. 10 Vertically	Un	U	PB/LP	#	FDC	Q
1305E	15¢ rose claret Holmes						
	(1288), 1978	.30	.05	1.65		.75	
1305C	$1 dull purple Eugene O'Neill						
	(1294), 1973	2.25	.20	6.50		3.00	
	Issues of 1966, Perf. 11						
1306	5¢ Migratory Bird Treaty, Mar. 16	.12	.05	.75	(4)	.75	116,835,000
1307	Humane Treatment of Animals,						
	Apr. 9	.12	.05	.90	(4)	.75	117,470,000
1308	5¢ Indiana Statehood, Apr. 16	.12	.05	.75	(4)	.75	123,770,000
1309	5¢ American Circus, May 2	.12	.05	.90	(4)	.75	131,270,000
	Sixth International Philatelic Exhibition Issue						
1310	5¢ Stamped Cover, May 21	.12	.05	.90	(4)	.75	122,285,000
	Imperf.						
1311	5¢ Souvenir Sheet, May 23	.30	.15			.75	14,680,000
	Perf. 11						
1312	5¢ Bill of Rights, July 1	.12	.05	.75	(4)	.75	114,160,000
	Perf. 10½ x 11						
1313	5¢ Polish Millennium, July 30	.12	.05	.90	(4)	.75	128,475,000
	Perf. 11						
1314	5¢ National Park Service, Aug. 25	.12	.05	.75	(4)	.75	119,535,000
1315	5¢ Marine Corps Reserve, Aug. 29	.12	.05	1.00	(4)	.75	125,110,000
1316	5¢ General Federation						
	of Women's Clubs, Sept. 12	.12	.05	1.00	(4)	.75	114,853,200
	American Folklore Issue, Sept. 24						
1317	5¢ Johnny Appleseed	.12	.05	1.00	(4)	.75	124,290,000
1318	5¢ Beautification of America, Oct. 5	.12	.05	1.00	(4)	.75	128,460,000
1319	5¢ Great River Road, Oct. 21	.12	.05	1.00	(4)	.75	127,585,000

Bill of Rights

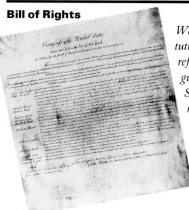

When the United States drafted its new constitution in 1787, Virginia delegate George Mason refused to sign it. According to him it did not guarantee "the rights of the people" (#1312). So he wrote a document that would ensure those rights for ages to come. His ideas ultimately became the first 10 amendments to our constitution, the Bill of Rights. They guarantee rights that Americans hold dear—freedom of religion, speech and the press.

	1966 continued, Perf. 11	Un	U	PB/LP	#	FDC	Q
1320	5¢ Savings Bond-Servicemen,						
	Oct. 26	.12	.05	1.00	(4)	.75	115,875,000
	Christmas Issue, Nov. 1						
1321	5¢ Madonna and Child, by						
	Hans Memling	.12	.05	.75	(4)	.75	1,173,547,000
1322	5¢ Mary Cassatt, Nov. 17	.20	.05	2.75	(4)	.75	114,015,000
	Issues of 1967						
1323	5¢ National Grange, Apr. 17	.12	.05	.90	(4)	.75	121,105,000
1324	5¢ Canada 100th Anniv., May 25	.12	.05	.90	(4)	.75	132,045,000
1325	5¢ Erie Canal, July 4	.12	.05	.90	(4)	.75	118,780,000
1326	5¢ Search for Peace-Lions, July 5	.12	.05	.90	(4)	.75	121,985,000
1327	5¢ Henry David Thoreau, July 12	.12	.05	.90	(4)	.75	111,850,000
1328	5¢ Nebraska Statehood, July, 29	.12	.05	.90	(4)	.75	117,225,000
1329	5¢ Voice of America, Aug. 1	.12	.05	1.00	(4)	.75	111,515,000
	American Folklore Issue, Davy Crockett, Aug. 17						
1330	5¢ Davy Crockett and Scrub Pine	.12	.05	1.00	(4)	.75	114,270,000
	Accomplishments in Space Issue, Sept. 29						
1331	5¢ Space Walking Astronaut	.90	.25			2.50	60,432,500
1331a	Attached pair, #1331-1332	2.00	1.50	8.00	(4)	8.00	
1332	5¢ Gemini 4 Capsule and Earth	.90	.25	8.00	(4)	2.50	60,432,500
1333	5¢ Urban Planning, Oct. 2	.15	.05	1.25	(4)	.75	110,675,000
1334	5¢ Finnish Independence, Oct. 6	.15	.05	1.25	(4)	.75	110,670,000
	Perf. 12						
1335	5¢ Thomas Eakins, Nov. 2	.18	.05	1.50	(4)	.75	113,825,000
	Perf. 11						
	Christmas Issue, Nov. 6						
1336	5¢ Madonna and Child, by						
	Hans Memling	.12	.05	.60	(4)	.75	1,208,700,000
1337	5¢ Mississippi Statehood, Dec. 11	.15	.05	1.00	(4)	.75	113,330,000
	Issues of 1968-71						
1338	6¢ Flag and White House,						
	Jan. 24, 1968	.12	.05	.60	(4)	.75	

U.S. Savings Bonds

The U.S. government offers one financial investment opportunity that is within the reach of every American—the U.S. savings bond (#1320). "Defense bonds" were introduced on April 30, 1941, at a fixed interest rate of 2.9%. Their name was changed to "war bonds" when we became involved in World War II. The bonds were offered in small denominations, beginning at $25, and were promoted as a way to invest in America and help the war effort. The bonds were meant to benefit our fighting forces in another way, as well: Military personnel were (and still are) encouraged to buy them as a way of saving money. Today savings bonds are issued in denominations up to $10,000.

1320

1321

1322

1323

1324

1325

1326

1327

1328

1329

1330

1331   1332

1333   1334

1335

1336

1337

1338

1339

1340

1341

1342

1343

1344

1345

1346

1347

1348

1349

1350

1351

1352

1353

1354

1355

1968-71 continued, Perf. 11x10½	Un	U	PB/LP	#	FDC	Q
1338D 6¢ dark blue, red & green						
(1338), Aug. 7, 1970	.20	.05	4.25	(20)	.75	
1338F 8¢ multicolored (1338),						
May 10, 1971	.20	.05	4.25	(20)	.75	
Coil Stamps of 1969-71, Perf. 10 Vertically						
1338A 6¢ dark blue, red & green						
(1338), May 30, 1969	.20	.05	—		.75	
1338G 8¢ multicolored (1338),						
May 10, 1971	.20	.05	—		.75	
Issues of 1968, Perf. 11						
1339 6¢ Illinois Statehood, Feb. 12	.18	.05	1.00	(4)	.75	141,350,000
1340 6¢ HemisFair '68, Mar. 30	.18	.05	1.00	(4)	.75	144,345,000
1341 $1 Airlift, Apr. 4	5.00	3.00	25.00	(4)	6.50	
1342 6¢ Support Our Youth-Elks, May 1	.18	.05	1.00	(4)	.75	147,120,000
1343 6¢ Law and Order, May 17	.18	.05	1.00	(4)	.75	130,125,000
1344 6¢ Register and Vote, June 27	.18	.05	1.00	(4)	.75	158,700,000
Historic Flag Series, July 4						
1345 6¢ Ft. Moultrie Flag, 1776	1.00	.50			4.00	23,153,000
1346 6¢ Ft. McHenry Flag, 1795-1818	1.00	.50			4.00	25,153,000
1347 6¢ Washington's Cruisers Flag,						
1775	.60	.50			4.00	23,153,000
1348 6¢ Bennington Flag, 1777	.60	.50			4.00	23,153,000
1349 6¢ Rhode Island Flag, 1775	.60	.45			4.00	23,153,000
1350 6¢ First Stars and Stripes Flag,						
1777	.60	.35			4.00	23,153,000
1351 6¢ Bunker Hill Flag, 1775	.60	.35			4.00	23,153,000
1352 6¢ Grand Union Flag, 1776	.60	.35			4.00	23,153,000
1353 6¢ Phila. Light Horse Flag, 1775	.80	.35			4.00	23,153,000
1354 6¢ First Navy Jack, 1775	.80	.40			4.00	23,153,000
Plate Block, #1345-1354			18.00	(20)		
1354a #1345-1354 printed se-tenant in						
vertical rows of 10	8.25	7.50				
Perf. 12						
1355 6¢ Walt Disney, Sept. 11	.20	.05	1.25	(4)	1.00	153,015,000

	1968 continued, Perf. 11	Un	U	PB/LP	#	FDC	Q
1356	6¢ Father Marquette, Sept. 20	.20	.05	1.00	(4)	.75	132,560,000
	American Folklore Issue, Daniel Boone, Sept. 26						
1357	6¢ Pennsylvania Rifle, Powder Horn,						
	Tomahawk, Pipe and Knife	.20	.05	1.00	(4)	.75	130,385,000
1358	6¢ Arkansas River, Oct. 1	.20	.05	1.00	(4)	.75	132,265,000
1359	6¢ Leif Erikson, Oct. 9	.20	.05	1.00	(4)	.75	128,710,000
	Perf. 11x10½						
1360	6¢ Cherokee Strip, Oct. 15	.20	.05	1.00	(4)	.75	124,775,000
	Perf. 11						
1361	6¢ John Trumbull, Oct. 18	.25	.05	1.25	(4)	.75	128,295,000
1362	6¢ Waterfowl Conservation,						
	Oct. 24	.25	.05	1.75	(4)	.75	142,245,000
	Christmas Issue, Nov. 1						
1363	6¢ "The Annunciation,"						
	by Jan van Eyck	.20	.05	2.75	(10)	.75	1,410,580,000
1364	6¢ American Indian, Nov. 4	.30	.05	1.35	(4)	.75	125,100,000
	Issues of 1969, Beautification of America Issue, Jan. 16						
1365	6¢ Capitol, Azaleas and Tulips	.90	.15	7.50	(4)	2.00	48,142,500
1366	6¢ Washington Monument,						
	Potomac River and Daffodils	.90	.15	7.50	(4)	2.00	48,142,500
1367	6¢ Poppies and Lupines						
	along Highway	.90	.15	7.50	(4)	2.00	48,142,500
1368	6¢ Blooming Crabapples						
	along Street	.90	.15	7.50	(4)	2.00	48,142,500
1368a	Block of four, #1365-1368	4.50	3.50			5.00	
1369	6¢ American Legion, Mar. 15	.20	.05	1.10	(4)	.75	148,770,000
	American Folklore Issue, Grandma Moses, May 1						
1370	6¢ "July Fourth"	.25	.05	1.35	(4)	.75	139,475,000
1371	6¢ Apollo 8, May 5	.30	.06	1.50	(4)	2.00	187,165,000
1372	6¢ W.C. Handy, May 17	.20	.05	1.00	(4)	.75	125,555,000

National Portrait Gallery

Officially authorized by Congress in 1962, the National Portrait Gallery opened its doors six years later. It is housed in the historic U.S. Patent Office Building and shares its home with the National Collection of Fine Arts and the Archives of American Art. All three are administered by the Smithsonian Institution.

As the name implies, the National Portrait Gallery is devoted to displaying the likenesses of those who shaped this country's history. The collection includes the great and the near-great captured in paintings, sculptures, drawings and prints. Chief Joseph (1840-1904), the legendary leader of the Nez Perce Indians, is among the illustrious Americans on display. His portrait (#1364) was chosen to celebrate the gallery's opening. Similar to eligibility guidelines for U.S. stamp subjects, portraits cannot be accepted as part of the permanent collection until 10 years after the subject's death. (They can, however, be exhibited before this.)

1356

1357

1358

1359

1360

1361

1362

1363

1364

1365   1366
1367   1368

1369

1370

1371

1372

1374

1375

1373

1381

1376
1378

1377
1379

1380

1382

1384

1383

1384a

1385

1386

	1969 continued, Perf. 11	Un	U	PB/LP	#	FDC	Q
1373	6¢ California Settlement, July 16	.20	.05	1.00	(4)	.75	144,425,000
1374	6¢ John Wesley Powell, Aug. 1	.20	.05	1.00	(4)	.75	135,875,000
1375	6¢ Alabama Statehood, Aug. 2	.20	.05	1.00	(4)	.75	151,110,000
	Botanical Congress Issue, Aug. 23						
1376	6¢ Douglas Fir (Northwest)	1.10	.15	8.50	(4)	2.00	39,798,750
1377	6¢ Lady's Slipper (Northeast)	1.10	.15	8.50	(4)	2.00	39,798,750
1378	6¢ Ocotillo (Southwest)	1.10	.15	8.50	(4)	2.00	39,798,750
1379	6¢ Franklinia (Southeast)	1.10	.15	8.50	(4)	2.00	39,798,750
1379a	Block of four, #1376-1379	5.50	5.00			7.00	
	Perf. 10½x11						
1380	6¢ Dartmouth College Case,						
	Sept. 22	.20	.05	1.35	(4)	.75	129,540,000
	Perf. 11						
1381	6¢ Professional Baseball, Sept. 24	.25	.05	1.75	(4)	1.50	130,925,000
1382	6¢ Intercollegiate Football,						
	Sept. 26	.25	.05	1.75	(4)	1.50	139,055,000
1383	6¢ Dwight D. Eisenhower, Oct. 14	.20	.05	1.00	(4)	.75	150,611,200
	Christmas Issue, Nov. 3, Perf. 11x10½						
1384	6¢ Winter Sunday in Norway, Maine	.18	.05	2.25	(10)	.75	1,709,795,000
1384a	Precanceled	.60	.06				
1385	6¢ Hope for Crippled, Nov. 20	.18	.05	1.00	(4)	.75	127,545,000
1386	6¢ William M. Harnett, Dec. 3	.18	.05	1.20	(4)	.75	145,788,800

College Football

When Princeton and Rutgers took the field in 1869 for the first official intercollegiate football contest (#1382), the sport they played was a far cry from the game we know today. Variations on the football theme had been played at American colleges as early as the 1820s, but it was not until after the Civil War that rules were developed. Prior to that time the game was so rough that playing it often was banned. Even after rules were established, what passed for football depended on where it was played...and by whom.

*For example, Rutgers and Princeton played two games one week apart. The first, at Rutgers, used the home team's rules, which were similar to what we call soccer. The second, at Princeton, looked more like the British game of rugby. But any way you played it, **foot**ball, as the name implies, was originally a kicking game. Passing was not legal until 1906, and even then you received more points for kicking (five for a field goal vs. two for a touchdown). Defense was emphasized, and scores were low by today's standards (20 points was considered a high score).*

	Issues of 1970	Un	U	PB/LP	#	FDC	Q
	Natural History Issue, May 6, Perf. 11						
1387	6¢ American Bald Eagle	.22	.12	1.75	(4)	2.00	50,448,550
1388	6¢ African Elephant Herd	.22	.12	1.75	(4)	2.00	50,448,550
1389	6¢ Tlingit Chief in						
	Haida Ceremonial Canoe	.22	.12	1.75	(4)	2.00	50,448,550
1390	6¢ Brontosaurus, Stegosaurus						
	and Allosaurus from Jurassic						
	Period	.22	.12	1.75	(4)	2.00	50,448,550
1390a	Block of four, #1387-1390	1.00	1.00			3.00	
1391	6¢ Maine Statehood, July 9	.18	.05	1.10	(4)	.75	171,850,000
	Perf. 10½x11						
1392	6¢ Wildlife Conservation, July 20	.18	.05	1.10	(4)	1.00	142,205,000
	Issues of 1970-74, Perf. 11x10½, 10½x11, 11						
1393	6¢ Dwight D. Eisenhower, 1970	.12	.05	.60	(4)	.75	
1393a	Booklet pane of 8	1.25	.50				
1393b	Booklet pane of 5 + label	1.20	.35				
1393D	7¢ Benjamin Franklin, 1972	.14	.05	1.35	(4)	.75	
1394	8¢ Eisenhower, 1971	.16	.05	1.00	(4)	.75	
1395	8¢ Eisenhower (1393), 1971	.16	.05			.75	
1395a	Booklet pane of 8, 1971	1.50	1.25				
1395b	Booklet pane of 6, 1971	1.00	.75				
1395c	Booklet pane of 4 + 2 labels,						
	1972	1.00	.50				
1395d	Booklet pane of 7 + label, 1972	1.75	1.00				
1396	8¢ U.S. Postal Service, 1971	.25	.05	5.00	(12)	.75	
1397	14¢ Fiorello H. LaGuardia, 1972	.32	.05	2.35	(4)	.85	
1398	16¢ Ernie Pyle, 1971	.35	.05	2.35	(4)	.75	
1399	18¢ Dr. Elizabeth Blackwell, 1974	.40	.06	2.25	(4)	1.25	
1400	21¢ Amadeo P. Giannini, 1973	.45	.06	2.25	(4)	1.00	
	Coil Stamps, Perf. 10 Vertically						
1401	6¢ dark blue gray Eisenhower						
	(1393), 1970	.20	.05	1.00		.75	
1402	8¢ deep claret Eisenhower						
	(1395), 1971	.22	.05	1.00		.75	
1403-04 not assigned.							
	Issues of 1970, Perf. 11						
1405	6¢ Edgar Lee Masters, Aug. 22	.18	.05	1.00	(4)	.75	137,660,000
1406	6¢ Woman Suffrage, Aug. 26	.18	.05	1.00	(4)	.75	135,125,000
1407	6¢ South Carolina, Sept. 12	.18	.05	1.00	(4)	.75	135,895,000
1408	6¢ Stone Mountain Mem., Sept. 19	.18	.05	1.00	(4)	.75	132,675,000
1409	6¢ Fort Snelling, Oct. 17	.18	.05	1.00	(4)	.75	134,795,000

AMERICAN BALD EAGLE

AFRICAN ELEPHANT HERD

1391

HAIDA CEREMONIAL CANOE

THE AGE OF REPTILES

1392

387
389

1388
1390

393

1393D

1394

1396

1397

398

1399

1400

EDGAR LEE MASTERS
AMERICAN POET

UNITED STATES 6¢

1405

1406

407

1408

1409

1414   1414a

1410
1412   1411
1413

1419

1420

1415
1417   1416
1418

1425

1421   1422   1423   1424

1426

1427 1428
1429 1430

	1970 continued	Un	U	PB/LP	#	FDC	Q
	Anti-Pollution Issue, Oct. 28, Perf. 11x10½						
1410	6¢ Save Our Soil	.45	.13	6.00	(10)	1.40	40,400,000
1411	6¢ Save Our Cities	.45	.13	6.00	(10)	1.40	40,400,000
1412	6¢ Save Our Water	.45	.13			1.40	40,400,000
1413	6¢ Save Our Air	.45	.13			1.40	40,400,000
1413a	Block of four, #1410, 1413	2.50	2.00			4.25	
	Christmas Issue, Nov. 5, Perf. 10½x11						
1414	6¢ Nativity, by Lorenzo Lotto	.20	.05	2.25	(8)	1.40	638,730,000
1414a	Precanceled	.35	.08				358,245,000
	Perf 11x10½						
1415	6¢ Tin and Cast Iron Locomotive	.85	.10	8.50	(8)	1.40	122,313,750
1415a	Precanceled	2.00	.15				109,912,500
1416	6¢ Toy Horse on Wheels	.85	.10	8.50	(8)	1.40	122,313,750
1416a	Precanceled	2.00	.15				109,912,500
1417	6¢ Mechanical Tricycle	.85	.10			1.40	122,313,750
1417a	Precanceled	2.00	.15				109,912,500
1418	6¢ Doll Carriage	.85	.10			1.40	122,313,750
1418a	Precanceled	2.00	.15				109,912,500
1418b	Block of 4, #1415, 1418	4.50	3.50			4.50	
1418c	Block of 4, #1415a, 1418b	9.00	6.00				
	Perf. 11						
1419	6¢ United Nations, Nov. 20	.18	.05	1.25	(4)	.75	127,610,000
1420	6¢ Landing of the Pilgrims, Nov. 21	.18	.05	1.25	(4)	.75	129,785,000
	Disabled Veterans and Servicemen Issue, Nov. 24						
1421	6¢ Disabled American Veterans Emblem	.20	.10	3.00	(4)	.75	67,190,000
1421a	Attached pair, #1421-1422	.50	.65			1.20	
1422	6¢ U.S. Servicemen	.20	.10	3.00	(4)	.75	67,190,000
	Issues of 1971						
1423	6¢ American Wool Industry, Jan. 19	.18	.05	1.00	(4)	.75	135,305,000
1424	6¢ Gen. Douglas MacArthur, Jan. 26	.18	.05	1.00	(4)	.75	134,840,000
1425	6¢ Blood Donors, Mar. 12	.18	.05	1.00	(4)	.75	130,975,000
	Perf. 11x10½						
1426	8¢ Missouri 150th Anniv., May 8	.20	.05	3.50	(12)	.75	161,235,000
	Wildlife Conservation Issue, June 12, Perf. 11						
1427	8¢ Trout	.30	.10	1.75	(4)	1.75	43,920,000
1428	8¢ Alligator	.30	.10	1.75	(4)	1.75	43,920,000
1429	8¢ Polar Bear and Cubs	.30	.10	1.75	(4)	1.75	43,920,000
1430	8¢ California Condor	.30	.10	1.75	(4)	1.75	43,920,000
1430a	Block of four #1427-1430	1.30	1.00			3.00	

	1971 continued, Perf. 11	Un	U	PB/LP	#	FDC	Q
1431	8¢ Antarctic Treaty, June 23	.25	.05	1.50	(4)	.75	138,700,000
1432	8¢ American Revolution						
	200th Anniversary, July 4	.50	.05	3.25	(4)	.75	138,165,000
1433	8¢ John Sloan, Aug. 2	.20	.05	1.50	(4)	.75	152,125,000
	Space Achievement Decade Issue, Aug. 2						
1434	8¢ Earth, Sun, Landing Craft						
	on Moon	.20	.10	1.75	(4)		88,147,500
1434a	Attached pair, #1434-1435	.50	.35			1.75	
1435	8¢ Lunar Rover and Astronauts	.20	.10	1.75	(4)		88,147,500
1436	8¢ Emily Dickinson, Aug. 28	.18	.05	1.25	(4)	.75	142,845,000
1437	8¢ San Juan, Sept. 12	.18	.05	1.25	(4)	.75	148,755,000
	Perf. 10½x11						
1438	8¢ Prevent Drug Abuse, Oct. 5	.18	.05	1.85	(6)	.75	139,080,000
1439	8¢ CARE, Oct. 27	.18	.05	2.10	(8)	.75	130,755,000
	Historic Preservation Issue, Oct. 29, Perf. 11						
1440	8¢ Decatur House,						
	Washington, D.C.	.25	.12	1.85	(4)	1.50	42,552,000
1441	8¢ Whaling Ship						
	Charles W. Morgan	.25	.12	1.85	(4)	1.50	42,552,000
1442	8¢ Cable Car, San Francisco	.25	.12	1.85	(4)	1.50	42,552,000
1443	8¢ San Xavier del Bac Mission,						
	Tucson, Arizona	.25	.12	1.85	(4)	1.50	42,552,000
1443a	Block of four, #1440-1443	1.20	1.20			3.00	
	Christmas Issue, Nov. 10, Perf. 10½x11						
1444	8¢ Adoration of the Shepherds,						
	by Giorgione	.18	.05	2.50	(12)	.75	1,074,350,000
1445	8¢ Partridge in a Pear Tree,						
	by Jamie Wyeth	.18	.05	2.50	(12)	.75	979,540,000
	Issues of 1972, Perf. 11						
1446	8¢ Sidney Lanier, Feb. 3	.18	.05	1.00	(4)	.75	137,355,000
	Perf. 10½x11						
1447	8¢ Peace Corps., Feb. 11	.18	.05	1.50	(6)	.75	150,400,000

American Revolution

The year was 1976, and the United States of America was celebrating its 200th anniversary as a nation. Festivities abounded—parades, fireworks—culminating on the big day, July 4, when the Declaration of Independence was signed. A celebration of that size needs some advance preparation. Postal patrons were introduced to the idea five years earlier, on July 4, 1971, when a new stamp (#1432) was issued bearing the Bicentennial logo that was to become ubiquitous by 1976.

Although unveiled early, the stamp did commemorate an anniversary of sorts. The United States declared its independence in 1776, but the military skirmishes leading to the main event already had begun. The American Revolution was well under way by July of 1771, it just had not been recognized.

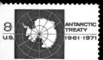

431

1433

AMERICAN
REVOLUTION
BICENTENNIAL
1776-1976

1432

434   1435

1436   1437

438   1439

HISTORIC PRESERVATION   HISTORIC PRESERVATION

HISTORIC PRESERVATION   HISTORIC PRESERVATION

1440   1441
1442   1443

444   1445   1446   1447

1452

1448
1450
1449
1451

1453

1454

1455

1456
1458
1457
1459

1460

1461

1462

1463

1464
1466
1465
1467

	1972 continued	Un	U	PB/LP	#	FDC	Q
	National Parks Centennial Issue, Apr. 5, Perf. 11, (See also #C84)						
1448	2¢ Hulk of Ship	.06	.06	1.60	(4)		172,730,000
1449	2¢ Cape Hatteras Lighthouse	.06	.06	1.60	(4)		172,730,000
1450	2¢ Laughing Gulls on Driftwood	.06	.06	1.60	(4)		172,730,000
1451	2¢ Laughing Gulls and Dune	.06	.06	1.60	(4)		172,730,000
1451a	Block of four, #1448-1451	.25	.30			1.25	
1452	6¢ Wolf Trap Farm, June 26	.16	.08	1.25	(4)	.75	104,090,000
1453	8¢ Yellowstone, Mar. 1	.18	.05	1.00	(4)	.75	164,096,000
1454	15¢ Mt. McKinley, July 28	.35	.22	2.75	(4)	.75	53,920,000
	Note: Beginning with this issue, the USPS began to offer stamp collectors first day cancellations affixed to 8"x 10½" souvenir pages. The pages are similar to the stamp announcements that have appeared on Post Office bulletin boards beginning with Scott #1132.						
1455	8¢ Family Planning, Mar. 18	.16	.05	1.00	(4)	.75	153,025,000
	American Bicentennial Issue, Colonial American Craftsmen, July 4, Perf. 11x10½						
1456	8¢ Glassmaker	.30	.08	1.75	(4)	1.00	50,472,500
1457	8¢ Silversmith	.30	.08	1.75	(4)	1.00	50,472,500
1458	8¢ Wigmaker	.30	.08	1.75	(4)	1.00	50,472,500
1459	8¢ Hatter	.30	.08	1.75	(4)	1.00	50,472,500
1459a	Block of four, #1456-1459	1.25	1.25			2.50	
	Olympic Games Issue, Aug. 17, (See also #C85)						
1460	6¢ Bicycling and Olympic Rings	.16	.12	2.25	(10)	.75	67,335,000
1461	8¢ Bobsledding	.16	.05	2.25	(10)	.85	179,675,000
1462	15¢ Running	.35	.18	4.50	(10)	1.00	46,340,000
1463	8¢ P.T.A. 75th Anniv., Sept. 15	.16	.05	1.00	(4)	.75	180,155,000
	Wildlife Conservation Issue, Sept. 20, Perf. 11						
1464	8¢ Fur Seals	.25	.08	1.40	(4)	2.00	49,591,200
1465	8¢ Cardinal	.25	.08	1.40	(4)	2.00	49,591,200
1466	8¢ Brown Pelican	.25	.08	1.40	(4)	2.00	49,591,200
1467	8¢ Bighorn Sheep	.25	.08	1.40	(4)	2.00	49,591,200
1467a	Block of 4, #1464-1467	1.10	.85			3.00	
	Note: With this issue the USPS introduced the "American Commemorative Series" Stamp Panels. Each panel contains a block of four mint stamps with text and background illustrations.						

National Parks

When the United States created Yellowstone National Park in 1872, it became the first country to set aside land as public preserves, protected from development or other man-made encroachments. (Since then, some 100 countries have created national parks and preserves.) Today there are 48 national parks encompassing almost 85,000 acres throughout the United States and the Virgin Islands. The system is administered by the National Park Service, created in 1916.

Yellowstone still is unique. Within the park, which encompasses parts of Wyoming, Montana and Idaho, are some 3,000 hot springs and 200 geysers. Caused by subsurface volcanic activity, geysers are rare. Old Faithful (#1453) is the most famous. As its name suggests, it erupts regularly—once every 60 minutes on average.

	1972 continued, Perf. 11x10½	Un	U	PB/LP	#	FDC	Q
1468	8¢ Mail Order 100th Anniversary,						
	Sept. 27	.16	.05	2.75	(12)	.75	185,490,000
	Perf. 10½x11						
1469	8¢ Osteopathic Medicine, Oct. 9	.16	.05	1.35	(5)	.75	162,335,000
	American Folklore Issue, Oct. 13, Perf. 11						
1470	8¢ Tom Sawyer, by Norman Rockwell	.16	.05	1.00	(4)	.75	162,789,950
	Christmas Issue, Nov. 9, Perf. 10½x11						
1471	8¢ Angels from "Mary, Queen of						
	Heaven," by the Master						
	of the St. Lucy Legend	.16	.05	2.75	(12)	.75	1,003,475,000
1472	8¢ Santa Claus	.16	.05	2.75	(12)	.75	1,017,025,000
	Perf. 11						
1473	8¢ Pharmacy, Nov. 11	.16	.05	1.00	(4)	.75	165,895,000
1474	8¢ Stamp Collecting, Nov. 17	.16	.05	1.00	(4)	.75	166,508,000
	Issues of 1973, Perf. 11x10½						
1475	8¢ Love, Jan. 26	.16	.05	1.35	(6)	.75	330,055,000
	This "special stamp for someone special" depicts "Love" by contemporary artist Robert Indiana.						
	American Revolution Bicentennial Issue, Communications in Colonial Times, Perf. 11						
1476	8¢ Printer and Patriots Examining						
	Pamphlet, Feb. 16	.20	.05	1.35	(4)	.75	166,005,000
1477	8¢ Posting a Broadside, Apr. 13	.20	.05	1.35	(4)	.75	163,050,000
1478	8¢ Post Rider, June 22	.20	.05	1.35	(4)	.75	159,005,000
1479	8¢ Drummer, Sept. 28	.20	.05	1.35	(4)	.75	147,295,000
	Boston Tea Party, July 4						
1480	8¢ British Merchantman	.20	.10	1.35	(4)	1.75	49,068,750
1481	8¢ British Three-master	.20	.10	1.35	(4)	1.75	49,068,750
1482	8¢ Boats and Ship's Hull	.20	.10	1.35	(4)	1.75	49,068,750
1483	8¢ Boat and Dock	.20	.10	1.35	(4)	1.75	49,068,750
1483a	Block of four, #1480-1483	.85	.80			3.75	
	American Arts Issue (See also #1485-1487)						
1484	8¢ George Gershwin, Feb. 28	.16	.05	2.75	(12)	.75	139,152,000

Mail Order

In 1872 Aaron Montgomery Ward had a good idea — suppose he sold his merchandise via the mail? After all, more than half the country's population was living on farms or in rural areas that had few stores nearby. Ward's first mail-order "catalog" actually was a single sheet of paper listing his wares and prices — quite different from today's elaborate publications. Other firms, such as Sears, Roebuck and Aldens and Spiegel soon jumped on the catalog bandwagon, selling life's necessities — clothing, housewares, farm equipment, even houses (which you had to assemble yourself) — via mail order. The 1972 commemorative stamp (#1468) honoring the 100th anniversary of the mail-order business depicts an event in the life of a rural family: going to the old-fashioned country store/post office to pick up mail-order merchandise.

468

1469

1470

1471

472

1473

1474

475

1476

1477

478

1479

480
482

1481
1483

1484

1485

1486

WILLA CATHER

1487

Copernicus
1473 - 1973

8¢US

1488

U.S. POSTAL SERVICE 8¢

Nearly 27 billion
U.S. stamps
are sold yearly
to carry
your letters to
every corner
of the world.

People Serving You

1489

Mail is
picked up
from nearly
a third of a million
local collection
boxes, as well
as your mailbox.

People Serving You

1490

More than
87 billion letters
and packages
are handled
yearly—almost
300 million every
delivery day.

People Serving You

1491

The People
in your
Postal Service
handle and
deliver more
than 500 million
packages yearly.

People Serving You

1492

Thousands of
machines, buildings,
and vehicles
must be operated
and maintained
to keep your
mail moving.

People Serving You

1493

U.S. POSTAL SERVICE 8¢

The skill
of sorting mail
manually
is still vital
to delivery of
your mail.

People Serving You

1494

Employees
use modern, high-
speed equipment
to sort and process
huge volumes of
mail in central
locations.

People Serving You

1495

Thirteen billion
pounds of mail are
handled yearly by
postal employees
as they speed
your letters and
packages.

People Serving You

1496

Our customers
include
54 million urban
and 12 million
rural families,
plus 9 million
businesses.

People Serving You

1497

Employees
cover
4 million miles
each delivery day
to bring mail to
your home or
business.

People Serving You

1498

	1973 continued	Un	U	PB/LP	#	FDC	Q
	American Arts Issue, Perf. 11 (See also #1484)						
1485	8¢ Robinson Jeffers, Aug. 13	.16	.05	2.75	(12)	.75	128,048,000
1486	8¢ Henry Ossawa Tanner, Sept. 10	.16	.05	2.75	(12)	.75	146,008,000
1487	8¢ Willa Cather, Sept. 20	.16	.05	2.75	(12)	.75	139,608,000
1488	8¢ Nicolaus Copernicus, Apr. 23	.16	.05	1.00	(4)	.75	159,475,000
	Postal Service Employees Issue, Apr. 30, Perf. 10½x11						
1489	8¢ Stamp Counter	.20	.12			1.10	48,602,000
1490	8¢ Mail Collection	.20	.12			1.10	48,602,000
1491	8¢ Letter Facing Conveyor	.20	.12			1.10	48,602,000
1492	8¢ Parcel Post Sorting	.20	.12			1.10	48,602,000
1493	8¢ Mail Canceling	.20	.12	2.25	(10)	1.10	48,602,000
1494	8¢ Manual Letter Routing	.20	.12			1.10	48,602,000
1495	8¢ Electronic Letter Routing	.20	.12			1.10	48,602,000
1496	8¢ Loading Mail on Truck	.20	.12			1.10	48,602,000
1497	8¢ Rural Mail Delivery	.20	.12	2.25	(10)	1.10	48,602,000
1498a	Strip of 10, #1489-1498	2.25	2.00	4.50	(20)	6.00	

Henry O. Tanner

Religion involves mystery, miracles and a sense of awe. In attempting to capture these qualities, black artist Henry O. Tanner (#1486) became famous. But Tanner's career was ordinary enough at first. He studied with American realist Thomas Eakins at the Pennsylvania Academy of Fine Arts and later traveled to Europe to learn about the popular new impressionist and abstract styles.

Tanner might have continued to be a follower, working in the mainstream, were it not for a trip to the Holy Land (his first of several) in the late 1890s. From then on his painting changed—in subject and style. He began to portray Biblical subjects, concentrating on the miraculous and supernatural. His paintings took on a surreal aspect and had a nocturnal quality. Tanner's breakthrough was recognized several years later, in 1908, when he became the first black painter to be elected to the National Academy of Design.

	1973 continued, Perf. 11	Un	U	PB/LP	#	FDC	Q
1499	8¢ Harry S. Truman, May 8	.16	.05	1.00	(4)	.75	157,052,800
	Electronics Progress Issue, July 10, (See also #C86)						
1500	6¢ Marconi's Spark Coil and Gap	.12	.10	1.25	(4)	.75	53,005,000
1501	8¢ Transistor and						
	Printed Circuit Board	.16	.05	1.00	(4)	.75	159,775,000
1502	15¢ Microphone, Speaker,						
	Vacuum Tube, TV Camera	.30	.20	3.00	(4)	.80	39,005,000
1503	8¢ Lyndon B. Johnson, Aug. 27	.16	.05	2.50	(12)	.75	152,624,000
	Issues of 1973-74, Rural America Centenary Issue						
1504	8¢ Angus and Longhorn Cattle,						
	by F.C. Murphy, Oct. 5, 1973	.16	.05	1.00	(4)	.75	145,840,000
1505	10¢ Chautauqua Tent and Buggies,						
	Aug. 6, 1974	.20	.05	1.00	(4)	.75	151,335,000
1506	10¢ Wheat Fields and Train,						
	Aug. 16, 1974	.20	.05	1.00	(4)	.75	141,085,000
	Christmas Issue, Nov. 7, 1973, Perf. 10½x11						
1507	8¢ Small Cowper Madonna,						
	by Raphael	.16	.05	2.10	(12)	.75	885,160,000
1508	8¢ Christmas Tree in Needlepoint	.16	.05	2.10	(12)	.75	939,835,000
	Issues of 1973-74, Perf. 11x10½						
1509	10¢ 50-Star and 13-Star Flags,						
	Dec. 8, 1973	.20	.05	5.50	(20)	.75	
1510	10¢ Jefferson Memorial						
	and Signature, Dec. 14, 1973	.20	.05	1.00	(4)	.75	
1510b	Booklet pane of 5 + label,						
	Dec. 14, 1973	1.50	*.30*				
1510c	Booklet pane of 8, Dec. 14, 1973	1.60	*.30*				
1510d	Booklet pane of 6, Aug. 5, 1974	2.50	*.30*				
1511	10¢ "ZIP Code,"						
	Jan. 4, 1974	.20	.05∘	2.25	(8)	.75	
	1512-1517 not assigned.						
	Coil Stamps, Perf. 10 Vertically						
1518	6.3¢ Bells, Oct. 1, 1974	.13	.07	.35		.75	
1519	10¢ red and blue Flags (1509),						
	Dec. 8, 1973	.25	.05	—		.75	
1520	10¢ blue Jefferson Memorial						
	(1510), Dec. 14, 1973	.20	.05	.50		.75	
	1521-24 not assigned.						

1499

1500

1501

1502

1503

1504

1505

1506

1507

1508

1509

1510

1511

1518

1519

1520

1525

Robert Frost
AMERICAN POET

1526

EXPO'74 · US10¢
PRESERVE THE ENVIRONMENT

1527

HORSE RACING
U.S. postage 10 cents

1528

US10¢
Skylab

1529

1530	1531	1532	1533
1534	1535	1536	1537

	Issues of 1974, Perf. 11	Un	U	PB/LP	#	FDC	Q
1525	10¢ VFW 75th Anniv., Mar. 11	.20	.05	1.25	(4)	.75	149,930,000
	Perf. 10½x11						
1526	10¢ Robert Frost, Mar. 26	.20	.05	1.00	(4)	.75	145,235,000
	Perf. 11						
1527	10¢ Expo '74, Apr. 18	.20	.05	2.60	(12)	.75	135,052,000
	Perf. 11x10½						
1528	10¢ Horse Racing Turn, May 4	.20	.05	2.60	(12)	.75	156,750,000
	Perf. 11						
1529	10¢ Skylab I, May 14	.20	.05	1.00	(4)	1.25	164,670,000
	Centenary of UPU Issue, June 6						
1530	10¢ Michelangelo, by Raphael	.20	.18			1.10	23,769,600
1531	10¢ "Five Feminine Virtues,"						
	by Hokusai	.20	.18			1.10	23,769,600
1532	10¢ "Old Scraps,"						
	by John Fredrick Peto	.20	.18			1.10	23,769,600
1533	10¢ "The Lovely Reader,"						
	by Jean Etienne Liotard	.20	.18			1.10	23,769,600
1534	10¢ "Lady Writing Letter,"						
	by Gerard Terborch	.20	.18			1.10	·23,769,600
1535	10¢ Inkwell and Quill, from						
	"Boy with a Top," by						
	Jean Baptiste Simeon Chardin	.20	.18			1.10	23,769,600
1536	10¢ Mrs. John Douglas,						
	by Thomas Gainsborough	.20	.18			1.10	23,769,600
1537	10¢ Don Antonio Noriega, by						
	Francisco de Goya	.20	.18			1.10	23,769,600
1537a	Block or strip of 8, #1530-37	1.60	2.00	3.40	(16)	4.25	

Veterans of Foreign Wars

The Spanish-American War (1898-99) was this country's first major foreign conflict fought outside the continental territories of the United States. In its aftermath, a new organization was formed to serve the needs of more than 306,000 veterans—the Veterans of Foreign Wars (VFW). In the years that followed, American fighting forces saw service in many parts of the world—Europe, Japan, Southeast Asia. Today more than two million veterans of these foreign military actions are members of the VFW (#1525).

Headquartered in Kansas City, Missouri, the VFW is primarily a patriotic organization. One of its principal aims is to ensure our nation's security through maximum military strength. It also is a service organization, providing benefits and assistance to disabled vets and their dependents. To meet its goals, the VFW maintains a lobbying office in Washington, D.C., as well as a benefits office that is open to members and nonmember veterans.

	1974 continued	Un	U	PB/LP	#	FDC	Q
	Mineral Heritage Issue, June 13, Perf. 11						
1538	10¢ Petrified Wood	.20	.10	1.50	(4)	1.50	41,803,200
1539	10¢ Tourmaline	.20	.10	1.50	(4)	1.50	41,803,200
1540	10¢ Amethyst	.20	.10	1.50	(4)	1.50	41,803,200
1541	10¢ Rhodochrosite	.20	.10	1.50	(4)	1.50	41,803,200
1541a	Block of 4, #1538-1541	.80	.80			3.00	
1542	10¢ First Kentucky Settlement,						
	June 15	.20	.05	1.20	(4)	.75	156,265,000
	American Revolution Bicentennial Issue, First Continental Congress, July 4						
1543	10¢ Carpenter's Hall	.20	.10	1.20	(4)	.90	48,896,250
1544	10¢ "We ask but for Peace,						
	Liberty and Safety"	.20	.10	1.20	(4)	.90	48,896,250
1545	10¢ "Deriving their Just Powers"	.02	.10	1.30	(4)	.90	48,896,250
1546	10¢ Independence Hall	.20	.10	1.20	(4)	.90	48,896,250
1546a	Block of 4, #1543-1546	.80	.80			2.75	
1547	10¢ Energy Conservation,						
	Sept. 22	.20	.05	1.00	(4)	.75	148,850,000
	American Folklore Issue, Legend of Sleepy Hollow, Oct. 10						
1548	10¢ Headless Horseman and Ichabod	.20	.05	1.00	(4)	.75	157,270,000
1549	10¢ Retarded Children, Oct. 12	.20	.05	1.00	(4)	.75	150,245,000
	Christmas Issue, Oct. 23						
1550	10¢ Angel	.20	.05	2.25	(10)	.75	835,180,000
1551	10¢ "The Road-Winter,"						
	by Currier and Ives	.20	.05	2.60	(12)	.75	882,520,000
1552	10¢ Weather Vane, Precanceled,						
	Imperf., Self-adhesive, Nov. 15	.20	.08	5.50	(20)	.75	213,155,000

Kentucky Settlement

Today the United States stretches from the Atlantic to the Pacific Oceans, but our nation's boundaries once were much narrower. In the 18th century Kentucky was considered the frontier, connected to the original colonies on the East Coast only by the "Wilderness Road" across the Cumberland Gap. Settlement of this area was perilous, due largely to a constant threat of Indian raids.

Although the territory first was explored in 1769, it was not until 1773 that Daniel Boone and a group of followers attempted to actually settle in Kentucky. They first were driven off by Indians who killed one of Boone's sons. Efforts to create a permanent settlement continued despite British aid to the Indians to prevent settlement. By 1775 the Americans had established three permanent settlements in Kentucky, including Fort Harrod (#1542) and Boonesborough, named after the famous frontiersman. Kentucky was considered part of the Virginia territory until 1792, when it was accepted as a state in its own right.

1538

1539

1540

1541

1542

543
1545

1544
1546

1547

1548

549

1550

1551

1552

American artist
10 cents U.S. postage

1553

American poet
10 cents U.S. postage

1554

1555

1556

1557

1558

Sybil Ludington — Youthful Heroine

YOUTHFUL HEROINE
On the dark night of April 26, 1777, 16-year-old Sybil Ludington rode her horse "Star" alone through the Connecticut countryside rallying her father's militia to repel a raid by the British on Danbury.

1559

Salem Poor — Gallant Soldier

Haym Salomon — Financial Hero

Peter Francisco — Fighter Extraordinary

GALLANT SOLDIER
The conspicuously courageous actions of black foot soldier Salem Poor at the Battle of Bunker Hill on June 17, 1775, earned him citations for his bravery and leadership ability.

FINANCIAL HERO
Businessman and broker Haym Salomon was responsible for raising most of the money needed to finance the American Revolution and later to save the new nation from collapse.

FIGHTER EXTRAORDINARY
Peter Francisco's strength and bravery made him a legend around campfires. He fought with distinction at Brandywine, Yorktown and Guilford Court House.

1560

1561

1562

Lexington & Concord 1775 by Sandham
US Bicentennial 10 cents

1563

Bunker Hill 1775 by Trumbull
US Bicentennial 10c

1564

	Issues of 1975	Un	U	PB/LP	#	FDC	Q
	American Arts Issue, Perf. 10½x11, 11 (1555)						
1553	10¢ Benjamin West, Feb. 10	.20	.05	2.20	(10)	.75	156,995,000
1554	10¢ Paul Laurence Dunbar, May 1	.20	.05	2.20	(10)	.75	146,365,000
1555	10¢ D.W. Griffith, May 27	.20	.05	1.00	(4)	.75	148,805,000
	Space Issues, Perf. 11						
1556	10¢ Pioneer 10 Passing Jupiter,						
	Feb. 28	.20	.05	1.00	(4)	1.25	173,685,000
1557	10¢ Mariner 10, Venus						
	and Mercury, Apr. 4	.20	.05	1.00	(4)	1.25	158,600,000
1558	10¢ Collective Bargaining,						
	Mar. 13	.20	.05	1.80	(8)	.75	153,355,000
	American Bicentennial Issue, Contributors to the Cause, Mar. 25, Perf. 11x10½						
1559	8¢ Sybil Ludington	.16	.13	2.00	(10)	.75	63,205,000
1560	10¢ Salem Poor	.20	.05	2.50	(10)	.75	157,865,000
1561	10¢ Haym Salomon	.20	.05	2.50	(10)	.75	166,810,000
1562	18¢ Peter Francisco	.36	.20	5.00	(10)	.75	44,825,000
	Battle of Lexington & Concord, Apr. 19, Perf. 11						
1563	10¢ "Birth of Liberty,"						
	by Henry Sandham	.20	.05	2.60	(12)	.75	144,028,000
	Battle of Bunker Hill, June 17, Perf. 11x10½						
1564	10¢ "Battle of Bunker Hill,"						
	by John Trumbull	.20	.05	2.60	(12)	.75	139,928,000

Paul Laurence Dunbar

There was a poetic aspect to the life of writer Paul L. Dunbar (#1554). This child of former slaves showed a talent for writing early on, composing his first poem at age 7 and producing his own plays in a church basement by the time he was 13. Dunbar was the only black student to attend Ohio's Dayton High School at the time, where he was editor of the school newspaper and graduated with honors. Despite his academic success, the best job he could find was as an elevator operator. He continued to write, however, and published his first volume of poetry at his own expense—Dunbar supposedly sold copies to his passengers.

*His early poems, written in Negro dialect, began to achieve some recognition. He became America's "first" black professional writer, supporting himself by what he wrote. Though successful, Dunbar resented being stereotyped by the dialect poems that had become so popular. He later described his struggles in the poems "We Wear the Mask" and "The Poet." By the late 1890s he had abandoned dialect poems and turned his attention to short stories and novels. **Sport of the Gods**, published in 1902, generally is considered his best work.*

Dunbar's personal life with Ruth Alice Moore, the woman he married, began when he saw her picture in a poetry journal. Despite its romantic beginnings, the marriage ended tragically when Dunbar succumbed to tuberculosis at the age of 34.

	1975 continued	Un	U	PB/LP	#	FDC	Q
	American Bicentennial Issue, Military Uniforms, July 4, Perf. 11						
1565	10¢ Soldier with Flintlock Musket,						
	Uniform Button	.20	.08	2.60	(12)	.90	44,963,750
1566	10¢ Sailor with Grappling Hook,						
	First Navy Jack, 1775	.20	.08			.90	44,963,750
1567	10¢ Marine with Musket,						
	Full-rigged Ship	.20	.08	2.60	(12)	.90	44,963,750
1568	10¢ Militiaman with Musket,						
	Powder Horn	.20	.08			.90	44,963,750
1568a	Block of 4, #1565-1568	.80	.80			2.40	
	Apollo Soyuz Space Issue, July 15, Perf. 11x10½						
1569	10¢ Apollo and Soyuz after						
	Docking, and Earth	.20	.10	2.60	(12)	1.00	80,931,600
1569a	Pair, #1569-1570	.40	.25			3.00	
1570	10¢ Spacecraft before Docking,						
	Earth and Project Emblem	.20	.10	3.40	(16)	1.00	80,931,600
1571	10¢ International Women's Year,						
	Aug. 26	.20	.05	1.40	(6)	.75	145,640,000
	Postal Service Bicentennial Issue, Sept. 3						
1572	10¢ Stagecoach and Trailer Truck	.20	.08	2.60	(12)	.75	42,163,750
1573	10¢ Old and New Locomotives	.20	.08	2.60	(12)	.75	42,163,750
1574	10¢ Early Mail Plane and Jet	.20	.08			.75	42,163,750
1575	10¢ Satellite for Transmission						
	of Mailgrams	.20	.08			.75	42,163,750
1575a	Block of 4, #1572-1575	.80	.80			2.40	
	Perf. 11						
1576	10¢ World Peace through Law,						
	Sept. 29	.20	.05	1.00	(4)	.75	146,615,000
	Banking and Commerce Issue, Oct. 6						
1577	10¢ Engine Turning, Indian Head						
	Penny and Morgan Silver Dollar	.20	.08	1.00	(4)	.75	73,098,000
1577a	Pair, #1577-1578	.40	.20			1.00	
1578	10¢ Seated Liberty Quarter,						
	$20 Gold (Double Eagle),						
	Engine Turning	.20	.08	1.00	(4)	.75	73,098,000

1569
1570

1565   1566
1567   1568

1571

1572   1573
1574   1575

1576

1577   1578

1579

1580

1582b

1581
1584

1582
1585

1591
1593

1592
1594

1595d

1596
1597

1618
1599

	1975 continued	Un	U	PB/LP	#	FDC	Q
	Christmas Issue, Oct. 14, Perf. 11						
1579	(10¢) Madonna and Child, by						
	Domenico Ghirlandaio	.20	.05	2.60	(12)	.75	739,430,000
1580	(10¢) Christmas Card,						
	by Louis Prang, 1878	.20	.05	2.60	(12)	.75	878,690,000
	Issues of 1975-81, Americana Issue, Perf. 11x10½						
1581	1¢ Inkwell & Quill, 1977	.05	.05	.25	(4)	.40	
1582	2¢ Speaker's Stand, 1977	.05	.05	.25	(4)	.40	
1583, 1586-89, 1600-02, 1607, 1609 not assigned.							
1584	3¢ Early Ballot Box, 1977	.06	.05	.30	(4)	.40	
1585	4¢ Books, Bookmark, Eyeglasses,						
	Size: 17½x20½mm, 1977	.08	.05	.40	(4)	.40	
1590	9¢ Capitol Dome (1591), 1977,						
	Single from booklet (see #1623a)	1.00	.20			1.00	
1590a	Booklet pane of 8 (1591), Perf. 10,						
	Size: 18½x22½mm	27.50	6.00				
1591	9¢ Capitol Dome, 1975	.18	.05	.90	(4)	.60	
1592	10¢ Contemplation of Justice, 1977	.20	.05	1.00	(4)	.60	
1593	11¢ Printing Press, 1975	.22	.05	1.10	(4)	.60	
1594	12¢ Torch, 1981	.24	.05	1.15	(4)	.60	
1595	13¢ Liberty Bell, 1975,						
	Single from booklet	.26	.05			.60	
1595a	Booklet pane of 6	1.60	.50				
1595b	Booklet pane of 7 + label	1.80	.50				
1595c	Booklet pane of 8	2.10	.50				
1595d	Booklet pane of 5 + label, 1976	1.30	.50				
	Perf. 11						
1596	13¢ Eagle and Shield, 1975	.26	.05	3.38	(12)	.60	
1597	15¢ Fort McHenry Flag, 1978	.30	.05	2.10	(6)	.65	
	Perf. 11x10½						
1598	15¢ Fort McHenry Flag						
	(1597), 1978, Single from booklet	.30	.05			.65	
1598a	Booklet pane of 8	4.25	.60				
1599	16¢ Head of Liberty, 1978	.32	.05	2.25	(4)	.65	
1603	24¢ Old North Church, 1975	.48	.09	2.75	(4)	.75	
1604	28¢ Fort Nisqually, 1978	.56	.08	3.25	(4)	1.20	
1605	29¢ Sandy Hook Lighthouse, 1978	.58	.08	3.25	(4)	1.10	
1606	30¢ One-room Schoolhouse, 1979	.60	.08	3.00	(4)	1.10	
1608	50¢ Whale Oil Lamp, 1979	1.00	.25	5.00	(4)	1.50	
1610	$1 Candle and Rushlight Holder,						
	1979	2.00	.25	9.00	(4)	3.00	
1611	$2 Kerosene Table Lamp, 1978	4.00	.50	18.00	(4)	5.00	
1612	$5 Railroad Lantern, 1979	10.00	2.00	45.00	(4)	10.00	

#1590 is on white paper, #1591 is on gray paper, #1590 and 1590a, 1595, 1598 issued only in booklets. Additional Americana Series, see #1613-19, 1623a-23d, 1811, 1813 and 1816.

	1975-81 continued	Un	U	PB/LP	#	FDC	Q
	Americana Issue, Coil Stamps, Perf. 10 Vertically						
1613	3.1¢ Guitar, 1979	.20	.10	1.75		.40	
1614	7.7¢ Saxhorns, 1976	.20	.08	1.00		.60	
1615	7.9¢ Drum, 1976	.20	.08	1.10		.60	
1615C	8.4¢ Piano, 1978	.25	.08	2.00		.60	
1616	9¢ Capitol Dome (1591), 1976	.22	.05	.90		.60	
1617	10¢ Contemplation of Justice						
	(1592), 1977	.20	.05	1.25		.60	
1618	13¢ Liberty Bell (1595), 1975	.26	.05	1.00		.65	
1618C	15¢ Fort McHenry Flag (1597),						
	1978	.40	.05	—		.65	
1619	16¢ Head of Liberty (1599), 1978	.32	.05	1.50		.60	
	Perf. 11x10½						
1622	13¢ Flag over Independence						
	Hall, 1975	.26	.05			.65	
1623	13¢ Flag over Capitol, 1977,	.26	.05			1.00	
	13¢ Single from booklet (1623a)	.26	.05			1.00	
1623a	Booklet pane of 8,						
	(1 #1590 and 7 #1623)	2.50	.60				
	Perf. 10						
1623b	(1623a) 13¢ Single from booklet	1.50	1.00				
1623c	Booklet pane of 8,						
	(1 #1590 and 7 #1623b)	40.00	—				
	#1623, 1623b issued only in booklets						
1623d	Se-tenant pair, #1590 and #1623	1.50					
1624 not assigned.							
	Coil Stamp, Perf. 10 Vertically						
1625	13¢ Flag over Independence Hall						
	(1622), 1975	.30	.05			.65	
	Issues of 1976, American Bicentennial Issue, The Spirit of '76, Jan. 1, Perf. 11						
1629	13¢ Drummer Boy	.26	.08			.65	
1630	13¢ Old Drummer	.26	.08			.65	
1631	13¢ Fifer	.26	.08			.65	
1631a	Strip of 3, #1629-1631	.78	.60	3.40	(12)	1.75	218,585,000
1632	13¢ Interphil 76	.26	.05	1.30	(4)	.65	157,825,000
	State Flags, Feb. 23						
1633	13¢ Delaware	.45	.30			1.75	8,720,100
1634	13¢ Pennsylvania	.45	.30			1.75	8,720,100
1635	13¢ New Jersey	.45	.30			1.75	8,720,100
1636	13¢ Georgia	.45	.30			1.75	8,720,100
1637	13¢ Connecticut	.45	.30			1.75	8,720,100
1638	13¢ Massachusetts	.45	.30			1.75	8,720,100

1613

1614

1615

1615c

1616

1622

1623a

1629   1630   1631

1632

1633

1634

1635

1636

1637

1638

183

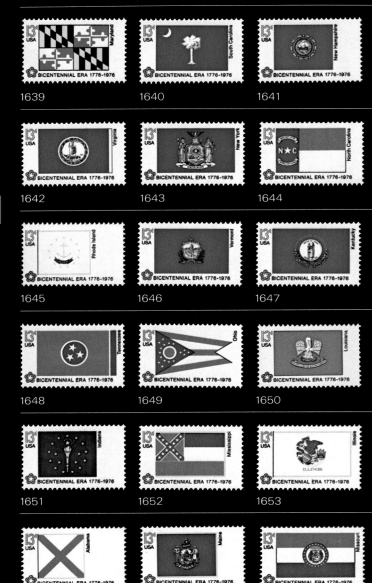

1639

1640

1641

1642

1643

1644

1645

1646

1647

1648

1649

1650

1651

1652

1653

1654

1655

1656

	1976 continued, Perf. 11	Un	U	PB/LP	#	FDC	Q
1639	13¢ Maryland	.45	.30			1.75	8,720,100
1640	13¢ South Carolina	.45	.30			1.75	8,720,100
1641	13¢ New Hampshire	.45	.30			1.75	8,720,100
1642	13¢ Virginia	.45	.30			1.75	8,720,100
1643	13¢ New York	.45	.30			1.75	8,720,100
1644	13¢ North Carolina	.45	.30			1.75	8,720,100
1645	13¢ Rhode Island	.45	.30			1.75	8,720,100
1646	13¢ Vermont	.45	.30			1.75	8,720,100
1647	13¢ Kentucky	.45	.30			1.75	8,720,100
1648	13¢ Tennessee	.45	.30			1.75	8,720,100
1649	13¢ Ohio	.45	.30			1.75	8,720,100
1650	13¢ Louisiana	.45	.30			1.75	8,720,100
1651	13¢ Indiana	.45	.30			1.75	8,720,100
1652	13¢ Mississippi	.45	.30			1.75	8,720,100
1653	13¢ Illinois	.45	.30			1.75	8,720,100
1654	13¢ Alabama	.45	.30			1.75	8,720,100
1655	13¢ Maine	.45	.30			1.75	8,720,100
1656	13¢ Missouri	.45	.30			1.75	8,720,100

New Hampshire State Flag

*The frigate **Raleigh** appears on New Hampshire's state flag (#1641). From its stern flies another flag, the emblem of the "United Colonies," adopted by the Continental Congress during the American Revolution. According to tradition, the **Raleigh** was the first ship to bear the banner in 1777. There are nine stars on the New Hampshire flag because it was the ninth colony to join the United States. The block of stone refers to its nickname, the "granite state," while the rising sun is a generic symbol of life and resurrection.*

*One unique feature of the New Hampshire flag is the date, "1776." Many state flags include the year that state was founded or admitted to the union, but New Hampshire chose to recognize the year the Declaration of Independence was signed. Although New Hampshire did not **officially** adopt this flag until 1909, it has been used since 1784.*

	1976 continued, Perf. 11	Un	U	PB/LP	#	FDC	Q
1657	13¢ Arkansas	.45	.30			1.75	8,720,100
1658	13¢ Michigan	.45	.30			1.75	8,720,100
1659	13¢ Florida	.45	.30			1.75	8,720,100
1660	13¢ Texas	.45	.30			1.75	8,720,100
1661	13¢ Iowa	.45	.30			1.75	8,720,100
1662	13¢ Wisconsin	.45	.30			1.75	8,720,100
1663	13¢ California	.45	.30			1.75	8,720,100
1664	13¢ Minnesota	.45	.30			1.75	8,720,100
1665	13¢ Oregon	.45	.30			1.75	8,720,100
1666	13¢ Kansas	.45	.30			1.75	8,720,100
1667	13¢ West Virginia	.45	.30			1.75	8,720,100
1668	13¢ Nevada	.45	.30			1.75	8,720,100
1669	13¢ Nebraska	.45	.30			1.75	8,720,100
1670	13¢ Colorado	.45	.30			1.75	8,720,100
1671	13¢ North Dakota	.45	.30			1.75	8,720,100
1672	13¢ South Dakota	.45	.30			1.75	8,720,100
1673	13¢ Montana	.45	.30			1.75	8,720,100
1674	13¢ Washington	.45	.30			1.75	8,720,100

American Bicentennial Issue

The National Council of Governors' meeting on February 23, 1976 probably would have consisted only of business as usual if it hadn't been the year of our country's 200th birthday. But because the bicentennial was something special, a special series of stamps was issued to coincide with that meeting (#1633-1682). Each stamp shows the flag of one of the 50 states.

This series was one of several stamp issues celebrating the United States' bicentennial. The occasion was first commemorated on stamps in 1971 with the American Revolution issue (#1432). The Bicentennial Series of 1976 is a multiple issue, or se-tenant, with each pane containing stamps of different designs. The Postal Service began issuing se-tenants in 1936.

1657   1658   1659

1660   1661   1662

1663   1664   1665

1666   1667   1668

1669   1670   1671

1672   1673   1674

1675

1676

1677

1678

1679

1680

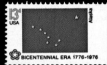

1681

1682

1683

1684

1685

The Surrender of Lord Cornwallis at Yorktown
From a Painting by John Trumbull

1686

	1976 continued, Perf. 11	Un	U	PB/LP	#	FDC	Q
1675	13¢ Idaho	.45	.30			1.75	8,720,100
1676	13¢ Wyoming	.45	.30			1.75	8,720,100
1677	13¢ Utah	.45	.30			1.75	8,720,100
1678	13¢ Oklahoma	.45	.30			1.75	8,720,100
1679	13¢ New Mexico	.45	.30			1.75	8,720,100
1680	13¢ Arizona	.45	.30			1.75	8,720,100
1681	13¢ Alaska	.45	.30			1.75	8,720,100
1682	13¢ Hawaii	.45	.30			1.75	8,720,100
1682a	Pane of 50, #1633-1682	25.00	—	25.00	(50)	32.50	
1683	13¢ Telephone Centennial, Mar. 10	.26	.05	1.30	(4)	.65	158,915,000
1684	13¢ Commercial Aviation, Mar. 19	.26	.05	2.90	(10)	.65	156,960,000
1685	13¢ Chemistry, Apr. 6	.26	.05	3.40	(12)	.65	158,470,000
	American Bicentennial Issue, Souvenir Sheets, May 29						
	Sheets of 5 Stamps Each, Perf. 11						
1686	13¢ Surrender of Cornwallis at						
	Yorktown, by John Trumbull	4.50	—			6.00	1,990,000
	a. 13¢ Two American Officers	.65	.40				1,990,000
	b. 13¢ Gen. Benjamin Lincoln	.65	.40				1,990,000
	c. 13¢ George Washington	.65	.40				1,990,000
	d. 13¢ John Trumbull, Col. Cobb,						
	von Steuben,						
	Lafayette, Thomas Nelson	.65	.40				1,990,000
	e. 13¢ Alexander Hamilton, John						
	Laurens, Walter Stewart	.65	.40				1,990,000

Telephone

Alexander Graham Bell is credited with inventing the first telephone (#1683). He was actually trying to improve the telegraph system. It was largely by accident that he and Thomas Watson, his associate, discovered voices could be transmitted as well as dots and dashes.

Bell's first message, "Mr. Watson, come here. I want you," was repeated almost 40 years later in the first transcontinental talk (1915). It took some time for Watson to "come here" because he was in San Francisco while Bell was in New York. In its early years, the telephone enjoyed steady growth. The device was patented in 1876, and by August of the following year there were 700 in service in the United States; that number increased by more than 100% in the next 10 years. More improvements were to come. In 1956 the first transatlantic cable was laid, allowing easy phone access to Europe. Today satellites are used to transmit messages worldwide and fiber optics allow more cable to be laid underground.

Although best remembered for his invention, Bell was actually a speech therapist. Most of his work was intended to benefit the hearing impaired. His wife, Mabel Hubbard Bell, was deaf. Helen Keller (#1824) is among those he helped.

	1976 continued, Perf. 11	Un	U	PB/LP	#	FDC	Q
1687	18¢ Declaration of Independence,						
	by John Trumbull	6.00	—			7.50	1,983,000
	a. 18¢ John Adams, Roger Sherman,						
	Robert R. Livingston	.80	.55				1,983,000
	b. 18¢ Thomas Jefferson, Benjamin						
	Franklin	.80	.55				1,983,000
	c. 18¢ Thomas Nelson, Jr., Francis						
	Lewis, John Witherspoon,						
	Samuel Huntington	.80	.55				1,983,000
	d. 18¢ John Hancock,						
	Charles Thomson	.80	.55				1,983,000
	e. 18¢ George Read, John						
	Dickinson, Edward Rutledge	.80	.55				1,983,000
1688	24¢ Washington Crossing the						
	Delaware, by Emanuel Leutze/						
	Eastman Johnson	7.50	—			8.50	1,953,000
	a. 24¢ Boatsmen	1.00	.75				1,953,000
	b. 24¢ George Washington	1.00	.75				1,953,000
	c. 24¢ Flagbearer	1.00	.75				1,953,000
	d. 24¢ Men in Boat	1.00	.75				1,953,000
	e. 24¢ Steersman, Men on Shore	1.00	.75				1,953,000
1689	31¢ Washington Reviewing Army						
	at Valley Forge, by William T. Trego	9.00	—			9.50	1,903,000
	a. 31¢ Two Officers	1.25	.90				1,903,000
	b. 31¢ George Washington	1.25	.90				1,903,000
	c. 31¢ Officer and Brown Horse	1.25	.90				1,903,000
	d. 31¢ Officer and White Horse	1.25	.90				1,903,000
	e. 31¢ Three Soldiers	1.25	.90				1,903,000

Washington at Valley Forge

By December of 1777 the fortunes of the Continental Army were at low ebb. The struggle to free the American colonies from British domination was not going well for the rebel forces, which had suffered serious setbacks at Brandywine and Germantown, Pennsylvania. When George Washington, commanding general, decided to take up winter quarters at Valley Forge, Pennsylvania (#1689), the British held Philadelphia — where, a year before, the colonies had proudly declared their independence. Worse was yet to come.

The winter was particularly severe. Supplies were dangerously low, and morale was even lower. Yet during that hard, bitter winter, Washington was able to turn his motley crew of underfed volunteers into a fighting force. With French aid and the military experience of Prussian Baron Friedrich von Steuben, the American forces began to turn the tide, beginning with a victory at Monmouth, New Jersey in June of the following year.

The Declaration of Independence, 4 July 1776 at Philadelphia
From a Painting by John Trumbull

1687

Washington Crossing the Delaware
From a Painting by Emanuel Leutze / Eastman Johnson

1688

Washington Reviewing His Ragged Army at Valley Forge
From a Painting by William T. Trego

1689

1690

1691   1692   1693   1694

1699

1700

1695   1696
1697   1698

1701

1702

1703

1705

1976 continued, Perf. 11	Un	U	PB/LP	#	FDC	Q
American Bicentennial Issue, Benjamin Franklin, June 1						
1690 13¢ Franklin and Map						
of North America, 1776	.26	.05	1.30	(4)	.65	164,890,000
Declaration of Independence, by John Trumbull, July 4						
1691 13¢	.26	.08	5.50	(20)	.65	51,008,750
1692 13¢	.26	.08			.65	51,008,750
1693 13¢	.26	.08			.65	51,008,750
1694 13¢	.26	.08	5.50	(20)	.65	51,008,750
1694a Strip of 4, #1691-1694	1.10	.75			2.00	
Olympic Games Issue, July 16						
1695 13¢ Diving	.26	.08	3.40	(12)	.75	46,428,750
1696 13¢ Skiing	.26	.08			.75	46,428,750
1697 13¢ Running	.26	.08	3.40	(12)	.75	46,428,750
1698 13¢ Skating	.26	.08			.75	46,428,750
1698a Block of 4, #1695-1698	1.10	1.00			2.00	
1699 13¢ Clara Maass, Aug. 18	.26	.06	3.40	(12)	.75	130,592,000
1700 13¢ Adolph S. Ochs, Sept. 18	.26	.05	1.30	(4)	.75	158,332,800
Christmas Issue, Oct. 27						
1701 13¢ Nativity,						
by John Singleton Copley	.26	.05	3.40	(12)	.65	809,955,000
1702 13¢ "Winter Pastime,"						
by Nathaniel Currier	.26	.05	3.00	(10)	.65	481,685,000
1703 13¢ as 1702	.26	.05	5.70	(20)	.65	481,685,000

#1702 has overall tagging. Lettering at base is black and usually ½mm. below design. As a rule, no "snowflaking" in sky or pond. Pane of 50 has margins on 4 sides with slogans. #1703 has block tagging the size of the printed area. Lettering at base is gray black and usually ¾mm. below design. "Snowflaking" generally in sky and pond. Pane of 50 has margin only at right or left and no slogans.

Issues of 1977, American Bicentennial Issue, Washington at Princeton, Jan. 3						
1704 13¢ Washington, Nassau Hall,						
Hessian Prisoners and 13-star Flag,						
by Charles Wilson Peale	.26	.05	2.90	(10)	.65	150,328,000
1705 13¢ Sound Recording, Mar. 23	.26	.05	1.30	(4)	.65	176,830,000

Sound Recording

We have come full circle in terms of recording sound. The first "records" were cylindrical discs with grooves that were read by a stylus or a needle. Since then, the familiar flat albums were developed and have been refined with high-fidelity, stereo and quadraphonic techniques. The latest innovation in sound recording is another circle—the compact disc that is read by a laser beam instead of a needle.

The first sound-recording device, the phonograph (#1705), was introduced in 1877 and is credited to famous inventor Thomas A. Edison. Ironically, Edison was hearing impaired. His invention used one of those cylindrical discs, as did many variations on the phonograph up until 1929. The flat record as we know it was introduced in 1893. Although we associate records with music, many of the early devices recorded human speech.

1977 continued, Perf. 11	Un	U	PB/LP	#	FDC	Q
American Folk Art Issue, Pueblo Pottery, Apr. 13, Perf. 11						
1706 13¢ Zia Pot	.26	.08	3.00	(10)	.75	48,994,000
1707 13¢ San Ildefonso Pot	.26	.08			.75	48,994,000
1708 13¢ Hopi Pot	.26	.08	5.00	(16)	.75	48,994,000
1709 13¢ Acoma Pot	.26	.08			.75	48,994,000
1709a Block of 4, #1706-1709	1.05	1.00			2.00	
1710 13¢ 50th Anniv. Lindbergh Flight,						
May 20	.26	.05	3.65	(12)	.75	208,820,000
1711 13¢ Colorado Statehood, May 21	.26	.05	3.65	(12)	.65	192,250,000
Butterfly Issue, June 6						
1712 13¢ Swallowtail	.26	.08	3.65	(12)	2.00	54,957,500
1713 13¢ Checkerspot	.26	.08	3.65	(12)	2.00	54,957,500
1714 13¢ Dogface	.26	.08			2.00	54,957,500
1715 13¢ Orange Tip	.26	.08			2.00	54,957,500
1715a Block of 4, #1712-1715	1.05	.90			2.00	
American Bicentennial Issue, Lafayette's Landing In South Carolina, June 13						
1716 13¢ Marquis de Lafayette	.26	.05	1.30	(4)	.65	159,852,000
Skilled Hands for Independence, July 4						
1717 13¢ Seamstress	.26	.08	3.65	(12)	.65	47,077,500
1718 13¢ Blacksmith	.26	.08	3.65	(12)	.65	47,077,500
1719 13¢ Wheelwright	.26	.08			.65	47,077,500
1720 13¢ Leatherworker	.26	.08			.65	47,077,500
1720a Block of 4, #1717-1720	1.05	.90			1.75	
Perf. 11x10½						
1721 13¢ Peace Bridge, Aug. 4	.26	.05	1.30	(4)	.65	163,625,000

Peace Bridge

Each year, thousands of U.S. and Canadian citizens freely cross the world's longest unpatrolled border. Many use Peace Bridge (#1721), which connects Buffalo, New York and Fort Erie, Ontario across the Niagara River. The bridge was erected in 1927 to commemorate 100 years of peace and friendship between the two nations, a tradition that continues to the present day. Peace Bridge is more than a monument; it connects two heavily industrialized countries to the power generated by the river and its waterfalls, making it a major link between the United States and Canada. And Peace Bridge carries more traffic and cargo than any other overland route.

Zia: Museum of New Mexico
Pueblo Art USA 13c

San Ildefonso: Denver Art Museum
Pueblo Art USA 13c

Hopi: Heard Museum Phoenix
Pueblo Art USA 13c

Acoma: School of American Research
Pueblo Art USA 13c

1706
1708

1707
1709

USA·13c

50th Anniversary Solo Transatlantic Flight

1710

COLORADO

13c
USA

THE CENTENNIAL STATE

1711

Swallowtail
USA**13**C *Papilio oregonius*

Checkerspot
USA**13**C *Euphydryas phaeton*

Dogface
USA**13**C *Colias eurydice*

Orange-Tip
USA**13**C *Anthocaris midea*

1712
1713

1714
1715

ℒafayette

US Bicentennial 13c

1716

the SEAMSTRESS
for INDEPENDENCE USA**13**c

the BLACKSMITH
for INDEPENDENCE USA**13**c

the WHEELWRIGHT
for INDEPENDENCE USA**13**c

the LEATHERWORKER
for INDEPENDENCE USA**13**c

1717
1719

1718
1720

Peace Bridge 1927-77

United States & Canada

USA13c

1721

Herkimer at Oriskany 1777 by Yohn
US Bicentennial 13 cents

1722

1723
1724

First Civil Settlement · Alta California · 1777

1725

1726

1727

Surrender at Saratoga 1777 by Trumbull
US Bicentennial 13 cents

1728

1729

1730

Carl Sandburg
USA 13c

1731

1732
1733

1734

US Postage

1735

1737

1738

1739

1740

1741   1742

	1977 continued,	Un	U	PB/LP	#	FDC	Q
	American Bicentennial Issue, Battle of Oriskany, Aug. 6, Perf. 11						
1722	13¢ Herkimer at Oriskany,						
	by Frederick Yohn	.26	.05	3.10	(10)	.65	156,296,000
	Energy Issue, Oct. 20						
1723	13¢ Energy Conservation	.26	.08	3.65	(12)	.65	79,338,000
1723a	Pair, #1723-1724	.52	.35			1.00	
1724	13¢ Energy Development	.26	.08			.65	79,338,000
1725	13¢ First Civil Settlement—						
	Alta, CA, Sept. 9	.26	.05	1.30	(4)	.65	154,495,000
	American Bicentennial Issue, Articles of Confederation, Sept. 30						
1726	13¢ Members of Continental						
	Congress in Conference	.26	.05	1.30	(4)	.65	168,050,000
1727	13¢ Talking Pictures, Oct. 6	.26	.05	1.30	(4)	.75	156,810,000
	American Bicentennial Issue, Surrender at Saratoga, Oct. 7						
1728	13¢ Surrender of Burgoyne,						
	by John Trumbull	.26	.05	3.10	(10)	.65	153,736,000
	Christmas Issue, Oct. 21						
1729	13¢ Washington at Valley Forge	.35	.05	5.70	(20)	.65	882,260,000
1730	13¢ Rural Mailbox	.26	.05	3.10	(10)	.65	921,530,000
	Issues of 1978						
1731	13¢ Carl Sandburg, Jan. 6	.26	.05	1.30	(4)	.65	156,580,000
	Capt. Cook Issue, Jan. 20						
1732	13¢ Capt. James Cook-Alaska,						
	by Nathanial Dance	.26	.08	1.30	(4)	.75	101,095,000
1732a	Pair, #1732-1733	.55	.30			1.50	
1733	13¢ "Resolution" and "Discovery,"						
	by John Webber	.26	.08	1.30	(4)	.75	101,095,000
1734	13¢ Indian Head Penny, Jan. 11	.26	.10	3.25	(4)	1.00	
1735	(15¢) A Stamp, May 22	.30	.05	1.50	(4)	.65	
	Perf. 11x10½						
1736	(15¢) orange Eagle (1735), May 22,						
	Single from booklet	.30	.05			.65	
1736a	Booklet pane of 8	2.40	.60				
	Perf. 10						
1737	15¢ Roses, July 11,						
	Single from booklet	.30	.06			.65	
1737a	Booklet pane of 8	2.40	.60				
	Issues of 1980, Windmills Issue, Feb. 7, Perf. 11						
1738	15¢ Virginia, 1720	.30	.05			.65	
1739	15¢ Rhode Island, 1790	.30	.05			.65	
1740	15¢ Massachusetts, 1793	.30	.05			.65	
1741	15¢ Illinois, 1860	.30	.05			.65	
1742	15¢ Texas, 1890	.30	.05			.65	
1742a	Booklet pane of 10, #1738-42	4.00	.60				
	#1736, 1737-42 issued only in booklets						

	1978 continued, Coil Stamp, **Perf. 10 Vertically**	Un	U	PB/LP	#	FDC	Q
1743	(15¢) orange Eagle (1735), May 22	.30	.05	1.00		.65	
	Black Heritage Issue, Feb. 1, Perf. 11						
1744	13¢ Harriet Tubman	.26	.05	3.65	(12)	1.00	156,555,000
	American Folk Art Issue, Quilts, Mar. 8						
1745	13¢ Basket design, red & orange	.26	.08	3.65	(12)	.75	41,295,600
1746	13¢ Basket design, red	.26	.08	3.65	(12)	.75	41,295,600
1747	13¢ Basket design, orange	.26	.08			.75	41,295,600
1748	13¢ Basket design, black	.26	.08			.75	41,295,600
1748a	Block of 4, #1745-1748	1.05	.75			2.00	
	American Dance Issue, Apr. 26						
1749	13¢ Ballet	.26	.08	3.65	(12)	.75	39,399,600
1750	13¢ Theater	.26	.08	3.65	(12)	.75	39,399,600
1751	13¢ Folk Dance	.26	.08			.75	39,399,600
1752	13¢ Modern Dance	.26	.08			.75	39,399,600
1752a	Block of 4, #1749-1752	1.05	.75			1.75	
	American Bicentennial Issue, French Alliance, May 4						
1753	13¢ King Louis XVI and Benjamin						
·	Franklin, by Charles G. Sauvage	.26	.05	1.30	(4)	.65	102,920,000
	Perf. 10½x11						
1754	13¢ Early Cancer Detection, May 18	.26	.05	1.30	(4)	.65	152,355,000
	Performing Arts Issue, Perf. 11						
1755	13¢ Jimmie Rodgers, May 24	.26	.05	3.65	(12)	.65	94,625,000
1756	15¢ George M. Cohan, July 3	.30	.05	4.20	(12)	.65	151,570,000

Early Cancer Detection

Cancer is the second largest cause of death in the United States, claiming 60,000 victims annually. As yet, there is no cure, but the prognosis is not always negative. With many types of cancer, if the disease is discovered early enough, a patient's chances of survival are an astoundingly good 90-95%. A key tool in the war against cancer is diagnostic testing, such as the Pap smear (#1754) for cervical cancer in women. Other forms of the disease, such as breast and colorectal cancer, can be arrested through surgery and chemical treatment if caught in early stages. The National Cancer Institute estimates the death rate could be halved by the year 2000 through proper screening. Obviously, early detection is important in combating cancer, a point the Postal Service has made on more than one occasion (#1263).

1744

1745   1746
1747   1748

1749

1750

1751

1752

1753

1754

1755

1756

1757a, b, c, d

1757e, f, g, h

1757

1758

1759

1760 1761

1762 1763

1764
1766

1765
1767

1768 1769

	1978 continued	Un	U	PB/LP	#	FDC	Q
	CAPEX '78, Souvenir Sheet, June 10, Perf. 11						
1757	13¢ Souvenir sheet of 8	2.10	2.10	2.75	(8)	3.00	15,170,400
1757a	13¢ Cardinal	.26	.10				
1757b	13¢ Mallard	.26	.10				
1757c	13¢ Canada Goose	.26	.10				
1757d	13¢ Blue Jay	.26	.10				
1757e	13¢ Moose	.26	.10				
1757f	13¢ Chipmunk	.26	.10				
1757g	13¢ Red Fox	.26	.10				
1757h	13¢ Raccoon	.26	.10				
1758	15¢ Photography, June 26	.30	.05	4.20	(12)	.65	163,200,000
1759	15¢ Viking Missions to Mars,						
	July 20	.30	.05	1.50	(4)	1.10	158,880,000
	American Owls Issue, Aug. 26						
1760	15¢ Great Gray Owl	.30	.08	1.50	(4)	.75	46,637,500
1761	15¢ Saw-whet Owl	.30	.08	1.50	(4)	.75	46,637,500
1762	15¢ Barred Owl	.30	.08	1.50	(4)	.75	46,637,500
1763	15¢ Great Horned Owl	.30	.08	1.50	(4)	.75	46,637,500
1763a	Block of 4, #1760-1763	1.25	.85			2.00	
	American Trees Issue, Oct. 9						
1764	15¢ Giant Sequoia	.30	.08	4.20	(12)	.75	42,034,000
1765	15¢ White Pine	.30	.08	4.20	(12)	.75	42,034,000
1766	15¢ White Oak	.30	.08			.75	42,034,000
1767	15¢ Gray Birch	.30	.08			.75	42,034,000
1767a	Block of 4, #1764-1767	1.25	.85			2.00	
	Christmas Issue, Oct. 18						
1768	15¢ Madonna and Child with Cherubim,						
	by Andrea della Robbia	.30	.05	4.20	(12)	.65	963,370,000
1769	15¢ Child on Hobby Horse and						
	Christmas Trees	.30	.05	4.20	(12)	.65	916,800,000

Owls

The faces on the "Wildlife Conservation" stamps (#1760-1763) suggest the wisdom of the ages, but they are those of predators: Owls are hunters. An "extra" digit on their claws lets them scoop up prey. Owls hunt at night. Especially acute hearing and vision allow them to locate any prey foolish enough to venture out after dark.

Owls have only one natural enemy. "Who?" you ask. Man. Much loved by farmers as an efficient form of pest control, the owl is hated by hunters and even fishermen for decimating their quarry. The inroads of civilization have destroyed many of its breeding grounds.

	Issues of 1979, Perf. 11	Un	U	PB/LP	#	FDC	Q
1770	15¢ Robert F. Kennedy, Jan. 12	.30	.05	1.50	(4)	.65	159,297,600
	Black Heritage Issue, Jan. 13						
1771	15¢ Martin Luther King, Jr., Jan. 13	.30	.05	4.20	(12)	.65	166,435,000
1772	15¢ International Year of the Child,						
	Feb. 15	.30	.05	1.50	(4)	.65	162,535,000
	Perf. 10½x11						
1773	15¢ John Steinbeck, Feb. 27	.30	.05	1.50	(4)	.65	155,000,000
1774	15¢ Albert Einstein, Mar. 4	.30	.05	1.50	(4)	.65	157,310,000
	American Folk Art Issue, Pennsylvania Toleware, Apr. 19, Perf. 11						
1775	15¢ Coffeepot	.30	.08	3.50	(10)	.75	43,524,000
1776	15¢ Tea Caddy	.30	.08			.75	43,524,000
1777	15¢ Sugar Bowl	.30	.08			.75	43,524,000
1778	15¢ Coffeepot	.30	.08			.75	43,524,000
1778a	Block or strip of 4, #1775-1778	1.25	.85			2.00	174,096,000
	American Architecture Issue, June 4						
1779	15¢ Virginia Rotunda,						
	by Thomas Jefferson	.30	.08	1.50	(4)	.75	41,198,400
1780	15¢ Baltimore Cathedral,						
	by Benjamin Latrobe	.30	.08	1.50	(4)	.75	41,198,400
1781	15¢ Boston State House,						
	by Charles Bulfinch	.30	.08	1.50	(4)	.75	41,198,400
1782	15¢ Philadelphia Exchange,						
	by William Strickland	.30	.08	1.50	(4)	.75	41,198,400
1782a	Block of 4, #1779-1782	1.25	.85			2.00	164,793,600
	Endangered Flora Issue, June 7						
1783	15¢ Persistent Trillium	.30	.08	4.20	(12)	.75	40,763,750
1784	15¢ Hawaiian Wild Broadbean	.30	.08			.75	40,763,750
1785	15¢ Contra Costa Wallflower	.30	.08	4.20	(12)	.75	40,763,750
1786	15¢ Antioch Dunes Evening Primrose	.30	.08			.75	40,763,750
1786a	Block of 4, #1783-1786	1.25	.85			2.00	163,055,000
1787	15¢ Seeing Eye Dogs, June 15	.30	.05	6.50	(20)	.65	161,860,000

Dr. Martin Luther King, Jr.

Dr. Martin Luther King, Jr. (#1771) had a dream—a dream of equality for black people. When King took up the gauntlet in 1955, blacks, especially in the South, were denied such basic dignities as a choice of seats on a bus or the right to use all public drinking fountains. King brought his cause to the American people through nonviolent demonstrations, such as sit-ins and marches. His efforts culminated in a Nobel Peace Prize (1964) and passage, in the same year, of the landmark Civil Rights Act that outlawed discrimination in public facilities.

Ironically, this man of peace met a violent end—the victim of an assassin's bullet at the age of 39. In the aftermath, much of Dr. King's dream died with him. Yet his contribution did not go unrecognized: His birthday is now observed as a federal holiday.

1770

1771

1772

1773

1774

1775   1776
1777   1778

1779   1780
1781   1782

1783   1784
1785   1786

1787

1788

1789

1790

1791   1792
1793   1794

1799

1800

1795   1796
1797   1798

1802

1801

1803

1804

	1979 continued, Perf. 11	Un	U	PB/LP #	FDC	Q
1788	15¢ Special Olympics, Aug. 9	.30	.05	3.50 (10)	.65	165,775,000
	American Bicentennial Issue, John Paul Jones, Sept. 23, Perf. 11x12					
1789	15¢ John Paul Jones,					
	by Charles Wilson Peale	.30	.05	3.50 (10)	.65	160,000,000
	Olympic Games Issue, Perf. 11 (see also #C97)					
1790	10¢ Javelin, Sept. 5	.25	.22	3.75 (12)	1.00	67,195,000
1791	15¢ Running, Sept. 28	.35	.08	4.75 (12)	.75	46,726,250
1792	15¢ Swimming, Sept. 28	.35	.08	4.75 (12)	.75	46,726,250
1793	15¢ Canoeing, Sept. 28	.35	.08		.75	46,726,250
1794	15¢ Equestrian, Sept. 28	.35	.08		.75	46,726,250
1794a	Block of 4, #1791-1794	1.50	.85		2.00	187,650,000
	Issues of 1980, Olympic Games Issue, Feb. 1, Perf. 11x10½					
1795	15¢ Speed Skating	.45	.08	6.50 (12)	.75	
1796	15¢ Downhill Skiing	.45	.08	6.50 (12)	.75	
1797	15¢ Ski Jump	.45	.08		.75	
1798	15¢ Hockey Goaltender	.45	.08		.75	
1798a	Block of 4, #1795-1798	1.90	.85		2.00	208,295,000
	1979 continued, Christmas Issue, Oct. 18, Perf. 11					
1799	15¢ Virgin and Child,					
	by Gerard David	.30	.05	4.25 (12)	.65	873,710,000
1800	15¢ Santa Claus,					
	Christmas Tree Ornament	.30	.05	4.25 (12)	.65	931,880,000
	Performing Arts Issue, Nov. 4					
1801	15¢ Will Rogers	.30	.05	4.25 (12)	.65	161,290,000
1802	15¢ Vietnam Veterans, Nov. 11	.30	.05	3.50 (10)	1.25	172,740,000
	Issues of 1980, Performing Arts Issue, Jan. 29					
1803	15¢ W.C. Fields	.30	.05	4.25 (12)	.65	168,995,000
	Black Heritage Issue, Feb. 15					
1804	15¢ Benjamin Banneker	.30	.05	4.25 (12)	.65	160,000,000

W.C. Fields

W.C. Fields (#1803) is one of the most popular film comedians. More than 40 years after his death, his movies still enjoy a strong following, especially among college students and film buffs. Comic talent notwithstanding, Fields billed himself as "the world's greatest juggler," a title he may well have deserved judging by the sleight of hand in his films. In fact, juggling gave Fields his start in show business.

After running away from home at the age of 11 and attempting a brief career as a petty thief, Fields (by then a mature 14) became a juggler in vaudeville. He may have been quick with his hands, but he was even quicker with his tongue. His banter with the audience soon turned the act into a comedy routine. The rest, as they say, is history. Fields ultimately went to Hollywood, where he not only starred in but also wrote, directed (and improvised) a number of movies, including two 1940 classics: **The Bank Dick** *and* **My Little Chickadee**.

	1980 continued	Un	U	PB/LP	#	FDC	Q
	Letter Writing Issue, Feb. 25, Perf. 11						
1805	15¢ Letters Preserve Memories	.30	.08	11.00	(36)	.65	
1806	15¢ P.S. Write Soon	.30	.08			.65	
1807	15¢ Letters Lift Spirits	.30	.08			.65	
1808	15¢ P.S. Write Soon	.30	.08			.65	
1809	15¢ Letters Shape Opinions	.30	.08			.65	
1810	15¢ P.S. Write Soon	.30	.08	11.00	(36)	.65	
1810a	Vertical Strip of 6, #1805-1810	2.75	1.25			3.00	233,598,000
	Americana Issue, Coil Stamps, Perf. 10 Vertically						
1811	1¢ Inkwell & Quill, March 6	.05	.05	.15		.40	
1813	3.5¢ Weaver Violins, June 23	.08	.05	.30		.50	
1816	12¢ Torch, Apr. 8	.24	.05	.75		.60	
	Perf. 11x10½						
1818	(18¢) B Stamp, Mar. 15	.36	.05	1.80	(4)	.75	
	Perf 10						
1819	(18¢) B Stamp (1818), Mar. 15,						
	Single from booklet	.36	.05			.75	
1819a	Booklet pane of 8	4.50	1.50				
	Coil Stamp, Perf. 10 Vertically						
1820	(18¢) B Stamp (1818), Mar. 15	.45	.05	1.00		.75	
	Perf. 10½x11						
1821	15¢ Frances Perkins, April 10	.30	.05	1.50	(4)	.65	163,510,000
	Perf. 11						
1822	15¢ Dolley Madison, May 20	.30	.05	1.50	(4)	.65	256,620,000
1823	15¢ Emily Bissell, May 31	.30	.05	1.50	(4)	.65	95,695,000
1824	15¢ Helen Keller/Anne Sullivan,						
	June 27	.30	.05	1.50	(4)	.80	153,975,000
1825	15¢ Veterans Administration,						
	July 21	.30	.05	1.50	(4)	.65	160,000,000
1826	15¢ General Bernardo de Galvez,						
	July 23	.30	.05	1.50	(4)	.65	103,855,000
	Coral Reefs Issue, Aug. 26						
1827	15¢ Brain Coral	.30	.08	4.50	(12)	.85	
1828	15¢ Elkhorn Coral	.30	.08			.85	
1829	15¢ Chalice Coral	.30	.08	4.50	(12)	.85	
1830	15¢ Finger Coral	.30	.08			.85	
1830a	Block of 4, #1827-1830	1.20	.85			2.00	205,165,000

1811

1813

1805
1806

1807
1808

1809
1810

1816

1818

1822

1821

1823

HELEN KELLER
ANNE SULLIVAN

1824

1825

1826

1827
1829

1828
1830

Organized Labor Proud and Free USA 15c

1831

1832

1833

Heiltsuk, Bella Bella **Indian Art** USA 15c

Chilkat Tlingit **Indian Art** USA 15c

Tlingit **Indian Art** USA 15c

Bella Coola **Indian Art** USA 15c

1834   1835
1836   1837

Benwick 1818-1895 Smithsonian Washington **Architecture** USA 15c

Richardson 1838-1886 Trinity Church Boston **Architecture** USA 15c

Furness 1839-1912 Penn Academy Philadelphia **Architecture** USA 15c

A.J.Davis 1803-1892 Lyndhurst Tarrytown NY **Architecture** USA 15c

Christmas USA 15c

USA 15c Season's Greetings

1842   1843

1838   1839
1840   1841

	1980 continued, Perf. 11	Un	U	PB/LP #	FDC	Q
1831	15¢ Organized Labor, Sept. 1	.30	.05	4.50 (12)	.65	166,590,000
	Literary Arts Issue, Sept. 5, Perf. 10½x11					
1832	15¢ Edith Wharton	.30	.05	1.50 (4)	.65	163,275,000
	Perf. 11					
1833	15¢ American Education, Sept. 12	.30	.05	2.25 (6)	.65	160,000,000
	American Folk Art Issue, Pacific Northwest Indian Masks, Sept. 25					
1834	15¢ Bella Bella	.30	.08		.75	
1835	15¢ Chilkat	.30	.08		.75	
1836	15¢ Tlingit	.30	.08		.75	
1837	15¢ Bella Coola	.30	.08		.75	
1837a	Block of 4, #1834-1837	1.20	.85	3.50 (10)	2.00	152,404,000
	American Architecture Issue, Oct. 9					
1838	15¢ Smithsonian Institution,					
	by Renwick	.30	.08		.75	
1839	15¢ Trinity Church, by Richardson	.30	.08		.75	
1840	15¢ Pennsylvania Academy of					
	Fine Arts, by Furness	.30	.08		.75	
1841	15¢ Lyndhurst, by A.J. Davis	.30	.08		.75	
1841a	Block of 4, #1838-1841	1.20	.85	1.50 (4)	2.00	155,024,000
	Christmas Issue, Oct. 31					
1842	15¢ Epiphany Window,					
	Washington Cathedral	.30	.05	4.25 (12)	.65	693,250,000
1843	15¢ Wreath and Toys	.30	.05	6.50 (20)	.65	718,715,000

Indian Art

The American Folk Art issue (#1834-1837) recognizes unique native American cultures in the Pacific Northwest that predate Eskimos by as much as 12,000 years.

The Indians of the Pacific Northwest settled a relatively narrow band of territory along the coast from the Gulf of Alaska, south through British Columbia into present-day California. Although divided into separate language groups, such as Tlingit, they all were related. The tribes supported themselves by hunting and, especially, fishing — for which they designed elaborately carved, seagoing canoes. Cedar and redwood were abundant in the area and, in addition to canoes, the tribes produced a variety of beautifully carved and elaborately decorated wooden objects. These included totem and burial poles; "potlatch" figures created for special ceremonies; and masks, such as the ones shown, that were used in tribal ceremonies or as home decorations.

	Issues of 1980-85	Un	U	PB/LP	#	FDC		Q
	Great Americans Issue, Perf. 11							
1844	1¢ Dorothea Dix, Sept. 23, 1983,	.05	.05	1.00	(20)	.60		
	Perf. 10½x11							
1845	2¢ Igor Stravinsky, Nov. 18, 1982	.05	.05	.20	(4)	.60		
1846	3¢ Henry Clay, July 13, 1983	.06	.05	.30	(4)	.60		
1847	4¢ Carl Schurz, June 3, 1983	.08	.05	.40	(4)	.60		
1848	5¢ Pearl Buck, June 25, 1983	.10	.05	.50	(4)	.60		
	Perf. 10½x11							
1849	6¢ Walter Lippman, Sept. 19, 1985	.12	.05	2.75	(20)	.60		
1850	7¢ Abraham Baldwin, Jan. 25, 1985	.14	.05	3.00	(20)	.60		
1851	8¢ Henry Knox, July 25, 1985	.16	.05	.80	(4)	.60		
1852	9¢ Sylvanus Thayer, June 7, 1985	.18	.05	4.00	(20)	.60		
	Perf. 11							
1853	10¢ Richard Russell, May 31, 1984	.20	.05	4.50	(20)	.65		
	Perf. 10½x11							
1854	11¢ Alden Partridge, Feb. 12, 1985	.22	.05	1.10	(4)	.65		
1855	13¢ Crazy Horse, Jan. 15, 1982	.26	.05	1.30	(4)	.65		
1856	14¢ Sinclair Lewis, Mar. 21, 1985	.28	.05	6.00	(20)	.65		
1857	17¢ Rachel Carson, May 28, 1981	.34	.05	1.75	(4)	.75		
1858	18¢ George Mason, May 7, 1981	.36	.05	1.75	(4)	.75		
1859	19¢ Sequoyah, Dec. 27, 1980	.38	.07	2.00	(4)	.80		
1860	20¢ Ralph Bunche, Jan. 12, 1982	.40	.05	2.00	(4)	.75		
1861	20¢ Thomas H. Gallaudet,							
	June 10, 1983	.40	.05	2.00	(4)	.75		
	Perf. 11							
1862	20¢ Harry S. Truman, Jan. 26, 1984	.40	.05	8.50	(20)	.75		
	Perf. 10½x11							
1863	22¢ John J. Audubon, Apr. 23, 1985	.44	.05	9.25	(20)	.80		
	Perf. 11							
1864	30¢ Frank C. Laubach,							
	Sept. 2, 1984	.60	.08	12.50	(20)	.85		
1865	35¢ Charles R. Drew, M.D,							
	June 3, 1981	.70	.08	3.50	(4)	1.00		
	Perf. 10½x11							
1866	37¢ Robert Millikan, Jan. 26, 1982	.75	.05	3.75	(4)	1.00		
1867	39¢ Grenville Clark, May 20, 1985	.80	.08	17.00	(20)	1.00		
	Perf. 11							
1868	40¢ Lillian M. Gilbreth,							
	Feb. 24, 1984	.80	.10	17.50	(20)	1.00		
	Perf. 10½x11							
1869	50¢ Chester W. Nimitz,							
	Feb. 22, 1985	1.00	.10	5.00	(4)	1.25		
	Issues of 1986, Perf. 11							
2168	1¢ Margaret Mitchell, June 30	.05	.05	.20	(4)	.80		
2170	3¢ Paul Dudley White, M.D, Sept. 15	.06	.05	.30	(4)	.80		

Dorothea Dix
USA 1c

Igor Stravinsky
USA 2c

Henry Clay
USA 3c

Carl Schurz
4c
USA

Pearl Buck
USA 5c

1844   1845   1846   1847   1848

Walter Lippmann
6 USA

Abraham Baldwin
USA 7

Henry Knox
USA 8

Sylvanus Thayer
USA 9

Richard Russell
USA 10c

1849   1850   1851   1852   1853

Alden Partridge
USA 11

USA 13c
Crazy Horse

Sinclair Lewis
USA 14

Rachel Carson
USA 17c

George Mason
USA 18c

1854   1855   1856   1857   1858

USA 19c
Sequoyah

Ralph Bunche
USA 20c

Thomas H Gallaudet
USA 20c

Harry S Truman
USA 20c

John J. Audubon
USA 22

1859   1860   1861   1862   1863

Frank C. Laubach
USA 30c

Charles R Drew MD
USA 35c

Robert Millikan
37c
USA

Grenville Clark
USA 39

Lillian M. Gilbreth
USA 40c

1864   1865   1866   1867   1868

USA 50
Chester W. Nimitz

Margaret Mitchell
USA 1

Paul Dudley White MD
USA 3

2171 2172 2179 2183 2191

2194 2195

	Issues of 1986	Un	U	PB/LP	#	FDC		Q
	Great Americans continued, Perf. 11							
2171	4¢ Father Flanagan, July 14	.08	.05	.40	(4)	.80		
2172	5¢ Hugo L. Black, Feb. 27	.10	.05	.50	(4)	.80		
2173-76, 2178 not assigned.								
2179	17¢ Belva Ann Lockwood,							
	June 18	.34	.06	1.75	(4)	.80		
2180-82 not assigned.								
2183	25¢ Jack London, Jan. 11	.50	.06	2.50	(4)	.85		
2184-90 not assigned.								
2191	56¢ John Harvard, Sept. 3	1.10	.08	5.50	(4)	1.25		
2192-93 not assigned.								
2194	$1 Bernard Revel, Sept. 23	2.00	.50	10.00	(4)	2.00		
2195	$2 William Jennings Bryan,							
	Mar. 19	4.00	.50	20.00	(4)	3.00		

	Issues of 1981, Perf. 11	Un	U	PB/LP	#	FDC	Q
1874	15¢ Everett Dirksen, Jan. 4	.30	.05	1.50	(4)	.65	160,155,000
	Black Heritage Issue, Jan. 30						
1875	15¢ Whitney Moore Young	.30	.05	1.50	(4)	.65	159,505,000
	Flower Issue, April 23						
1876	18¢ Rose	.36	.08			.75	52,658,250
1877	18¢ Camellia	.36	.08			.75	52,658,250
1878	18¢ Dahlia	.36	.08			.75	52,658,250
1879	18¢ Lily	.36	.08			.75	52,658,250
1879a	Block of 4, #1876-1879	1.50	.85	1.75	(4)	2.50	
	Wildlife Issue, May 14						
1880	18¢ Bighorn Sheep	.36	.05			.75	
1881	18¢ Puma	.36	.05			.75	
1882	18¢ Harbor Seal	.36	.05			.75	
1883	18¢ Bison	.36	.05			.75	
1884	18¢ Brown Bear	.36	.05			.75	
1885	18¢ Polar Bear	.36	.05			.75	
1886	18¢ Elk (Wapiti)	.36	.05			.75	
1887	18¢ Moose	.36	.05			.75	
1888	18¢ White-Tailed Deer	.36	.05			.75	
1889	18¢ Prong Horned Antelope	.36	.05			.75	
1889a	Booklet pane of 10 (#1880-1889)	7.50					
	Flag Issue, April 24						
1890	18¢ Flag and Anthem, "…For amber waves of grain"	.36	.05	7.50	(20)	.75	
	Coil Stamp, Perf. 10 Vertically						
1891	18¢ Flag and Anthem, "…From sea to shining sea"	.36	.05			.75	
	Perf. 11						
1892	6¢ USA Circle of Stars, Single from booklet (1893a)	.50	.10			.75	
1893	18¢ Flag and Anthem, "…For purple mountain majesties," Single from booklet (1893a)	.36	.05			.75	
1893a	Booklet pane of 8, (2 #1892 & 6 #1893)	3.50	—				
1894	20¢ Flag over Supreme Court, Dec. 17	.40	.05	8.50	(20)	.75	
	Coil Stamp, Perf. 10 Vertically						
1895	20¢ Flag over Supreme Court, Dec. 17	.40	.05	—		.75	
	Perf. 11x10½						
1896	20¢ Flag over Supreme Court, Single from booklet	.40	.05	—		.75	
1896a	Booklet pane of 6, Dec. 17	2.50					

USA 15c
Everett Dirksen

1874

WhitneyMooreYoung

Black Heritage USA 15c

1875

Rose USA 18c

Camellia USA 18c

Dahlia USA 18c

Lily USA 18c

1876   1877
1878   1879

1889a

USA 18c

...for amber waves of grain

1890

USA 18c

...from sea to shining sea

1891

1893a

1894

1895

Omnibus 1880s 1 USA — 1897

Locomotive 1870s USA 2c — 1897A

Handcar 1880s USA 3c — 1898

Stagecoach 1890s USA 4c — 1898A

Motorcycle 1913 USA 5c — 1899

Sleigh 1880s USA 5.2c Auth Nonprofit Org — 1900

Bicycle 1870s USA 5.9c — 1901

Baby Buggy 1880s USA 7.4c — 1902

Mail Wagon 1880s USA 9.3c Bulk Rate — 1903

Hansom Cab 1890s USA 10.9c Bulk Rate — 1904

RR Caboose 1890s USA 11c Bulk Rate — 1905

Electric Auto 1917 USA 17c — 1906

Surrey 1890s USA 18c — 1907

Fire Pumper 1860s USA 20c — 1908

School Bus 1920s 3.4 USA — 2123

Buckboard 1880s USA 4.9 — 2124

Star Route Truck 5.5 USA 1910s — 2125

Tricycle 1880s 6 USA — 2126

Ambulance 1860s 8.3 USA — 2128

Oil Wagon 1890s 10.1 USA — 2130

Stutz Bearcat 1933 11 USA — 2131

Stanley Steamer 1909 USA 12 — 2132

Pushcart 1880s 12.5 USA — 2133

Iceboat 1880s USA 14 — 2134

Dog Sled 1920s 17 USA — 2135

Bread Wagon 1880s 25 USA — 2136

	Issues of 1981-86	Un	U	Pl# strip of 3	FDC	Q
	Transportation Issue, Coil Stamps, Perf. 10 Vertically					
1897	1¢ Omnibus, Aug. 19, 1983	.05	.05	.85	.60	
1897A	2¢ Locomotive 1870s,					
	May 20, 1982	.10	.05	.75	.60	
1898	3¢ Railroad Handcar,					
	Mar. 25, 1983	.15	.05	1.00	.60	
1898A	4¢ Stagecoach 1890s,					
	Aug. 19, 1982	.12	.05	2.00	.60	
1899	5¢ Motorcycle, Oct. 10, 1983	.15	.05	2.00	.60	
1900	5.2¢ Antique Sleigh,					
	Mar. 21, 1983	.20	.05	4.00	.60	
1901	5.9¢ Bicycle 1870s, Feb. 17, 1981	.20	.05	3.00	.60	
1902	7.4¢ Baby Buggy 1880s,					
	April 7, 1984	.20	.08	3.50	.65	
1903	9.3¢ Mail Wagon, Dec. 15, 1981	.20	.08	4.00	.65	
1904	10.9¢ Hansom Cab 1890s,					
	Mar. 26, 1982	.25	.05	4.00	.65	
1905	11¢ Railroad Caboose, Feb. 3, 1984	.25	.08	4.00	.65	
1906	17¢ Electric Auto, June 25, 1981	.34	.05	4.00	.75	
1907	18¢ Surrey, May 15, 1981	.36	.05	4.00	.75	
1908	20¢ Fire Pumper, Dec. 10, 1981	.40	.05	6.00	.65	
2123	3.4¢ School Bus 1920s,					
	June 8, 1985	.08	.05	1.25	.60	
2124	4.9¢ Buckboard 1880s,					
	June 21, 1985	.10	.05	1.25	.60	
2125	5.5¢ Star Route Truck, Nov. 3, 1986	.11	.05			
2126	6¢ Tricycle 1880s, May 6, 1985	.12	.05	1.50	.60	
2128	8.3¢ Ambulance 1860s,					
	June 21, 1985	.18	.05	3.00	.60	
2130	10.1¢ Oil Wagon 1890s,					
	Apr. 18, 1985	.22	.05	3.50	.65	
2131	11¢ Stutz Bearcat 1933,					
	June 11, 1985	.22	.05	2.50	.65	
2132	12¢ Stanley Steamer 1909,					
	Apr. 2, 1985	.24	.05	2.50	.65	
2133	12.5¢ Pushcart 1880s, Apr. 18, 1985	.25	.05	3.00	.65	
2134	14¢ Iceboat 1880s, Mar. 23, 1985	.28	.05	1.50	.65	
2135	17¢ Dog Sled 1920s, Aug. 20, 1986	.34	.05		.75	
2136	25¢ Bread Wagon, Nov. 22, 1986	.50	.05			
2225	1¢ Re-engraved Omnibus, 1986	.05	.05			
2228	4¢ Re-engraved Stagecoach, 1986	.08	.05			

	Issue of 1983, Perf. 10 Vertically	Un	U	PB/LP	#	FDC	Q
1909	$9.35 Express Mail,						
	Single from booklet, Aug. 12	20.00	6.00	—		25.00	
1909a	Booklet pane of 3	62.50	—				
	Issues of 1981, Perf. 11x10½						
1910	18¢ American Red Cross, May 1	.36	.05	1.75	(4)	.75	165,175,000
	Perf. 11						
1911	18¢ Savings and Loan, May 8	.36	.05	1.75	(4)	.75	107,240,000
	Space Achievement Issue, May 21						
1912	18¢ Exploring the Moon	.36	.10			.75	42,227,375
1913	18¢ Benefiting Mankind	.36	.10			.75	42,227,375
1914	18¢ Benefiting Mankind	.36	.10			.75	42,227,375
1915	18¢ Understanding the Sun	.36	.10			.75	42,227,375
1916	18¢ Probing the Planets	.36	.10			.75	42,227,375
1917	18¢ Benefiting Mankind	.36	.10			.75	42,227,375
1918	18¢ Benefiting Mankind	.36	.10			.75	42,227,375
1919	18¢ Comprehending the						
	Universe	.36	.10			.75	42,227,375
1919a	Block of 8, #1912-1919	3.00	2.25	3.50	(8)	5.00	

Red Cross

The Red Cross was founded in 1859 by Jean Henri Dutant, a native of Switzerland. Originally devoted to helping victims of war, the Red Cross now provides relief for those suffering as a result of many types of disaster, including fires, floods and earthquakes. A truly international organization, it has affiliates in virtually every country.

Clara Barton introduced the Red Cross in America in 1881; this milestone is commemorated by stamps recognizing its 50th (#702) and 100th (#1910) anniversaries. Postage also has been used in other ways to recognize the contributions of the Red Cross: The United States has used cancellations to encourage donations, and in 1889 Portugal began giving free postage to the Red Cross. During World War I special Red Cross stamps were sold with proceeds going to the organization—at one time, 47 countries were selling these issues, and the practice has continued.

1909

1910

1911

1912   1913   1914   1915
1916   1917   1918   1919

1920

1925

1921 1922
1923 1924

1926

1927

1981 continued, Perf. 11	Un	U	PB/LP	#	FDC	Q
1920 18¢ Professional Management,						
June 18	.36	.05	1.75	(4)	.75	99,420,000
Preservation of Wildlife Habitats Issue, June 26						
1921 18¢ Save Wetland Habitats	.36	.08			.75	46,732,500
1922 18¢ Save Grassland Habitats	.36	.08			.75	46,732,500
1923 18¢ Save Mountain Habitats	.36	.08			.75	46,732,500
1924 18¢ Save Woodland Habitats	.36	.08			.75	46,732,500
1924a Block of 4, #1921-1924	1.50	.85	1.75	(4)	2.50	
1925 18¢ International Year of the						
Disabled, June 29	.36	.05	1.75	(4)	.75	100,265,000
1926 18¢ Edna St. Vincent Millay,						
July 10	.36	.05	1.75	(4)	.75	99,615,000
1927 18¢ Alcoholism, Aug. 19	.45	.05	25.00	(20)	.75	97,535,000

Joseph Wharton

When the Wharton School of Business and Economics at the University of Pennsylvania opened its doors in 1881, the idea of learning how to manage was a novelty. Management was a seat-of-the-pants operation, the ultimate in on-the-job training. Joseph Wharton, the man who founded the nation's first business school, knew this all too well. Although Wharton was academically trained (he had a bachelor's degree in chemistry and a doctorate in law), he gained his business experience by working. He began in a dry goods operation and later moved into the mining and metal industry, where he ultimately established one of the nation's industrial giants, Bethlehem Steel.

Learning the hard way left Wharton with the belief that it was possible to train people for leadership positions. He founded the school that today bears his name to prepare students for careers in civil service and business—to turn management into a profession (#1920). Although the idea was slow to take hold, by the turn of the century "scientific management" had become a popular catchphrase.

1981 continued	Un	U	PB/LP	#	FDC	Q
American Architecture Issue, Aug. 28, Perf. 11						
1928 18¢ NYU Library,						
by Sanford White	.36	.08			.75	41,827,000
1929 18¢ Biltmore House,						
by Richard Morris Hunt	.36	.08			.75	41,827,000
1930 18¢ Palace of the Arts,						
by Bernard Maybeck	.36	.08			.75	41,827,000
1931 18¢ National Farmer's Bank,						
by Louis Sullivan	.36	.08			.75	41,827,000
1931a Block of 4, #1928-1931	1.50	.85	1.75	(4)	2.00	
American Sports Issue, Sept. 22, Perf. 10½x11						
1932 18¢ Babe Zaharias	.36	.05	1.75	(4)	.75	101,625,000
1933 18¢ Bobby Jones	.36	.05	1.75	(4)	.75	99,170,000
Perf. 11						
1934 18¢ Frederic Remington, Oct. 9	.36	.05	1.75	(4)	.75	101,155,000
1935 18¢ James Hoban, Oct. 13	.50	.25	3.00	(4)	.75	101,200,000
1936 20¢ James Hoban, Oct. 13	.40	.05	2.00	(4)	.75	167,360,000
American Bicentennial Issue, Yorktown-Virginia Capes, Oct. 16						
1937 18¢ Battle of Yorktown 1781	.36	.06			.75	81,210,000
1938 18¢ Battle of Virginia Capes 1781	.36	.06			.75	81,210,000
1938a Pair, #1937-1938	.72	.15	1.75	(4)	1.00	
Christmas Issue, Oct. 28						
1939 20¢ Madonna and Child,						
by Botticelli	.40	.05	2.00	(4)	.75	597,720,000
1940 20¢ Felt Bear on Sleigh	.40	.05	2.00	(4)	.75	792,600,000
1941 20¢ John Hanson, Nov. 5	.40	.05	2.00	(4)	.75	167,130,000

John Hanson

Was John Hanson (#1941) really our first president? George Washington is given the honor, but it was Hanson who presided over our country's first government, the Continental Congress. Convened in 1774, the Congress included delegates from 12 of the original 13 colonies who were intent on airing their differences with England. By the time they were through, independence was declared and a new constitution, the Articles of Confederation (1781), was drafted.

Hanson, who had served as president of the Continental Congress, also took over the reins of the new government. According to historians, however, Washington wins the race for first on a technicality: Hanson was president of a congress; when Washington was elected, after a new constitution was drafted in 1787, he served as chief executive of the entire nation.

1928   1929

1930   1931

1932   1933

1934   1935   1936

1937   1938   1939

1940

1941

1946

1942

1943
1944

1945

1950

1949

1951

	1981 continued	Un	U	PB/LP	#	FDC	Q
	Desert Plants Issue, Dec. 11, Perf. 11						
1942	20¢ Barrel Cactus	.40	.06			.75	47,890,000
1943	20¢ Agave	.40	.06			.75	47,890,000
1944	20¢ Beavertail Cactus	.40	.06			.75	47,890,000
1945	20¢ Saguaro	.40	.06			.75	47,890,000
1945a	Block of 4, #1942-1945	1.60	.85	2.00	(4)	2.50	
	Perf. 11x10½						
1946	(20¢) C Stamp, Oct. 11	.40	.05	2.00	(4)	.75	
	Coil Stamp, Perf. 10 Vert.						
1947	(20¢) C Stamp, Oct. 11	.40	.05	1.00		.75	
	Perf. 11x10½						
1948	(20¢) C Stamp (1946),						
	Single from booklet, Oct. 11	.40	.05			.75	
1948a	Booklet pane of 10	4.25	—				
	Issues of 1982, Perf. 11						
1949	20¢ Bighorn Sheep,						
	Single from booklet, Jan. 8	.40	.05			.75	
1949a	Booklet pane of 10	5.50	—				
1950	20¢ Franklin D. Roosevelt, Jan. 3	.40	.05	2.00	(4)	.75	163,939,200
	Perf. 11x10½						
1951	20¢ Love, Feb. 1	.40	.05	2.00	(4)	.75	
	Perf. 11						
1952	20¢ George Washington, Feb. 22	.40	.05	2.00	(4)	.75	180,700,000

Stamp Booklets

Booklets, such as the ones issued in 1981 featuring the bighorn sheep stamp (#1949), make life simple for stamp users—they store well, and it's easy to see how many stamps are left. But the booklet idea took a while to catch on...

The first stamp booklets were issued in the 1870s by telegraph companies. A.W. Cooke of Boston patented the idea of using booklets for postage stamps in 1884. The first book of stamps was issued in Luxembourg in 1895. The first U.S. stamp book was introduced in 1898. A surcharge of one cent was placed on the books—the price of convenience. In the early years of this century, booklets were issued with varying denominations; for example, one-cent and two-cent stamps might be included in the same book.

Booklets originally were cut from ordinary stamp sheets. Today special sheets usually are printed to accommodate the booklet format, which is why the stamps have no perforations on the outside edges. The number of stamps in a booklet pane depends on size and format. The United States has offered outsized panes with the sheet folded to fit the cover. U.S. booklets are bound at the top and stapled. A few countries offer issues bound at the side; some, such as Canada, have used thread to sew booklets together.

	1982 continued	Un	U	PB/LP	#	FDC	Q
	State Birds & Flowers Issue, Apr. 14, Perf. 10½x11						
1953	20¢ Alabama	.40	.25			1.00	13,339,900
1954	20¢ Alaska	.40	.25			1.00	13,339,900
1955	20¢ Arizona	.40	.25			1.00	13,339,900
1956	20¢ Arkansas	.40	.25			1.00	13,339,900
1957	20¢ California	.40	.25			1.00	13,339,900
1958	20¢ Colorado	.40	.25			1.00	13,339,900
1959	20¢ Connecticut	.40	.25			1.00	13,339,900
1960	20¢ Delaware	.40	.25			1.00	13,339,900
1961	20¢ Florida	.40	.25			1.00	13,339,900
1962	20¢ Georgia	.40	.25			1.00	13,339,900
1963	20¢ Hawaii	.40	.25			1.00	13,339,900
1964	20¢ Idaho	.40	.25			1.00	13,339,900
1965	20¢ Illinois	.40	.25			1.00	13,339,900
1966	20¢ Indiana	.40	.25			1.00	13,339,900
1967	20¢ Iowa	.40	.25			1.00	13,339,900
1968	20¢ Kansas	.40	.25			1.00	13,339,900
1969	20¢ Kentucky	.40	.25			1.00	13,339,900
1970	20¢ Louisiana	.40	.25			1.00	13,339,900
1971	20¢ Maine	.40	.25			1.00	13,339,900
1972	20¢ Maryland	.40	.25			1.00	13,339,900

Cardinal

What's the most popular bird in the United States? You might guess the old, familiar bluebird or robin. But just a glance at the State Birds and Flowers series (#1953-2002) will show you how popular the cardinal is. Seven states — Illinois (#1965), Indiana (#1966), Kentucky (#1969), North Carolina (#1985), Ohio (#1987), Virginia (#1998) and West Virginia (#2000) — have chosen this familiar red bird as theirs.

It is not surprising that these states are in the East. The cardinal, also called the cardinal grosbeak or simply redbird, is indigenous to North America east of the Rocky Mountains. Not everyone would agree that all seven states chose the same bird. Two states claim a particular cardinal as uniquely theirs — the Kentucky and Virginia cardinals. Well known as songbirds, cardinals were once popular as pets, but it is now illegal to export them for this purpose. The birds pictured are males; female cardinals are a much duller, brownish-red color.

If you're counting, next in popularity are the mockingbird and western meadowlark, tied with five states each. One state chose a true original, the Rhode Island Red. Another original, the Baltimore Oriole, loaned its name to a major league baseball team. So did the cardinal (St. Louis), although Missouri's state bird is a bluebird.

Alabama
USA 20c
Yellowhammer & Camellia
1953

Alaska
USA 20c
Willow Ptarmigan &
1954

Arizona
USA 20c
Cactus Wren & Saguaro Cactus Blossom
1955

Arkansas
USA 20c
Mockingbird & Apple Blossom
1956

California
USA 20c
California Quail & California Poppy
1957

Colorado
USA 20c
Lark Bunting & Rocky Mountain Columbine
1958

Connecticut
USA 20c
Robin & Mountain Laurel
1959

Delaware
USA 20c
Blue Hen Chicken & Peach Blossom
1960

Florida
USA 20c
Mockingbird & Orange Blossom
1961

Georgia
USA 20c
Brown Thrasher & Cherokee Rose
1962

Hawaii
USA 20c
Hawaiian Goose & Hibiscus
1963

Idaho
USA 20c
Mountain Bluebird & Syringa
1964

Illinois
USA 20c
Cardinal & Violet
1965

Indiana
USA 20c
Cardinal & Peony
1966

Iowa
USA 20c
Eastern Goldfinch & Wild Rose
1967

Kansas
USA 20c
Western Meadowlark & Sunflower
1968

Kentucky
USA 20c
Cardinal & Goldenrod
1969

Louisiana
USA 20c
Brown Pelican & Magnolia
1970

Maine
USA 20c
Chickadee & White Pine Cone and Tassel
1971

Maryland
USA 20c
Baltimore Oriole & Black-Eyed Susan
1972

Massachusetts USA 20c — Black-Capped Chickadee & Mayflower — 1973

Michigan USA 20c — Robin & Apple Blossom — 1974

Minnesota USA 20c — Common Loon & Showy Lady Slipper — 1975

Mississippi USA 20c — Mockingbird & Magnolia — 1976

Missouri USA 20c — Eastern Bluebird & Red Hawthorn — 1977

Montana USA 20c — Western Meadowlark & Bitterroot — 1978

Nebraska USA 20c — Western Meadowlark & Goldenrod — 1979

Nevada USA 20c — Mountain Bluebird & Sagebrush — 1980

New Hampshire USA 20c — Purple Finch & Lilac — 1981

New Jersey USA 20c — American Goldfinch & Violet — 1982

New Mexico USA 20c — Roadrunner & Yucca Flower — 1983

New York USA 20c — Eastern Bluebird & Rose — 1984

North Carolina USA 20c — Cardinal & Flowering Dogwood — 1985

North Dakota USA 20c — Western Meadowlark & Wild Prairie Rose — 1986

Ohio USA 20c — Cardinal & Red Carnation — 1987

Oklahoma USA 20c — Scissor-tailed Flycatcher & Mistletoe — 1988

Oregon USA 20c — Western Meadowlark & Oregon Grape — 1989

Pennsylvania USA 20c — Ruffed Grouse & Mountain Laurel — 1990

Rhode Island USA 20c — Rhode Island Red & Violet — 1991

South Carolina USA 20c — Carolina Wren & Carolina Jessamine — 1992

	1982 continued, Perf. 10½x11	Un	U	PB/LP	#	FDC	Q
1973	20¢ Massachusetts	.40	.25			1.00	13,339,900
1974	20¢ Michigan	.40	.25			1.00	13,339,900
1975	20¢ Minnesota	.40	.25			1.00	13,339,900
1976	20¢ Mississippi	.40	.25			1.00	13,339,900
1977	20¢ Missouri	.40	.25			1.00	13,339,900
1978	20¢ Montana	.40	.25			1.00	13,339,900
1979	20¢ Nebraska	.40	.25			1.00	13,339,900
1980	20¢ Nevada	.40	.25			1.00	13,339,900
1981	20¢ New Hampshire	.40	.25			1.00	13,339,900
1982	20¢ New Jersey	.40	.25			1.00	13,339,900
1983	20¢ New Mexico	.40	.25			1.00	13,339,900
1984	20¢ New York	.40	.25			1.00	13,339,900
1985	20¢ North Carolina	.40	.25			1.00	13,339,900
1986	20¢ North Dakota	.40	.25			1.00	13,339,900
1987	20¢ Ohio	.40	.25			1.00	13,339,900
1988	20¢ Oklahoma	.40	.25			1.00	13,339,900
1989	20¢ Oregon	.40	.25			1.00	13,339,900
1990	20¢ Pennsylvania	.40	.25			1.00	13,339,900
1991	20¢ Rhode Island	.40	.25			1.00	13,339,900
1992	20¢ South Carolina	.40	.25			1.00	13,339,900

Ohio and Carnations

The red carnation was adopted by the Ohio legislature as the state flower in 1904 (#1987). It was selected because it was the favorite flower of William McKinley— U.S. President, state governor, and Buckeye native.

Carnations are associated with motherhood. According to legend, they first grew from the tears the Virgin Mary wept at the crucifixion of Jesus. Today, the pink carnation is the official flower of Mother's Day.

In England carnations are called "gillyflowers," which means clove flowers. Their distinctive odor and taste made them a popular flavoring for beer and wine in the 16th century. They were also used to disguise the taste of medicine.

	1982 continued, Perf. 10½x11	Un	U	PB/LP	#	FDC	Q
1993	20¢ South Dakota	.40	.25			1.00	13,339,900
1994	20¢ Tennessee	.40	.25			1.00	13,339,900
1995	20¢ Texas	.40	.25			1.00	13,339,900
1996	20¢ Utah	.40	.25			1.00	13,339,900
1997	20¢ Vermont	.40	.25			1.00	13,339,900
1998	20¢ Virginia	.40	.25			1.00	13,339,900
1999	20¢ Washington	.40	.25			1.00	13,339,900
2000	20¢ West Virginia	.40	.25			1.00	13,339,900
2001	20¢ Wisconsin	.40	.25			1.00	13,339,900
2002	20¢ Wyoming	.40	.25			1.00	13,339,900
2002b	Sheet of 50	20.00	—				
	Perf. 11						
2003	20¢ USA/Netherlands, Apr. 20	.40	.05	8.50	(20)	.75	109,245,000
2004	20¢ Library of Congress, Apr. 21	.40	.05	2.00	(4)	.75	112,535,000
	Coil Stamp, Perf. 10 Vertically						
2005	20¢ Consumer Education,						
	Apr. 27	.50	.05	1.10		.75	
	World's Fair Issue, Apr. 29, Perf. 11						
2006	20¢ Solar Energy	.40	.08			.75	31,160,000
2007	20¢ Synthetic Fuels	.40	.08			.75	31,160,000
2008	20¢ Breeder Reactor	.40	.08			.75	31,160,000
2009	20¢ Fossil Fuels	.40	.08			.75	31,160,000
2009a	Block of 4, #2006-2009	1.60	.85	2.00	(4)	2.50	
2010	20¢ Horatio Alger, Apr. 30	.40	.05	2.00	(4)	.75	107,605,000
2011	20¢ Aging Together, May 21	.40	.05	2.00	(4)	.75	173,160,000
	Performing Arts Issue, June 8						
2012	20¢ The Barrymores	.40	.05	2.00	(4)	.75	107,285,000

Library of Congress

In 1800 the U.S. capital was moved from Philadelphia to Washington, D.C. As part of the move, space was set aside for a small congressional library consisting of 740 volumes and a few maps. That modest collection grew into the largest library in the world—the Library of Congress (#2004). Housed in three buildings, the library includes more than 16 million books, not to mention periodicals, prints, sheet music and photographs. Much more than a congressional resource, the Library of Congress is used by scholars from all over the world and provides services for libraries throughout the country. It houses copies of all copyrighted material published in this country as well as vast collections in foreign languages, particularly Chinese and Russian. It also is the repository for valuable historical documents, including a Gutenberg Bible and the diaries of George Washington, Thomas Jefferson and Abraham Lincoln.

South Dakota
USA 20c

Ring-Necked Pheasant &

Tennessee
USA 20c

Mockingbird &

Texas
USA 20c

Mockingbird &

Utah
USA 20c

California Gull &

Vermont
USA 20c

Hermit Thrush &

1993   1994   1995   1996   1997

Virginia
USA 20c

Cardinal &

Washington
USA 20c

American Goldfinch &

West Virginia
USA 20c

Cardinal &

Wisconsin
USA 20c

Robin &

Wyoming
USA 20c

Western Meadowlark &

1998   1999   2000   2001   2002

20c
1782·1982·USA·THE NETHERLANDS

Library of Congress
USA 20c

Wise shoppers
stretch dollars
Consumer
Education
USA 20c

2003   2004   2005

USA 20c
Breeder reactor Knoxville World's Fair

USA 20c
Solar energy Knoxville World's Fair

USA 20c
Fossil fuels Knoxville World's Fair

USA 20c
Synthetic fuels Knoxville World's Fair

Horatio Alger

USA 20c

THE BARRYMORES

Performing Arts USA 20c

2006   2007   2010   2012
2008   2009

Aging
together
USA
20c

2011

Dr. Mary Walker
Army Surgeon

Medal of Honor
USA 20c

2013

International Peace Garden

1932
1982   USA 20c

2014

America's
A B C
Libraries
X Y Z
USA 20c
Legacies To Mankind

2015

Jackie Robinson

Black Heritage USA 20c

2016

Touro   USA 20c
Synagogue
Newport RI 1763

To bigotry,
no sanction.
To persecution,
no assistance.
George Washington

2017

Frank Lloyd Wright 1867-1959 Fallingwater Mill Run PA
Architecture USA 20c

Mies van der Rohe 1886-1969 Illinois Inst Tech Chicago
Architecture USA 20c

Walter Gropius 1883-1969 Gropius House Lincoln MA
Architecture USA 20c

Eero Saarinen 1910-1961 Dulles Airport Washington DC
Architecture USA 20c

USA 20c

Wolf Trap Farm Park
for the performing arts

2018

2019   2020
2021   2022

FRANCIS OF ASSISI 1182-1982 USA 20c

2023

Ponce de León   USA 20c

2024

USA 13c

2025

Christmas USA 20c

Tiepolo: National Gallery of Art

2026

Season's Greetings USA 20c   Season's Greetings USA 20c

Season's Greetings USA 20c   Season's Greetings USA 20c

2027   2028
2029   2030

	1982 continued, Perf. 11	Un	U	PB/LP	#	FDC	Q
2013	20¢ Dr. Mary Walker, June 10	.40	.05	2.00	(4)	.75	109,040,000
2014	20¢ International Peace Garden,						
	June 30	.40	.05	2.00	(4)	.75	183,270,000
2015	20¢ America's Libraries, July 13	.40	.05	2.00	(4)	.75	169,495,000
	Black Heritage Issue, Aug. 2, Perf. 11x10½						
2016	20¢ Jackie Robinson	.40	.05	2.00	(4)	.75	164,235,000
	Perf. 11						
2017	20¢ Touro Synagogue, Aug. 22	.40	.05	8.50	(20)	.85	110,130,000
2018	20¢ Wolf Trap Farm Park,						
	Sept. 1	.40	.05	2.00	(4)	.75	110,995,000
	American Architecture Issue, Sept. 30						
2019	20¢ Fallingwater,						
	by Frank Lloyd Wright	.40	.08			.75	41,335,000
2020	20¢ Illinois Institute of Technology,						
	by Mies van der Rohe	.40	.08			.75	41,335,000
2021	20¢ Gropius House,						
	by Walter Gropius	.40	.08			.75	41,335,000
2022	20¢ Dulles Airport,						
	by Eeno Saarinen	.40	.08			.75	41,335,000
2022a	Block of 4, #2019-2022	1.60	.85	2.00	(4)	2.50	
2023	20¢ Francis of Assisi, Oct. 7	.40	.05	2.00	(4)	.75	174,180,000
2024	20¢ Ponce de Leon, Oct. 2	.40	.05	8.50	(20)	.75	110,261,000
	Christmas Issue						
2025	13¢ Puppy and Kitten, Nov. 3	.26	.05	1.30	(4)	.75	
2026	20¢ Madonna and Child,						
	by Tiepolo, Oct. 28	.40	.05	8.50	(20)	.75	703,295,000
	Seasons Greetings Issue, Oct. 28						
2027	20¢ Sledding	.40	.05			.75	197,220,000
2028	20¢ Snowman	.40	.05			.75	197,220,000
2029	20¢ Skating	.40	.05			.75	197,220,000
2030	20¢ Tree	.40	.05			.75	197,220,000
2030a	Block of 4, #2027-2030	1.60	.85	2.00	(4)	2.50	

Dogs and Cats

A puppy and a kitten playing in the snow helped the United States celebrate Christmas in 1982 (#2025). That's not surprising. Dogs, especially, have been popular subjects for stamps: In addition to a stamp series featuring dogs specifically (#2098-2101), an all-American mutt was used to plead for humane treatment of animals (#1307).

Dogs and cats have another connection with the mail. At one time, they were used to deliver it. Unlikely as it may seem, in 1879 cats were enlisted as mail carriers in Liege, Belgium. As you might suspect, the independent felines proved unreliable and were "fired" within a short time. Dogs have served longer. As late as the 1950s sled teams were used to deliver mail in parts of Alaska. They're still pressed into occasional duty today.

	Issues of 1983, Perf. 11	Un	U	PB/LP	#	FDC	Q
2031	20¢ Science & Industry, Jan. 19	.40	.05	2.00	(4)	.75	118,555,000
	Balloons Issue, March 31						
2032	20¢ Intrepid	.40	.08			.75	
2033	20¢ Hot Air Ballooning	.40	.08			.75	
2034	20¢ Hot Air Ballooning	.40	.08			.75	
2035	20¢ Explorer	.40	.08			.75	
2035a	Block of 4, #2032-2035	1.60	.85	2.00	(4)	2.50	226,128,000
2036	20¢ U.S./Sweden Treaty,						
	Mar. 24	.40	.05	2.00	(4)	.75	118,225,000
2037	20¢ Civilian Conservation Corps,						
	Apr. 5	.40	.05	2.00	(4)	.75	114,290,000
2038	20¢ Joseph Priestley, Apr. 13	.40	.05	2.00	(4)	.75	165,000,000
2039	20¢ Voluntarism, Apr. 5	.40	.05	8.50	(20)	.75	120,430,000
2040	20¢ German Immigration,						
	Apr. 29	.40	.05	2.00	(4)	.75	117,025,000
2041	20¢ Brooklyn Bridge, May 5	.40	.05	2.00	(4)	.75	181,700,000
2042	20¢ TVA, May 18	.40	.05	8.50	(20)	.75	114,250,000
2043	20¢ Physical Fitness, May 14	.40	.05	8.50	(20)	.75	111,775,000

Brooklyn Bridge

The Brooklyn Bridge (#2041) was the work of father and son. John and Washington Rowling shared the dream of connecting the New York City boroughs of Manhattan and Brooklyn across the East River. After 14 years of construction, the $9 million bridge was completed in 1883, but the effort cost the father-and-son team dearly. John Rowling died while supervising the final surveys for the bridge. Washington, his son, was crippled while laying the underwater caissons that anchor the bridge. He continued to supervise the work through binoculars, using his wife, Emily, as courier to the construction crew.

The sacrifices may have been substantial, but the result was the longest bridge in the world at the time (1,595 feet) and an engineering feat—the first suspension bridge to use steel wire cables and pneumatic caisson foundations. The Brooklyn Bridge still is regarded as one of the world's most beautiful structures, and it was given National Landmark status in 1964.

Science & Industry
USA 20c

2031

INTREPID

USA
20c

Hot air ballooning

Hot air ballooning

Intrepid 1861

Explorer I 1935

USA
20c

USA
20c

USA
20c

USA
20c

2032

2033

2034

2035

20c
USA
TREATY OF AMITY
AND COMMERCE
BETWEEN USA AND
SWEDEN 1783

2036

1933-1983
Civilian Conservation Corps USA 20c

2037

Joseph Priestley
USA 20c

2038

Volunteer
lend a hand

USA 20c

2039

Concord 1683   USA 20c

German
Immigration
Tricentennial

2040

Brooklyn Bridge
1883 1983
USA 20c

2041

Tennessee
Valley
Authority
USA 20c

2042

Physical Fitness

USA
20c

2043

2044

2045

2046

2047

2048
2050

2049
2051

2052

2053

2054

2055
2057

2056
2058

	1983 continued	Un	U	PB/LP	#	FDC	Q
	Black Heritage Issue, June 9, Perf. 11						
2044	20¢ Scott Joplin	.40	.05	2.00	(4)	.75	115,200,000
2045	20¢ Medal of Honor, June 7	.40	.05	2.00	(4)	.75	108,820,000
	American Sports Issue, July 6, Perf. 10½x11						
2046	20¢ George Herman "Babe" Ruth	.40	.05	2.00	(4)	.75	184,950,000
	Literary Arts Issue, July 8, Perf. 11						
2047	20¢ Nathaniel Hawthorne,						
	by Cephus Giovanni Thompson	.40	.05	2.00	(4)	.75	110,925,000
	Olympic Games Issue, July 28 (see also #C101-112)						
2048	13¢ Discus	.26	.05			.75	
2049	13¢ High Jump	.26	.05			.75	
2050	13¢ Archery	.26	.05			.75	
2051	13¢ Boxing	.26	.05			.75	
2051a	Block of 4, #2048-2051	1.05	.65	1.30	(4)	2.50	
	American Bicentennial Issue, Treaty of Paris, Sept. 2						
2052	20¢ Signing of Treaty of Paris,						
	by Benjamin West	.40	.05	2.00	(4)	.75	104,340,000
2053	20¢ Civil Service, Sept. 9	.40	.05	8.50	(20)	.75	114,725,000
2054	20¢ Metropolitan Opera, Sept. 14	.40	.05	2.00	(4)	.75	112,525,000
	American Inventors Issue, Sept. 14						
2055	20¢ Charles Steinmetz	.40	.08			.75	
2056	20¢ Edwin Armstrong	.40	.08			.75	
2057	20¢ Nikola Tesla	.40	.08			.75	
2058	20¢ Philo T. Farnsworth	.40	.08			.75	
2058a	Block of 4, #2055-2058	1.60	.85	2.00	(4)	2.50	193,055,000

Congressional Medal of Honor

*The Medal of Honor, America's highest and most precious decoration for military valor, was established in late 1861. In more than 125 years, less than 3,400 of these honors have been bestowed. Small wonder…the requirements are quite stiff. The Medal is awarded—often posthumously—for "courage above and beyond the call of duty"; in 1918 Congress restricted it to persons who perform the most extraordinary acts of heroism. The Medal of Honor was the first decoration to be approved in this country after the Revolutionary War and the **only** medal approved until World War I.*

More than 1,900 U.S. servicemen received the Medal during the Civil War and the Indian Wars. The Medal was presented to the "unknown soldiers" of World Wars I and II and Korea as a tribute to the efforts of America's fighting forces during these conflicts. At least two Medal earners—Army General Douglas MacArthur (#1424) and Dr. Mary E. Walker, Civil War army-contract surgeon (#2013)—appear on U.S. stamps. The Medals of Honor pictured on the stamp (#2045) are presented to deserving Army, Air Force and Navy personnel (the Marine Corps uses Navy decorations).

	1983 continued	Un	U	PB/LP	#	FDC	Q
	Streetcars Issue, Oct. 8, Perf. 11						
2059	20¢ First American Streetcar	.40	.08			.75	
2060	20¢ Early Electric Streetcar	.40	.08			.75	
2061	20¢ "Bobtail" Horsecar	.40	.08			.75	
2062	20¢ St. Charles Streetcar	.40	.08			.75	
2062a	Block of 4, #2059-2062	1.60	.85	2.00	(4)	2.50	207,725,000
	Christmas Issue, Oct. 28						
2063	20¢ Niccolini-Cowper Madonna						
	by Raphael	.40	.05	2.00	(4)	.75	
2064	20¢ Santa Claus	.40	.05	8.50	(20)	.75	
2065	20¢ Martin Luther, Nov. 11	.40	.05	2.00	(4)	.75	
	Issues of 1984						
2066	20¢ Alaska Statehood, Jan. 3	.40	.05	2.00	(4)	.75	
	Olympic Games Issue, Jan. 6, Perf. 10½x11 (see also #C101-112)						
2067	20¢ Ice Dancing	.40	.08			.75	
2068	20¢ Alpine Skiing	.40	.08			.75	
2069	20¢ Nordic Skiing	.40	.08			.75	
2070	20¢ Hockey	.40	.08			.75	
2070a	Block of 4, #2067-2070	1.60	.85	2.00	(4)	2.50	
	Perf. 11						
2071	20¢ Federal Deposit Insurance Corp,						
	Jan. 12	.40	.05	2.00	(4)	.75	
	Perf. 11x10½						
2072	20¢ Love, Jan. 31	.40	.05	8.50	(20)	.75	

Ice Dancing

When Jane Torvill and Christopher Dean took the ice at the Winter Olympic Games in Sarajevo, Yugoslavia in 1984, they had been the reigning world champions of ice dancing for three consecutive years. As expected, the British couple waltzed off with the gold medal, garnering a record number of perfect scores in the process.

*At the time, ice dancing (#2067) was a relatively new Olympic sport. Although the winter games date back to 1924, ice dancing was not introduced until 1976. As the name suggests, the sport is closer to ballroom dancing than to the more familiar figure-skating competitions that feature jumps and spins. Like figure skating, ice dancing is a three-part competition: prescribed compulsory dances, an original set pattern performed to a specified tempo but composed by the couple, and a four-minute free dance. Free dance, worth 50% of the overall score, is the high point for spectators and competitors. Torvill and Dean were known especially for their innovation in this event. The couple had choreographed routines to scores from Broadway shows such as **Barnum** and **Mack and Mabel**.*

First American streetcar, New York City, 1832
Early electric streetcar, Montgomery, Ala., 1886

Christmas USA 20c

Raphael, 1483-1983, National Gallery

2063

"Bobtail" horsecar, Sulphur Rock, Ark., 1926
St. Charles streetcar, New Orleans, La., 1923

2059
2061

2060
2062

Season's Greetings USA 20c

2064

Martin Luther

1483-1983   USA 20c

2065

USA 20c

1959-1984
Alaska Statehood

2066

Olympics 84
USA 20c

Olympics 84
USA 20c

FEDERAL DEPOSIT
INSURANCE
CORPORATION

USA 50TH ANNIVERSARY 20c

2071

LO♥E
LO♥E
LO♥E
LO♥E
LO♥E
USA 20c

2072

Olympics 84
USA 20c

Olympics 84
USA 20c

2067
2069

2068
2070

2073   2074   2075

2080

2076   2077
2078   2079

2086

2081

2087

2082
2084

2083
2085

	1984 continued	Un	U	PB/LP	#	FDC	Q
	Black Heritage Issue, Feb. 1, Perf. 11						
2073	20¢ Carter G. Woodson	.40	.05	2.00	(4)	.75	
2074	20¢ Soil and Water Conservation,						
	Feb. 6	.40	.05	2.00	(4)	.75	
2075	20¢ Credit Union Act, Feb. 10	.40	.05	2.00	(4)	.75	
	Orchids Issue, Mar. 5						
2076	20¢ Wild Pink	.40	.05			.75	
2077	20¢ Yellow Lady's-slipper	.40	.05			.75	
2078	20¢ Spreading Pogonia	.40	.05			.75	
2079	20¢ Pacific Calypso	.40	.05			.75	
2079a	Block of 4, #2076-2079	1.60	.85	2.00	(4)	2.50	
2080	20¢ Hawaii Statehood, Mar. 12	.40	.05	2.00	(4)	.75	
2081	20¢ National Archives, Apr. 16	.40	.05	2.00	(4)	.75	
	Olympic Games Issue, May 4 (see also #C101-112)						
2082	20¢ Diving	.40	.08			.75	
2083	20¢ Long Jump	.40	.08			.75	
2084	20¢ Wrestling	.40	.08			.75	
2085	20¢ Kayak	.40	.08			.75	
2085a	Block of 4, #2082-2085	1.60	.85	2.00	(4)	2.50	
2086	20¢ Louisiana World Exposition,						
	May 11	.40	.05	2.00	(4)	.75	
2087	20¢ Health Research, May 17	.40	.05	2.00	(4)	.75	

Carter Woodson

*When Carter Woodson received his Ph.D. from Harvard in 1912, there was no such thing as Black Studies. The contributions of black people to American life and culture were ignored because of stereotyping and prejudice. This black historian (#2073) devoted his life to redressing the imbalance. Through his efforts, black contributions were specifically recognized during Negro History Week. He also founded the Association for the Study of Negro Life and the **Journal of Negro History**.*

*A quick glance through **The Postal Service Guide to U.S. Stamps** indicates the extensive, diverse contributions of black Americans. Were it not for the pioneering efforts of Carter Woodson, knowledge of many of these persons and their corresponding heritage might have been lost forever.*

	1984 continued	Un	U	PB/LP	#	FDC	Q
	Performing Arts Issue, May 23, Perf. 11						
2088	20¢ Douglas Fairbanks	.40	.05	8.50	(20)	.75	
	American Sports Issue, May 24						
2089	20¢ Jim Thorpe	.40	.05	2.00	(4)	.75	
	Performing Arts Issue, June 6						
2090	20¢ John McCormack	.40	.05	2.00	(4)	.75	
2091	20¢ St. Lawrence Seaway,						
	June 26	.40	.05	2.00	(4)	.75	
2092	20¢ Migratory Bird Hunting &						
	Preservation Act, July 2	.40	.05	2.00	(4)	.75	
2093	20¢ Roanoke Voyages, July 13	.40	.05	2.00	(4)	.75	
	Literary Arts Issue, Aug. 1						
2094	20¢ Herman Melville, by J. Eaton	.40	.05	2.00	(4)	.75	
2095	20¢ Horace Moses, Aug. 6	.40	.05	8.50	(20)	.75	
2096	20¢ Smokey the Bear, Aug. 13	.40	.05	2.00	(4)	.75	
	American Sports Issue, Aug. 17						
2097	20¢ Roberto Clemente	.40	.05	2.00	(4)	.75	
	American Dogs Issue, Sept. 7						
2098	20¢ Beagle and Boston Terrier	.40	.08			.75	
2099	20¢ Chesapeake Bay Retriever						
	and Cocker Spaniel	.40	.08			.75	
2100	20¢ Alaskan Malamute and Collie	.40	.08			.75	
2101	20¢ Black and Tan Coonhound						
	and American Foxhound	.40	.08			.75	
2101a	Block of 4, #2098-2101	1.60	.85	2.00	(4)	2.50	

Roberto Clemente

Baseball great Roberto Clemente was a superstar outside the ballpark as well as on the diamond. "Number 21" of the Pittsburgh Pirates played with a zeal that earned the respect and admiration of millions of fans. In his 18 seasons with the Pirates, Clemente captured 11 Golden Glove Awards, racked up a career batting average of .317 (the best among active players at the time) and played in 12 All Star Games. He also was a five-time National League Batting Champion and had a career total of 3,000 hits.

Clemente's death at the age of 38 made him a hero in another way. When his plane crashed on New Year's Eve 1972, he was on a mission of mercy, flying medical supplies to victims of a devastating earthquake in Nicaragua. His sacrifice was recognized by the governor of Puerto Rico, Carlos Romero Barcelo, and by Postmaster General William F. Bolger. This stamp (#2097), the fourth in the Sports Series, was dedicated by both men at the Roberto Clemente Sports Center in the hero's birthplace of Carolina, Puerto Rico.

DOUGLAS FAIRBANKS

Jim Thorpe

JOHN McCORMACK

USA 20c 1959-1984 Saint Lawrence Seaway

Performing Arts USA 20c

USA 20c

Performing Arts USA 20c

2091

2088

2089

2090

Preserving Wetlands
1934
1984

Roanoke Voyages
North
Carolina
1584

Herman Melville

Horace Moses
Founder, Junior Achievement
USA 20c

USA 20c

USA 20c

USA 20c

2092

2093

2094

2095

SMOKEY

USA 20c

Roberto Clemente

USA 20c

USA 20c

USA 20c

Beagle, Boston Terrier

Chesapeake Bay Retriever, Cocker Spaniel

USA 20c

USA 20c

Alaskan Malamute, Collie

Black and Tan Coonhound, American Foxhound

2096

2097

2098

2099

2102

2103

2104

2105

2106

2107

2108

2109

2110

2111

2114

2116

	1984 continued, Perf. 11	Un	U	PB/LP	#	FDC	Q
2102	20¢ Crime Prevention, Sept. 26	.40	.05	2.00	(4)	.75	
2103	20¢ Hispanic Americans, Oct. 31	.40	.05	2.00	(4)	.75	
2104	20¢ Family Unity, Oct. 1	.40	.05	8.50	(20)	.75	
2105	20¢ Eleanor Roosevelt, Oct. 11	.40	.05	2.00	(4)	.75	
2106	20¢ A Nation of Readers, Oct. 16	.40	.05	2.00	(4)	.75	
	Christmas Issue, Oct. 30						
2107	20¢ Madonna and Child,						
	by Fra Filippo Lippi	.40	.05	2.00	(4)	.75	
2108	20¢ Santa Claus	.40	.05	2.00	(4)	.75	
	Perf. 10½						
2109	20¢ Vietnam Veteran's Memorial,						
	Nov. 10	.40	.05	2.00	(4)	.75	
	Issues of 1985, Performing Arts Issue, Jan. 23, Perf. 11						
2110	22¢ Jerome Kern	.44	.05	2.20	(4)	.80	
2111	(22¢) D Stamp, Feb. 1	.44	.05	9.25	(20)	.80	
	Coil Stamp, Perf. 10 Vertically						
2112	(22¢) D Stamp (2111), Feb. 1	.44	.05			.80	
	Perf. 11						
2113	(22¢) D Stamp (2111),						
	Single from booklet, Feb. 1	.44	.05			.80	
2113a	Booklet pane of 10	5.50	—				
2114	22¢ Flag Over Capitol Dome,						
	Mar. 29	.44	.05	2.20	(4)	.80	
	Coil Stamp, Perf. 10 Vertically						
2115	22¢ Flag Over Capitol Dome (2114)						
	Mar. 29	.44	.05			.80	
	Perf. 10 Horizontally						
2116	22¢ Flag Over Capitol Dome,						
	Single from booklet, Mar. 29	.44	.05			.80	
2116a	Booklet pane of 5	2.20	—				

Vietnam War Memorial

More than eight million American military personnel served in the Vietnam War between 1960 and 1975 in an attempt to prevent a communist-backed government from taking control of the tiny Southeast Asian country. At home, many persons questioned whether the United States had the right to intervene in another country's political struggles. Protestors took to the streets to oppose American involvement—sometimes violently. Some 10,000 Americans of draft age fled the country rather than fight in a war in which they did not believe. Vietnam veterans returned home bitter and disillusioned at this lack of support, feeling that their sacrifice—nearly 58,000 killed and more than 153,000 wounded—went unrecognized. Although the war officially ended in 1975, for many, the emotional and psychological wounds it created did not begin to heal until a memorial, "The Wall" (#2109), was dedicated in Washington, D.C. some seven years later. Inscribed on it are the names of those killed or missing in action in Vietnam.

1985 continued	Un	U	PB/LP	#	FDC	Q
Seashells Issue, Apr. 4, Perf. 10						
2117 22¢ Frilled Dogwinkle	.44	.05			.80	
2118 22¢ Reticulated Helmet	.44	.05			.80	
2119 22¢ New England Neptune	.44	.05			.80	
2120 22¢ Calico Scallop	.44	.05			.80	
2121 22¢ Lightning Whelk	.44	.05			.80	
2121a Booklet pane of 10, #2117-21	4.40	—				
#2117-21 issued only in booklet form						
Perf. 10 Vertically						
2122 $10.75 Express Mail,						
Single from booklet, Apr. 29	22.00	—			30.00	
2122a Booklet pane of 3	67.50	—				
Black Heritage Issue, Mar. 5, Perf. 11						
2137 22¢ Mary McLeod Bethune	.44	.05	2.20	(4)	.80	
American Folk Art Issue, Duck Decoys, Mar. 22						
2138 22¢ Broadbill	.44	.08			.80	
2139 22¢ Mallard	.44	.08			.80	
2140 22¢ Canvasback	.44	.08			.80	
2141 22¢ Redhead	.44	.08			.80	
2141a Block of 4, #2138-2141	1.80	1.00	2.20	(4)	2.75	

Mary McLeod Bethune

In 1904 Mary McLeod Bethune, the daughter of emancipated slaves, opened a school in Daytona, Florida for black children that provided vocational and academic training at the primary and secondary levels. It ultimately evolved into Bethune-Cookman College, and she served as its president until 1942. Following ratification of women's suffrage in 1920, Bethune launched a voter registration drive aimed principally at black women. In 1935 she founded the National Council of Negro Women (NCNW)—the first national coalition intended to aid this minority group.

Bethune won the 1935 Spingarn Medal of achievement from the National Association for the Advancement of Colored People (NAACP). And U.S. Presidents Calvin Coolidge, Herbert Hoover and Harry S. Truman appointed her to various government posts. She served as Franklin D. Roosevelt's Special Advisor on Minority Affairs (1935-1944) and as director of the National Youth Administration's Division of Negro Affairs (1936-1944). The latter appointment made her the first black woman to head a federal agency division.

USA 22 — Frilled Dogwinkle

USA 22 — Reticulated Helmet

USA 22 — New England Neptune

USA 22 — Calico Scallop

USA 22 — Lightning Whelk

2121a

USA $10.75

2122

Mary McLeod Bethune

Black Heritage USA 22

2137

Broadbill Decoy — Folk Art USA 22

Mallard De— Folk Art USA 2

Canvasback Decoy — Folk Art USA 22

Redhead De— Folk Art USA 2

2138
2140

2139
2141

Winter Special Olympics

2142

2143

Rural Electrification Administration

2144

2145

2146

F.A. Bartholdi, Statue of Liberty Sculptor

2147

2149

2150

2152

2153

	1985 continued, Perf. 11	Un	U	PB/LP	#	FDC	Q
2142	22¢ Winter Special Olympics,						
	Mar. 25	.44	.05	2.20	(4)	.80	
2143	22¢ Love, Apr. 17	.44	.05	2.20	(4)	.80	
2144	22¢ Rural Electrification						
	Administration, May 11	.44	.05	9.25	(20)	.80	
2145	22¢ AMERIPEX '86, May 25	.44	.05	2.20	(4)	.80	
2146	22¢ Abigail Adams, June 14	.44	.05	2.20	(4)	.80	
2147	22¢ Frederic A. Bartholdi, July 18	.44	.05	2.20	(4)	.80	
	Perf. 10 Vertically						
2149	18¢ George Washington,						
	Washington Monument, Nov. 6	.36	.08			.80	
2150	21.1¢ Sealed Envelopes, Oct. 22	.45	.08			.80	
	Perf. 11						
2152	22¢ Korean War Veterans, July 26	.44	.05	2.20	(4)	.80	
2153	22¢ Social Security Act, Aug. 14	.44	.05	2.20	(4)	.80	

REA

Just flip a switch and you have light. Your phone rings—maybe too often. These are things we often take for granted. Just 50 years ago, however, thousands of American families regarded these devices as luxuries. Persons living in rural areas had to travel to use a phone. When it got dark, they lit a kerosene lamp.

In 1935 President Franklin D. Roosevelt created a federal agency, the Rural Electrification Administration (REA), to provide these essential services to rural America. At the time, only one in 10 farm families had the electricity needed to run a water pump or light a house. Since then, the REA has approved nearly $60 billion in loans to assist millions of electricity consumers and telephone service subscribers. However, it did more than provide electricity and phone services: Created in the midst of the Great Depression, the REA (#2144) also provided needed jobs for thousands of unemployed Americans.

1985 continued, Perf. 11	Un	U	PB/LP	#	FDC	Q
2154 22¢ World War I Veterans,						
Aug. 26	.44	.05	2.20	(4)	.80	
American Horses Issue, Sept. 25						
2155 22¢ Quarter Horse	.44	.08			.80	
2156 22¢ Morgan	.44	.08			.80	
2157 22¢ Saddlebred	.44	.08			.80	
2158 22¢ Appaloosa	.44	.08			.80	
2158a Block of 4, #2155-2158	1.80	1.00	2.20	(4)	2.75	
2159 22¢ Public Education, Oct. 1	.44	.05	2.20	(4)	.80	
International Youth Year Issue, Oct. 7						
2160 22¢ YMCA Youth Camping	.44	.08			.80	
2161 22¢ Boy Scouts	.44	.08			.80	
2162 22¢ Big Brothers/Big Sisters	.44	.08			.80	
2163 22¢ Camp Fire	.44	.08			.80	
2163a Block of 4, #2160-2163	1.80	1.00	2.20	(4)	2.75	
2164 22¢ Help End Hunger, Oct. 16	.44	.05	2.20	(4)	.80	
Christmas Issue, Oct. 31						
2165 22¢ Genoa Madonna,						
by Luca della Robbia	.44	.05	2.20	(4)	.80	
2166 22¢ Poinsettias	.44	.05	2.20	(4)	.80	

Public Education

Millions of American children currently enjoy the benefits of public education (#2159). When Boston Latin School, the first publicly supported educational institution in this country, opened its doors in 1635, free universal education was more a dream than a reality. Although several public schools flourished in New England from colonial times, the idea was slow to take hold in the rest of the country. After the American Revolution, land was provided to support schools in the territory west of the Appalachians; but in most of the original 13 colonies, children still were educated at home or sent to private schools. It took another 50 years and the efforts of activists such as Horace Mann (#869) to establish our free public school system. One of the arguments against public education was the expense. Today's taxpayers contribute more than $103 billion annually to educate our children, an investment most of us believe is well worth it.

2154

2155
2157

2156
2158

2159

2160
2162

2161
2163

2164

2165

2166

2167

2198   2199   2200   2201

Issues of 1986, Perf. 11	Un	U	PB/LP	#	FDC	Q
2167 Arkansas Statehood	.44	.05	2.25	(4)	.80	
United States-Sweden Stamp Collecting, Jan. 23, Perf. 10 Vert.						
2198 22¢ Handstamped Cover	.44	.05			.80	
2199 22¢ Boy Examining Stamp Collection	.44	.05			.80	
2200 22¢ #836 Under Magnifying Glass	.44	.05			.80	
2201 22¢ 1986 Presidents Miniature Sheet	.44	.05			.80	
2201a Booklet pane of 4, #2198-2201	1.80					
2202 22¢ Love, Jan. 30	.44	.05	2.25	(4)	.80	
Black Heritage Issue						
2203 22¢ Sojourner Truth, Feb. 4	.44	.05	2.25	(4)	.80	
2204 22¢ Republic of Texas						
150th Anniversary, Mar. 2	.44	.05	2.20	(4)	.80	

Stamp Collecting

"In addition to the fun of it, [stamp collecting] has kept up my interest in history and geography, past and present. I really believe that it makes one a better citizen." That's how Franklin D. Roosevelt, who began his collection at age 10 and continued the interest throughout his life, felt about his hobby. Roosevelt shared this passion with millions of people. The 1986 issue commemorating the 100th anniversary of the American Philatelic Society (#2198-2201) celebrates the most popular hobby in the world. In the United States alone, there are some 19 million stamp collectors ranging from school children to senior citizens and from generalists (like Roosevelt) to those with highly specialized collections.

For any collector, the range is virtually unlimited. Since the first "official" U.S. postage stamp appeared in 1847, more than 150,000 stamps have been issued by over 800 countries and postal administrations. Today there are roughly 240 stamp-issuing entities ranging in size and population from the People's Republic of China to tiny Pitcairn Island (population 80).

If you already collect stamps, you are aware of their appeal. What you may not realize is you are in some pretty classy company. Besides Roosevelt, notable collectors included King George V of England and Theodore Steinway of piano fame.

	1986 continued	Un	U	PB/LP	#	FDC	Q
	Fish Issue, Mar. 21, Perf. 10 Horiz.						
2205	22¢ Muskellunge	.44	.05			.80	
2206	22¢ Atlantic Cod	.44	.05			.80	
2207	22¢ Largemouth Bass	.44	.05			.80	
2208	22¢ Bluefin Tuna	.44	.05			.80	
2209	22¢ Catfish	.44	.05			.80	
2209c	Booklet pane of 5, #2205-09	2.25					
	Perf. 11						
2210	22¢ Public Hospitals, Apr. 11	.44	.05	2.20	(4)	.80	
	Performing Arts Issue, Apr. 29						
2211	22¢ Duke Ellington	.44	.05	2.20	(4)	.80	
	AMERIPEX '86 Issue, Presidents Miniature Sheets, May 22						
2216	Sheet of 9	4.00				3.00	
2216a	22¢ George Washington						
2216b	22¢ John Adams						
2216c	22¢ Thomas Jefferson						
2216d	22¢ James Madison						
2216e	22¢ James Monroe						
2216f	22¢ John Quincy Adams						
2216g	22¢ Andrew Jackson						
2216h	22¢ Martin Van Buren						
2216i	22¢ William H. Harrison						
	a-i, any single	.44	.20			.80	
2217	Sheet of 9	4.00				3.00	
2217a	22¢ John Tyler						

Public Hospitals

New York City's Bellevue Hospital Center is the oldest operating public hospital (#2210) in the United States. Opened 251 years ago as a center for the treatment of infectious disease, it soon gained notoriety as a receiving center for indigent alcoholics and the mentally unbalanced. Yet even in those early days, Bellevue was more than a psychiatric ward.

By the 1870s it provided 24-hour (horse-drawn) ambulance service and had established one of the first nursing schools in the country. Innovations continued. The first cardiopulmonary laboratory in the world was established at Bellevue in 1940. Work done at the lab led to a new surgical procedure that was awarded a Nobel Prize in 1956. Today the "new" Bellevue, which was remodeled in 1973, continues as a research and teaching facility (in affiliation with New York University Medical School) as well as providing a full range of medical services. As one of the largest hospitals in the United States, it has come a long way from a six-bed infirmary in 1736.

Muskellunge

2205

Atlantic Cod

2206

Largemouth Bass

2207

Bluefin Tuna

2208

Carfish

2209

2210

Duke Ellington 22 USA

2211

USA 22
George Washington 1789-1797

2216a

USA 22
John Adams 1797-1801

2216b

USA 22
Thomas Jefferson 1801-1809

2216c

USA 22
James Madison 1809-1817

2216d

USA 22
James Monroe 1817-1825

2216e

USA 22
John Quincy Adams 1825-1829

2216f

USA 22
Andrew Jackson 1829-1837

2216g

USA 22
Martin Van Buren 1837-1841

2216h

USA 22
William Henry Harrison 1841-1841

2216i

USA 22
John Tyler 1841-1845

2217a

James K. Polk 1845-1849   Zachary Taylor 1849-1850   Millard Fillmore 1850-1853   Franklin Pierce 1853-1857   James Buchanan 1857-1861

2217b   2217c   2217d   2217e   2217f

Abraham Lincoln 1861-1865   Andrew Johnson 1865-1869   Ulysses S. Grant 1869-1877   Rutherford B. Hayes 1877-1881   James A. Garfield 1881-1881

2217g   2217h   2217i   2218a   2218b

Chester A. Arthur 1881-1885   Grover Cleveland 1885-89, 1893-97   Benjamin Harrison 1889-1893   William McKinley 1897-1901   Theodore Roosevelt 1901-1909

2218c   2218d   2218e   2218f   2218g

William H. Taft 1909-1913   Woodrow Wilson 1913-1921   Warren G. Harding 1921-1923   Calvin Coolidge 1923-1929   Herbert C. Hoover 1929-1933

2218h   2218i   2219a   2219b   2219c

	1986 continued, Perf. 11	Un	U	PB/LP	#	FDC	Q
2217b	22¢ James Polk						
2217c	22¢ Zachary Taylor						
2217d	22¢ Millard Fillmore						
2217e	22¢ Franklin Pierce						
2217f	22¢ James Buchanan						
2217g	22¢ Abraham Lincoln						
2217h	22¢ Andrew Johnson						
2217i	22¢ Ulysses S. Grant						
	a-i, any single	.44	.20			.80	
2218	Sheet of 9	4.00				3.00	
2218a	22¢ Rutherford B. Hayes						
2218b	22¢ James A. Garfield						
2218c	22¢ Chester A. Arthur						
2218d	22¢ Grover Cleveland						
2218e	22¢ Benjamin Harrison						
2218f	22¢ William McKinley						
2218g	22¢ Theodore Roosevelt						
2218h	22¢ William H. Taft						
2218i	22¢ Woodrow Wilson						
	a-i, any single	.44	.20			.80	
2219	Sheet of 9	4.00				3.00	
2219a	22¢ Warren G. Harding						
2219b	22¢ Calvin Coolidge						
2219c	22¢ Herbert Hoover						

Presidential Series

From the time the U.S. began issuing stamps in 1847, presidential portraits have been the single most popular subject for U.S. postage. That does not mean that every former chief executive got equal time. For the first 15 years of our philatelic history, stamps showed only George Washington and Thomas Jefferson, along with first Postmaster General Benjamin Franklin. In 1861 Presidents Andrew Jackson and Abraham Lincoln joined the group. Other chief executives were gradually added, but 70 years later there were still 12 presidents who had never appeared on stamps.

It was Franklin D. Roosevelt, a stamp collector himself, who suggested a series showing all deceased presidents. (Portraits of living people are never shown on U.S. stamps.) The result was the Presidential series of 1938 (#803-834). In 1986 the idea was repeated with a new wrinkle. Most presidential stamps, including the 1938 series, were regular issues. The new Presidential series (#2216-2219) is commemorative, issued to coincide with AMERIPEX '86, an international philatelic exposition.

	1986 continued, Perf. 11	Un	U	PB/LP	#	FDC	Q
2219d	22¢ Franklin D. Roosevelt						
2219e	22¢ White House						
2219f	22¢ Harry S. Truman						
2219g	22¢ Dwight D. Eisenhower						
2219h	22¢ John F. Kennedy						
2219i	22¢ Lyndon B. Johnson						
	a-i, any single	.44	.20			.80	
	Polar Explorers Issue, May 28						
2220	22¢ Elisha Kent Kane	.44	.05			.80	
2221	22¢ Adolphus W. Greely	.44	.05			.80	
2222	22¢ Vilhjalmur Stefansson	.44	.05			.80	
2223	22¢ Robert E. Peary, Matthew Henson	.44	.05			.80	
2223a	Block of 4, #2220-23	1.80	1.00			2.75	
2224	22¢ Statue of Liberty Centennial,						
	July 4	.44	.05	2.20	(4)	.80	
2225-27 not assigned							
2229-34 not assigned							
	American Folk Art Issue, Sept. 4						
2235	22¢ Navajo Blanket	.44	.08			.80	
2236	22¢ Navajo Blanket	.44	.08			.80	
2237	22¢ Navajo Blanket	.44	.08			.80	
2238	22¢ Navajo Blanket	.44	.08			.80	
2238a	Block of 4, #2235-38	1.80	1.00			2.75	
	Literary Arts Issue, Sept. 26						
2239	22¢ T.S. Eliot	.44	.05	2.20	(4)		

T.S. Eliot

One of England's most famous writers was an American. Poet and playwright T.S. Eliot (#2239) achieved his success in Great Britain, but he was born in St. Louis and educated at Harvard. Eliot first went to England in 1914. Initially he was prevented from returning home by the outbreak of World War I. By the end of the war he had settled in England permanently, becoming a British subject in 1927. In the intervening years, Eliot began to write seriously, attracting the attention of poet Ezra Pound and publishing his first book of verse.

Although Eliot, who was awarded the Nobel Prize for literature in 1948, lived and worked in England for the rest of his life, he never completely severed his ties with this country. He returned from time to time to lecture and read his work. During one noteworthy tour, in 1934, Eliot was reunited with his family for the first time in 10 years.

2219d

2219e

2219f

2219g

2219h

2219i

Elisha Kent Kane
Adolphus W. Greely

Vilhjalmur Stefansson
Robert E. Peary, Matthew Henson

2220
2222

2221
2223

Liberty
1886-1986
USA 22
2224

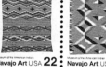
Navajo Art USA 22
Navajo Art USA 22
Navajo Art USA 22
Navajo Art USA 22

2235
2237

2236
2238

T.S.Eliot
22 USA
2239

2244

2245

2240
2242

2241
2243

	1986 continued	Un	U	PB/LP	#	FDC		Q
	American Folk Art Issue, Woodcarved Figurines, Oct. 1, Perf. 11							
2240	22¢ Highlander Figure	.44	.08			.80		
2241	22¢ Ship Figurehead	.44	.08			.80		
2242	22¢ Nautical Figure	.44	.08			.80		
2243	22¢ Cigar Store Figure	.44	.08			.80		
2243a	Block of 4, #2240-43	1.80	1.00	2.20	(4)	2.75		
	Christmas Issue, Oct. 24							
2244	22¢ Madonna,							
	by Perugino	.44	.05	2.20	(4)	.80		
2245	22¢ Village Scene	.44	.05	2.20	(4)	.80		

Perugino's Madonna and Child

The Madonna and child pictured in stamp #2244 was painted by Perugino (1450-1523), one of the masters of the Italian Renaissance. Yet you may not be familiar with his name. Even in his own day, his reputation was eclipsed by more famous contemporaries — Michelangelo, Leonardo da Vinci and Raphael.

When he began his career, Perugino's talent was recognized enough so that he was allowed to include his own portrait in one of his frescoes, a rare honor. He was also commissioned to work at the Vatican in Rome. Nonetheless, his fame was fleeting. Just a few years after they were completed, some of Perugino's frescoes in the Sistene Chapel were destroyed to make room for the greater genius of Michelangelo's "Last Judgment."

One of Perugino's last commissions was to finish some paintings in the church of San Severo, Perugia. This was not unusual for the Renaissance. Often a master would begin a work, leaving his assistants to finish the job. What was ironic in this case is the "master" who left Perugino to fill in the blanks was Raphael, a former student of his.

1987 Issues

Tow Truck (8.5¢, #2129)
Type: Definitive (Transportation Series)
Date of Issue: January 24, 1987
Place of Issue: Tucson, Arizona
Designer: William H. Bond
Printing: Intaglio
Color: Dark Grey (Red Overprint on Precancel)

Since automobiles appeared in significant numbers, "wreckers" have cleared roadways of disabled vehicles.

Michigan Statehood (22¢, #2246)
Type: Commemorative
Date of Issue: January 26, 1987
Place of Issue: Lansing, Michigan
Designer: Robert Wilbert
Printing: Gravure
Colors: Magenta, Cyan, Yellow, Black,
   Special Green

Michigan, our 26th state, celebrates 150 years of statehood in 1987.

Pan American Games (22¢, #2247)
Type: Commemorative
Date of Issue: January 29, 1987
Place of Issue: Indianapolis, Indiana
Designer: Lon Busch
Printing: Gravure
Colors: Special Red, Special Blue, Yellow, Black,
   Special Silver

This past August, Indianapolis hosted the year's biggest international athletic event and an important prelude to the 1988 Summer Olympics: the 10th Pan American Games.

Love (22¢, #2248)
Type: Special
Date of Issue: January 30, 1987
Place of Issue: San Francisco, California
Designer: John Alcorn
Printing: Gravure
Colors: Yellow, Orange, Blue, Green

The most recognizable symbol of love…

Tractor (7.1¢, #2127)
Type: Definitive (Transportation Series)
Date of Issue: February 6, 1987
Place of Issue: Sarasota, Florida
Designer: Ken Dallison
Printing: Intaglio
Colors: Dark Red (Mint); Dark Red, Black
      (Precanceled)

The tractor (*trac*tion and *motor*) revolutionized U.S. agricultural production.

Julia Ward Howe (14¢, #2177)
Type: Definitive (Great Americans Series)
Date of Issue: February 12, 1987
Place of Issue: Boston, Massachusetts
Designer: Ward Brackett
Printing: Intaglio
Color: Red

Howe's "The Battle Hymn of the Republic" was first published 125 years ago.

Jean Baptiste Pointe Du Sable (22¢, #2249)
Type: Commemorative (Black Heritage USA Series)
Date of Issue: February 20, 1987
Place of Issue: Chicago, Illinois
Designer: Thomas Blackshear
Printing: Gravure
Colors: Magenta, Cyan, Yellow, Black Tone,
      Black Type

Issued during Black History Month in Chicago's sesquicentennial year, this stamp honors that city's first settler.

Enrico Caruso (22¢, #2250)
Type: Commemorative (Performing Arts Series)
Date of Issue: February 27, 1987
Place of Issue: New York, New York
Designer: Jim Sharpe
Printing Gravure
Colors: Yellow, Magenta, Process Black,
      Line Black

Caruso, an Italian tenor with one of the most brilliant voices in the history of music, mastered at least 67 opera roles, and his repertoire included about 500 songs.

Mary Lyon (2¢, #2169)
Type: Definitive (Great Americans Series)
Date of Issue: February 28, 1987
Place of Issue: South Hadley, Massachusetts
Designer: Ron Adair
Printing: Intaglio
Color: Blue

Lyon organized Wheaton College (Norton, Massachusetts) in 1834 and founded Mount Holyoke Seminary three years later.

Reengraved Locomotive (2¢, #2226)
Type: Definitive (Transportation Series)
Date of Issue: March 6, 1987
Place of Issue: Milwaukee, Wisconsin
Designer: David Stone
Printing: Intaglio
Color: Black

After five years, the original locomotive stamp had to be reengraved because the Bureau of Engraving and Printing no longer uses Cottrell presses.

Girl Scouts (22¢, #2251)
Type: Commemorative
Date of Issue: March 12, 1987
Place of Issue: Washington, D.C.
Designer: Richard D. Sheaff
Printing: Offset/Intaglio
Colors: Magenta, Yellow, Cyan, Black,
       Green (Offset); Black, Red (Intaglio)

This stamp salutes the 75th anniversary of Girl Scouting in the United States.

Canal Boat (10¢, #2259)
Type: Definitive (Transportation Series)
Date of Issue: April 11, 1987
Place of Issue: Buffalo, New York
Designer: William H. Bond
Printing: Intaglio
Color: Blue

For 60 years after the opening of the Erie Canal in 1825, canal boats carried freight and passengers on waterways that crisscrossed the Middle Atlantic and Great Lakes states.

Special Occasions (22¢, #2267-2274, single stamps; #2268-2271, 2273-2274 and two each 2267 and 2272, booklet pane of 10)

Type: Special
Date of Issue: April 20, 1987
Place of Issue: Atlanta, Georgia
Designer: Oren Sherman
Printing: Gravure (Andreotti Press), BEP
Colors: Lavender, Red, Blue, Yellow, Black, Special Blue

These eight stamps are intended to convey important messages to loved ones and friends, especially on occasions such as Mother's Day, Father's Day, birthdays, weddings and graduations.

United Way (22¢, #2275)

Type: Commemorative
Date of Issue: April 28, 1987
Place of Issue: Washington, D.C.
Designer: Jerry Pinkney
Printing: Offset/Intaglio
Colors: Magenta, Yellow, Cyan, Purple, Black (Offset); Purple (Intaglio)

This stamp, which commemorates the 100th anniversary of the United Way, depicts people of various ages and races from all walks of life — a sampling of the diversity of the millions of people who contribute to and benefit from volunteer work.

Flag with Fireworks (22¢, #2276)

Type: Definitive
Date of Issue: May 9, 1987
Place of Issue: Denver, Colorado
Designer: Peter Cocci
Printing: Gravure
Colors: Yellow, Red, Royal Blue, Background Blue

This stamp replaces the Flag Over the Capitol (#2114) in regular sheet form.

Pre-Phosphored Paper
Flag Over Capitol (22¢)
Type: Special
Date of Issue: May 23, 1987
Place of Issue: Secaucus, New Jersey
Designer: Frank Waslick
Printing: Intaglio
Colors: Red, Blue, Black

Delaware Statehood (22¢, #2336)
Type: Commemorative
Date of Issue: July 4, 1987
Place of Issue: Dover, Delaware
Designer: Richard Sheaff
Printing: Offset/Intaglio
Colors: Black, Magenta, Cyan, Yellow (Offset);
Red, Black (Intaglio)

On December 7, 1787 Delaware became the *first* state to ratify the U.S. Constitution. The state's motto is "Liberty and Independence."

Friendship with Morocco (22¢, #2349)
Type: Commemorative
Date of Issue: July 17, 1987
Place of Issue: Washington, D.C.
Designer: Howard E. Paine
Printing: Offset/Intaglio
Colors: Red, Black

A joint issue celebrated 200 years of friendly diplomatic relations with the Kingdom of Morocco.

William Faulkner (22¢, #2350)
Type: Commemorative (Literary Arts Series)
Date of Issue: August 3, 1987
Place of Issue: Oxford, Mississippi
Designer: Bradbury Thompson
Printing: Intaglio
Color: Green

Faulkner, a leading American author of the 1900s, is remembered for such novels as *The Sound and the Fury* and *Absalom, Absalom!*

Lacemaking USA 22 Lacemaking USA 22
Lacemaking USA 22 Lacemaking USA 22

Lacemaking (22¢, #2351-2354)
Type: Commemorative
Date of Issue: August 14, 1987
Place of Issue: Ypsilanti, Michigan
Designer: Libby Thiel
Printing: Offset/Intaglio
Colors: Blue (Offset); White
    (Intaglio)
These four stamps are based on creations of modern lacemakers in Michigan.

Bret Harte

USA $5

Bret Harte ($5, #2196)
Type: Definitive (Great Americans Series)
Date of Issue: August 25, 1987
Place of Issue: Twain Harte, California
Designer: Arthur Lidov
Printing: Intaglio
Color: Brown

By the early 1870s, Harte had become America's favorite Western epic writer.

Design not available at press time.

Pennsylvania Statehood (22¢, #2337)
Type: Commemorative
Date of Issue: August 26, 1987
Place of Issue: Philadelphia, Pennsylvania
Designer: Richard Sheaff
Printing: Gravure
Colors: Line Red, Yellow, Magenta, Cyan, Black

This stamp features another of the 13 original states, Pennsylvania, in its bicentennial year.

See stamp designs on pages 268-269.

American Wildlife (22¢, #2286-2335)
Type: Commemorative
Date of Issue: June 13, 1987
Place of Issue: Toronto, Ontario, Canada
Designer: Chuck Ripper
Printing: Gravure
Colors: Magenta, Cyan, Yellow, Tone Black

This pane of 50 stamps reflects the geographic and biologic diversity of animals native to North America. All areas of the United States are represented, including Alaska and Hawaii.

 Barn Swallow 22 USA

 Monarch 22 USA

 Bighorn Sheep 22 USA

 Broad-tailed Hummingbird 22 USA

 Cottontail 22 USA

 Armadillo 22 USA

 Eastern Chipmunk 22 USA

 Moose 22 USA

 Black Bear 22 USA

 Tiger Swallowtail 22 USA

 Scarlet Tanager 22 USA

 Woodchuck 22 USA

 Roseate Spoonbill 22 USA

 Bald Eagle 22 USA

 Alaskan Brown Bear 22 USA

 Beaver 22 USA

 White-tailed Deer 22 USA

 Blue Jay 22 USA

 Pika 22 USA

 Bison 22 USA

 Box Turtle 22 USA

 Wolverine 22 USA

 American Elk 22 USA

 California Sea Lion 22 USA

 Mockingbird 22 USA

Osprey

Mountain Lion

Luna Moth

Mule Deer

Gray Squirrel

Bobwhite

Ringtail

Red-winged Blackbird

American Lobster

Black-tailed Jack Rabbit

Iiwi

Badger

Pronghorn

River Otter

Ladybug

Snowy Egret

Gray Wolf

Mountain Goat

Deer Mouse

Black-tailed Prairie Dog

Raccoon

Bobcat

Black-footed Ferret

Canada Goose

Red Fox

The Bicentennial
of the Constitution of
the United States
of America
1787-1987   USA **22**

We the people
of the United States,
in order to form
a more perfect Union...
Preamble, U.S. Constitution   USA **22**

Establish justice,
insure domestic tranquility,
provide for the common defense,
promote the general welfare...
Preamble, U.S. Constitution   USA **22**

And secure
the blessings of liberty
to ourselves
and our posterity...
Preamble, U.S. Constitution   USA **22**

Do ordain
and establish this
Constitution for the
United States of America.
Preamble, U.S. Constitution   USA **22**

Drafting of the U.S. Constitution
(22¢, #2355-2359)
Type: Commemorative
Date of Issue: August 28, 1987
Place of Issue: Washington, D.C.
Designer: Bradbury Thompson
Printing: Gravure
Colors: Black, Red, Light Blue, Yellow
These stamps, featuring the Preamble to the
U.S. Constitution, were issued as part of the
Postal Service's philatelic recognition of that
great document's bicentennial.

Red Cloud (10¢, #2176)
Type: Definitive (Great
    Americans Series)
Date of Issue: August 15, 1987
Place of Issue: Red Cloud,
    Nebraska
Designer: Robert Anderson
Printing: Intaglio
Color: Brown Red

---

*Design not available
at press time.*

New Jersey Statehood (22¢, #2338)
Type: Commemorative
Date of Issue: September 11, 1987
Place of Issue: Trenton, New Jersey
Designer: Jim Lamb
Printing: Gravure
Colors: Beige, Yellow, Red, Blue, Black

New Jersey became the third state on December 18, 1787.

Signing of the U.S. Constitution (22¢, #2360)
Type: Commemorative
Date of Issue: September 17, 1987
Place of Issue: Philadelphia, Pennsylvania
Designer: Howard Koslow
Printing: Offset/Intaglio
Colors: Yellow, Magenta, Cyan, Black, Dark Blue
    (Offset); Black (Intaglio)

Fifty-two of the Constitutional Convention's 55 delegates signed the document
on September 17, 1787.

Certified Public Accountants (22¢, #2361)
Type: Commemorative
Date of Issue: September 21, 1987
Place of Issue: New York, New York
Designer: Lou Nolan
Printing: Offset/Intaglio
Colors: Olive, Red, Green, Line Black

The American Association of Public Accountants was created 100 years ago.

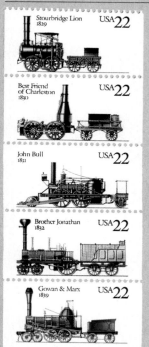

Locomotives (22¢, #2362-2366)
Type: Commemorative
Date of Issue: October 1, 1987
Place of Issue: Baltimore, Maryland
Designer: Richard Leech
Printing: Offset/Intaglio

Christmas Traditional
Type: Special   (22¢, #2367)
Date of Issue: October 23, 1987
Place of Issue: Washington, D.C.
Designer: Bradbury Thompson
Printing: Gravure
Colors: Black, Magenta, Cyan,
Yellow, Green

Design not available at press time.

Christmas Contemporary
Type: Special   (22¢, #2368)
Date of Issue: October 23, 1987
Place of Issue: Holiday, California
Designer: James Dean
Printing: Gravure
Colors: Black, Red, Blue,
Yellow, Green

Design not available at press time.
Racing Car (17.5¢, #2264)
Type: Definitive (Transportation Series)
Date of Issue: September 25, 1987
Place of Issue: Indianapolis, IN
Designer: Tom Broad
Printing: Intaglio

Design not available at press time.
Milk Wagon (5¢, #2255)
Type: Definitive
(Transportation Series)
Date of Issue: September 25, 1987
Place of Issue: Indianapolis, IN
Designer: Lou Nolan
Printing: Intaglio

Airmail/Special Delivery

1918-1935

C1   C2   C3   C3a

C4   C5   C6

C7   C10   C11

C12   C13

C14   C15

C18

Airmail Stamps	Un	U	PB/LP	#	FDC	Q
For prepayment of postage on all mailable matter sent by airmail. All unwatermarked.						
Issues of 1918, Perf. 11						
C1 6¢ Curtiss Jenny, Dec. 10	120.00	45.00	1,250.00	(6)	*16,000.00*	3,395,854
C2 16¢ Curtiss Jenny, July 11	160.00	52.50	2,500.00	(6)	*16,000.00*	3,793,887
C3 24¢ Curtiss Jenny, May 13	160.00	65.00	775.00	(4)	*19,000.00*	2,134,888
C3a Center Inverted	*115,000.00*					
Issues of 1923						
C4 8¢ Wooden Propeller and						
Engine Nose, Aug. 15	45.00	20.00	600.00	(6)	350.00	6,414,576
C5 16¢ Air Svc. Emblem, Aug. 17	160.00	50.00	3,500.00	(6)	750.00	5,309,275
C6 24¢ De Havilland Biplane, Aug. 21	200.00	40.00	4,500.00	(6)	900.00	5,285,775
Issues of 1926-27						
C7 10¢ Map of U.S. and						
Two Mail Planes, Feb. 13, 1926	4.50	.50	60.00	(6)	65.00	42,092,800
C8 15¢ olive brown (C7), Sept. 18, 1926	5.50	2.75	75.00	(6)	75.00	15,597,307
C9 20¢ yellow green (C7),						
Jan. 25, 1927	16.00	2.25	175.00	(6)	115.00	17,616,350
Issues of 1927						
C10 10¢ Lindbergh's "Spirit of						
St. Louis," June 18	13.00	3.00	200.00	(6)	25.00	20,379,179
C10a Booklet pane of 3, May 26	110.00	*60.00*				
#C1-10 inclusive also were available for ordinary postage.						
Issues of 1928						
C11 5¢ Beacon on Rocky Mountains,						
July 25	6.00	.65	70.00	(6)	50.00	106,887,675
C12 5¢ Winged Globe, Feb. 10	17.50	.45	250.00	(6)	20.00	97,641,200
Issues of 1930, Graf Zeppelin Issue, Apr. 19						
C13 65¢ Zeppelin over Atlantic	350.00	250.00	3,500.00	(6)	1,850.00	93,536
C14 $1.30 Zeppelin between						
Continents	850.00	550.00	8,000.00	(6)	1,400.00	72,428
C15 $2.60 Zeppelin Passing Globe	1,350.00	800.00	13,500.00	(6)	2,000.00	61,296
Issued for use on mail carried on the first Europe Pan-American round-trip flight of Graf Zeppelin, May 1930.						
Issues of 1931-32, Perf. 10½x11						
C16 5¢ violet (C12), Aug. 19, 1931	10.00	.50	150.00	(4)	200.00	57,340,050
C17 8¢ olive bistre (C12), Sept. 26, 1932	4.00	.30	50.00	(4)	20.00	76,648,803
Issue of 1933, Century of Progress Issue, Oct. 2, Perf. 11						
C18 50¢ Zeppelin, Federal Building						
at Chicago Exposition and						
Hangar at Friedrichshafen	110.00	95.00	1,250.00	(6)	275.00	324,070
Issue of 1934, Perf. 10½x11						
C19 6¢ dull orange (C12), July 1	4.25	.12	27.50	(4)	*200.00*	302,205,100

	Issue of 1935,	Un	U	PB/LP	#	FDC	Q
	Trans-Pacific Issue, Nov. 22, Perf. 11						
C20	25¢ China Clipper over Pacific	1.50	1.25	27.50	(6)	40.00	10,205,400
	Issues of 1937, Trans-Pacific Issue, Feb. 15, Perf. 11						
C21	20¢ China Clipper over Pacific	15.00	2.25	160.00	(6)	40.00	12,794,600
C22	50¢ carmine (C21)	14.00	6.50	150.00	(6)	40.00	9,285,300
	Issue of 1938						
C23	6¢ Eagle Holding Shield, Olive						
	Branch, and Arrows, May 14	.50	.06	11.00	(4)	15.00	349,946,500
	Issue of 1939, Trans-Atlantic Issue, May 16						
C24	30¢ Winged Globe	16.00	1.50	225.00	(6)	45.00	19,768,150
	Issues of 1941-44, Perf. 11x10½						
C25	6¢ Twin-motor Transport Plane, 1941	.15	.05	1.00	(4)	2.25	4,476,527,700
C25a	Booklet pane of 3, (C25), 1943	6.50	1.00				
	Singles of #C25a are imperf. at sides or imperf. at sides and bottom.						
C26	8¢ olive green (C25), 1944	.20	.05	1.50	(4)	3.75	1,744,876,650
C27	10¢ violet (C25), 1941	1.65	.20	14.00	(4)	7.00	67,117,400
C28	15¢ brown carmine (C25), 1941	3.75	.35	20.00	(4)	10.00	78,434,800
C29	20¢ bright green (C25), 1941	2.75	.30	16.50	(4)	10.00	42,359,850
C30	30¢ blue (C25), 1941	3.50	.30	18.50	(4)	16.00	59,880,850
C31	50¢ orange (C25), 1941	20.00	4.00	110.00	(4)	40.00	11,160,600
	Issue of 1946						
C32	5¢ DC-4 Skymaster, Sept. 25	.15	.05	.75	(4)	2.00	864,753,100
	Issues of 1947, Perf. 10½x11						
C33	5¢ DC-4 Skymaster, Mar. 26	.12	.05	.75	(4)	2.00	971,903,700
	Perf. 11x10½						
C34	10¢ Pan American Union Building,						
	Washington, D.C., Aug. 30	.30	.06	2.25	(4)	2.00	207,976,550
C35	15¢ Statue of Liberty/						
	N.Y. Skyline, Aug. 20	.35	.05	2.50	(4)	2.75	756,186,350
C36	25¢ Plane over San Francisco-						
	Oakland Bay Bridge, July 30	1.60	.12	7.50	(4)	3.50	132,956,100
	Issues of 1948, Coil Stamp, Perf. 10 Horizontally						
C37	5¢ carmine (C33), Jan. 15	2.00	1.10	13.50		2.00	Unlimited
	Perf. 11x10½						
C38	5¢ New York City, July 31	.18	.18	20.00	(4)	1.75	38,449,100
	Issues of 1949, Perf. 10½x11						
C39	6¢ carmine (C33), Jan. 18	.18	.05	.85	(4)	1.50	5,070,095,200
C39a	Booklet pane of 6	12.00	5.00				
	Perf. 11x10½						
C40	6¢ Alexandria Bicentennial, May 11	.16	.10	.95	(4)	1.25	75,085,000
	Coil Stamp, Perf. 10 Horizontally						
C41	6¢ carmine (C33), Aug. 25	4.50	.05	20.00		1.25	Unlimited
	Universal Postal Union Issue, Perf. 11x10½						
C42	10¢ Post Office Dept. Bldg., Nov. 18	.35	.35	3.25	(4)	1.75	21,061,300

 C20

 C21

 C23

 C24

 C25

 C32

 C33

 C34

 C35

 C36

 C38

 C40

 C42

275

C43

C44

C45

C46

C47

C48

C49

C51

C53

C54

C55

C56

C57

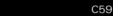

C58

C59

C60

	1949 continued, Perf. 11x10½	Un	U	PB/LP	#	FDC	Q
C43	15¢ Globe and Doves Carrying						
	Messages, Oct. 7	.50	.50	2.75	(4)	2.25	36,613,100
C44	25¢ Boeing Stratocruiser						
	and Globe, Nov. 30	.85	.85	11.00	(4)	2.75	16,217,100
C45	6¢ Wright Brothers, Dec. 17	.16	.10	1.00	(4)	3.75	80,405,000
	Issue of 1952						
C46	80¢ Diamond Head, Honolulu,						
	Hawaii, Mar. 26	11.00	1.50	62.50	(4)	17.50	18,876,800
	Issue of 1953						
C47	6¢ Powered Flight, May 29	.16	.10	.85	(4)	1.50	78,415,000
	Issue of 1954						
C48	4¢ Eagle in Flight, Sept. 3	.12	.08	5.00	(4)	.75	50,483,600
	Issue of 1957						
C49	6¢ Air Force, Aug. 1	.16	.10	1.50	(4)	1.75	63,185,000
	Issues of 1958						
C50	5¢ rose red (C48), July 31	.22	.15	5.00	(4)	.80	72,480,000
	Perf. 10½x11						
C51	7¢ Jet Airliner, July 31	.22	.05	1.30	(4)	.75	532,410,300
C51a	Booklet pane of 6	15.00	6.50				1,326,960,000
	Coil Stamp, Perf. 10 Horizontally						
C52	7¢ blue (C51)	4.50	.20	22.50		.90	157,035,000
	Issues of 1959, Perf. 11x10½						
C53	7¢ Alaska Statehood, Jan. 3	.25	.12	1.50	(4)	.65	90,055,200
	Perf. 11						
C54	7¢ Balloon Jupiter, Aug. 17	.25	.12	1.50	(4)	1.10	79,290,000
	Issued for the 100th anniversary of the carrying of mail by the balloon Jupiter from Lafayette to Crawfordsville, Indiana.						
	Perf. 11x10½						
C55	7¢ Hawaii Statehood, Aug. 21	.25	.12	1.50	(4)	1.00	84,815,000
	Perf. 11						
C56	10¢ Pan American Games, Aug. 27	.40	.40	5.00	(4)	.90	38,770,000
	Issues of 1959-60						
C57	10¢ Liberty Bell, June 10, 1960	3.00	1.00	15.00	(4)	1.50	39,960,000
C58	15¢ Statue of Liberty,						
	Nov. 20, 1959	.75	.06	4.00	(4)	1.10	Unlimited
C59	25¢ Abraham Lincoln,						
	Apr. 22, 1960	.75	.06	4.00	(4)	1.50	Unlimited
	Issues of 1960, Perf. 10½x11						
C60	7¢ Jet Airliner, Aug. 12	.30	.05	1.50	(4)	.70	289,460,000
C60a	Booklet pane of 6	20.00	7.00				
	Coil Stamp, Perf. 10 Horizontally						
C61	7¢ carmine (C60), Oct. 22	8.00	.25	50.00		1.00	87,140,000

		Un	U	PB/LP	#	FDC	Q
C62	**Issues of 1961, Perf. 11**						
C62	13¢ Liberty Bell, June 28	.65	.10	7.00	(4)	.80	Unlimited
C63	15¢ Statue of Liberty, Jan. 13	.40	.08	2.25	(4)	1.00	Unlimited
	#C63 has a gutter between the two parts of the design; #C58 does not.						
	Issues of 1962, Perf. 10½x11						
C64	8¢ Jetliner over Capitol, Dec. 5	.22	.05	1.10	(4)	.60	Unlimited
C64b	Booklet pane of 5 + label	7.50	1.25				
	Coil Stamp, Perf. 10 Horizontally						
C65	8¢ carmine (C64), Dec. 5	.50	.08	4.00		.80	Unlimited
	Issues of 1963, Perf. 11						
C66	15¢ Montgomery Blair, May 3	1.30	.75	7.00	(4)	1.35	42,245,000
	Perf. 11x10½						
C67	6¢ Bald Eagle, July 12	.20	.15	3.50	(4)	.50	Unlimited
	Perf. 11						
C68	8¢ Amelia Earhart, July 24	.30	.15	3.00	(4)	2.50	63,890,000
	Issue of 1964						
C69	8¢ Robert H. Goddard, Oct. 5	.90	.15	5.00	(4)	2.75	65,170,000
	Issues of 1967						
C70	8¢ Alaska Purchase, Mar. 30	.45	.20	4.00	(4)	.70	64,710,000
C71	20¢ "Columbia Jays," by Audubon,						
	Apr. 26 (see also #1241)	1.50	.15	8.50	(4)	2.00	165,430,000
	Issues of 1968, Perf. 11x10½						
C72	10¢ 50-Star Runway, Jan. 5	.30	.05	2.25	(4)	.60	Unlimited
C72b	Booklet pane of 8	4.00	.75				
C72c	Booklet pane of 5 + label	2.50	.75				
	Coil Stamp, Perf. 10 Vertically						
C73	10¢ carmine (C72)	.65	.05	4.50		.60	Unlimited
	Perf. 11						
C74	10¢ U.S. Air Mail Service, May 15	.60	.15	5.00	(4)	1.50	74,180,000
C75	20¢ USA and Jet, Nov. 22	.85	.06	5.00	(4)	1.10	Unlimited
	Issue of 1969						
C76	10¢ Moon Landing, Sept. 9	.30	.15	2.50	(4)	3.50	152,364,800
	Issues of 1971-73, Perf. 10½x11, 11x10½						
C77	9¢ Plane, May 15, 1971	.22	.15	2.00	(4)	.50	Unlimited
C78	11¢ Silhouette of Jet, May 7, 1971	.30	.05	1.75	(4)	.50	Unlimited
C78a	Booklet pane of 4 + 2 labels	1.50	.40				
C79	13¢ Winged Airmail Envelope,						
	Nov. 16, 1973	.32	.10	1.65	(4)	.55	Unlimited
C79a	Booklet pane of 5 + label,						
	Dec. 27, 1973	1.35	.70				
	Perf. 11						
C80	17¢ Statue of Liberty, July 13, 1971	.55	.15	2.75	(4)	.60	Unlimited
	Perf. 11x10½						
C81	21¢ red, blue and black,						
	May 21, 1971	.55	.10	2.75	(4)	.75	Unlimited

C62

C63

C64

C66

C67

C68

C69

C68

C70

C71

C72

C74

C75

C76

C77

C78   C79   C80   C81

279

C84

C85

C86

C87

C88

C89

C90

C91
C92

C93
C94

C95
C96

C97

C98

C99

C100

	1971-73 continued, Coil Stamps, **Perf. 10 Vertically**	Un	U	PB/LP	#	FDC	Q
C82	11¢ Silhouette of Jet (C78),						
	May 7, 1971	.40	.06	2.25		.50	Unlimited
C83	13¢ red (C79), Dec. 27, 1973	.40	.10	2.10		.50	
	Issues of 1972, National Parks Centennial Issue, May 3, Perf. 11 (see also #1448-54)						
C84	11¢ City of Refuge, National Park,						
	Hawaii	.30	.15	2.00	(4)	.65	78,210,000
	Olympic Games Issue, Aug. 7, Perf. 11x10½ (see also #1460-62)						
C85	11¢ Skiing and Olympic Rings	.30	.15	3.50	(10)	.50	96,240,000
	Issue of 1973, Electronics Progress Issue, July 10, Perf. 11 (see also #1500-02)						
C86	11¢ De Forest Audions	.30	.15	1.75	(4)	.50	58,705,000
	Issues of 1974						
C87	18¢ Statue of Liberty, Jan. 11	.45	.45	2.50	(4)	.65	Unlimited
C88	26¢ Mt. Rushmore National						
	Memorial, Jan. 2	.60	.15	2.85	(4)	.85	Unlimited
	Issues of 1976						
C89	25¢ Plane & Globes, Jan. 2	.60	.18	3.25	(4)	.85	
C90	31¢ Plane, Globes & Flag, Jan. 2	.62	.10	3.25	(4)	.85	
	Issues of 1978, Wright Brothers Issue, Sept. 23						
C91	31¢ Orville & Wilbur Wright						
	& Flyer A	.90	.15			1.15	
C92	31¢ Orville & Wilbur Wright,						
	Flyer A & Shed	.90	.15	5.00	(4)	1.15	
C92a	Pair, #C91-C92	1.85	.65	5.00	(4)	2.30	
	Issues of 1979, Octave Chanute Issue, March 29						
C93	21¢ Chanute and Biplane Hang-glider	1.25	.32			1.00	
C94	21¢ Biplane Hang-glider and Chanute	1.25	.32			1.00	
C94a	Pair, #C93-C94	2.60	.75	5.00	(4)	2.00	
	Wiley Post Issue, Nov. 20						
C95	25¢ Wiley Post & "Winnie Mae"	1.50	.35			1.00	
C96	25¢ NR-105-W, Post in Pressurized						
	Suit, Portrait	1.50	.35	5.00	(4)	1.00	
C96a	Pair, #C95-C96	3.10	.85	5.00	(4)	2.00	
	Olympic Games Issue, Nov. 1 (see also #1790-94)						
C97	31¢ High Jump	.90	.30	12.00	(12)	1.15	47,200,000
	Issues of 1980						
C98	40¢ Philip Mazzei, Oct. 13	.90	.30	12.00	(12)	1.35	80,935,000
C99	28¢ Blanche Stuart Scott, Dec. 30	.70	.15	9.00	(12)	1.10	20,190,000
C100	35¢ Glenn Curtiss, Dec. 30	.75	.15	10.00	(12)	1.25	22,945,000

	Issues of 1983	Un	U	PB/LP	#	FDC	Q
	Olympic Games Issue, June 17, Perf. 11 (see also #2048-51, 2067-70, 2082-85)						
C101	28¢ Gymnastics	.56	.28			1.10	
C102	28¢ High Jump	.56	.28			1.10	
C103	28¢ Basketball	.56	.28			1.10	
C104	28¢ Soccer	.56	.28	2.75	(4)	1.10	
C104a	Block of 4, #C101-C104	2.25	1.75			3.75	Unlimited
	Olympic Games Issue, April 8						
C105	40¢ Shotput	.80	.40			1.35	
C106	40¢ Gymnastics	.80	.40			1.35	
C107	40¢ Swimming	.80	.40			1.35	
C108	40¢ Weightlifting	.80	.40	4.00	(4)	1.35	
C108a	Block of 4, #C105-C108	3.50	2.00			5.00	Unlimited
	Olympic Games Issue, Nov. 4						
C109	35¢ Fencing	.70	.35			1.25	
C110	35¢ Bicycling	.70	.35			1.25	
C111	35¢ Volleyball	.70	.35			1.25	
C112	35¢ Pole Vault	.70	.35	3.50	(4)	1.25	
C112a	Block of 4, #C109-C112	3.00	1.85			4.50	
	Issues of 1985						
C113	33¢ Alfred V. Verville, Feb. 13	.66	.20	3.50	(4)	1.25	
C114	39¢ Lawrence & Elmer Sperry,						
	Feb. 13	.78	.20	4.00	(4)	1.35	
C115	44¢ Transpacific Airmail, Feb. 15	.88	.20	4.50	(4)	1.35	
C116	44¢ Junipero Serra, Aug. 22	.88	.20	4.50	(4)	1.35	
	Airmail Special Delivery Stamps						
	Issue of 1934						
CE1	16¢ dark blue						
	Great Seal of the United States	.75	.85	27.50	(6)	25.00	
	For imperforate variety see #771.						
	Issue of 1936						
CE2	16¢ carmine and blue Great Seal						
	of the United States	.40	.25	12.00	(4)	17.50	

C105
C107
C106
C108

C101
C103
C102
C104

C113

C109
C111
C110
C112

C114

C115

C116

CE1

CE2

	Special Delivery Stamps	Un	U	PB/LP	#	FDC	Q
	Issue of 1885, Oct. 1, Unwmkd., Perf. 12						
E1	10¢ Messenger Running	275.00	30.00	*12,000.00*	(8)	*8,000.00*	
	Issue of 1888, Sept. 6						
E2	10¢ blue (E3)	275.00	7.50	*12,000.00*	(8)		
	Issue of 1893, Jan. 24						
E3	10¢ Messenger Running	175.00	14.00	*7,250.00*	(8)		
	Issue of 1894, Line under "Ten Cents," Oct. 10						
E4	10¢ Messenger Running	750.00	17.50	*14,500.00*	(6)		
	Issue of 1895, Aug. 16, Wmkd. (191)						
E5	10¢ blue (E4)	135.00	2.50	*4,500.00*	(6)		
	Issue of 1902, Dec. 9						
E6	10¢ Messenger on Bicycle	90.00	2.50	*2,750.00*	(6)		
	Issue of 1908, Dec. 12						
E7	10¢ Mercury Helmet and						
	Olive Branch	60.00	27.50	925.00	(6)		
	Issue of 1911, Jan., Wmkd. (190)						
E8	10¢ ultramarine (E6)	90.00	4.00	*2,750.00*	(6)		
	Issue of 1914, Sept., Perf. 10						
E9	10¢ ultramarine (E6)	175.00	5.25	*5,000.00*	(6)		
	Issue of 1916, Oct. 19, Unwmkd.						
E10.	10¢ ultramarine (E6)	325.00	21.00	6,250.00	(6)		
	Issue of 1917, May 2, Perf. 11						
E11	10¢ ultramarine (E6)	15.00	.30	200.00	(6)		
	Issue of 1922, July 12						
E12	10¢ Postman and Motorcycle	22.50	.15	375.00	(6)	550.00	
	Issues of 1925						
E13	15¢ Postman and Motorcycle,						
	Apr. 11	24.00	.65	250.00	(6)	275.00	
E14	20¢ Post Office Truck, Apr. 25	3.00	1.75	37.50	(6)	150.00	
	Issue of 1927, Nov. 29, Perf. 11x10½						
E15	10¢ Postman and Motorcycle	.70	.05	5.25	(4)	100.00	
	Issue of 1931, Aug. 13						
E16	15¢ orange (E12)	.80	.08	6.50	(4)	135.00	
	Issues of 1944, Oct. 30						
E17	13¢ Postman and Motorcycle	.65	.06	4.00	(4)	12.00	
E18	17¢ Postman and Motorcycle	5.00	2.25	28.50	(4)	12.00	
	Issue of 1951, Nov. 30						
E19	20¢ black (E14)	2.00	.12	12.00	(4)	5.00	
	Issues of 1954-57						
E20	20¢ Delivery of Letter,						
	Oct. 13, 1954	.60	.08	4.00	(4)	3.00	
E21	30¢ Delivery of Letter, Sept. 3, 1957	.90	.05	5.00	(4)	2.25	
	Issues of 1969-71, Perf. 11						
E22	45¢ Arrows, Nov. 21, 1969	2.25	.20	11.00	(4)	3.50	
E23	60¢ Arrows, May 10, 1971	1.20	.12	5.50	(4)	3.50	

E1

E3

E4

E6

E7

E12

E13

E14

E15

E17

E18

E20

E21

E22

E23

285

Registration, Certified Mail, Postage Due

1879-1959

F1

FA1

JQ1

JQ5

J2

J19

J25

J33

J69

J78

J88

J98

J101

Registration Stamp

Issued for the prepayment of registry; not usable for postage. Sale discontinued May 28, 1913.

	Issue of 1911, Wmkd. (190), Perf. 12	Un	U	PB/LP	#	FDC	Q
F1	10¢ Bald Eagle, Dec. 1	75.00	4.50	*1,850.00*	(6)	*9,000.00*	

Certified Mail Stamp

For use on First-class mail for which no indemnity value was claimed, but for which proof of mailing and proof of delivery were available at less cost than registered mail.

	Issue of 1955, Perf. 10½x11						
FA1	15¢ Letter Carrier, June 6	.50	.30	6.25	(4)	3.25	54,460,300

Postage Due Stamps

For affixing by a postal clerk to any mail to denote amount to be collected from addressee because of insufficient prepayment of postage.

Issues of 1879,
Printed by American Bank Note Co.,
Design of J2, Perf. 12, Unwmkd.

		Un	U
J1	1¢ brown	27.50	5.00
J2	2¢ Figure of Value	175.00	4.00
J3	3¢ brown	20.00	2.50
J4	5¢ brown	275.00	20.00
J5	10¢ brown, Sept. 19	325.00	10.00
J6	30¢ brown, Sept. 19	150.00	20.00
J7	50¢ brown, Sept. 19	200.00	30.00

Special Printing, Soft, Porous Paper

J8	1¢ deep brown	*5,500.00*	—
J9	2¢ deep brown	*3,500.00*	—
J10	3¢ deep brown	*3,250.00*	—
J11	5¢ deep brown	*2,750.00*	—
J12	10¢ deep brown	*1,600.00*	—
J13	30¢ deep brown	*1,600.00*	—
J14	50¢ deep brown	*1,600.00*	—

Issues of 1884-89,
Design of J19

		Un	U
J15	1¢ red brown	25.00	2.50
J16	2¢ red brown	32.50	2.50
J17	3¢ red brown	450.00	100.00
J18	5¢ red brown	200.00	12.50
J19	10¢ Figure of Value,		
	Mar. 15, 1887	165.00	5.00
J20	30¢ red brown	90.00	22.50
J21	50¢ red brown	900.00	125.00

Issues of 1891, Design of J25

J22	1¢ bright claret	10.00	.50
J23	2¢ bright claret	12.50	.45
J24	3¢ bright claret	27.50	3.50
J25	5¢ Figure of Value	30.00	3.50
J26	10¢ bright claret	60.00	10.00
J27	30¢ bright claret	225.00	85.00
J28	50¢ bright claret	225.00	85.00

Issues of 1894,
Printed by the Bureau of Engraving and
Printing, Design of J33, Perf. 12

J29	1¢ vermilion	500.00	95.00
J30	2¢ vermilion	225.00	45.00

Parcel Post Postage Due Stamps

For affixing by a postal clerk to any parcel post package to denote the amount to be collected from the addressee because of insufficient prepayment of postage.

Beginning July 1, 1913 these stamps were valid for use as regular postage due stamps.

Issues of 1912,
Design of JQ1 and JQ5, Perf. 12

JQ1	1¢ Figure of Value	9.00	3.00
JQ2	2¢ dark green	80.00	15.00
JQ3	5¢ dark green	11.50	3.50
JQ4	10¢ dark green	150.00	35.00
JQ5	25¢ Figure of Value	75.00	3.50

	Issues of 1894-95, Design of J33, Unwmkd., Perf. 12	Un	U	PB/LP	#	FDC	Q
J31	1¢ deep claret, Aug. 14, 1894	17.50	3.00	375.00	(6)		
J32	2¢ deep claret, July 20, 1894	15.00	1.75	325.00	(6)		
J33	3¢ Figure of Value, Apr. 27, 1895	65.00	17.50	850.00	(6)		
J34	5¢ deep claret, Apr. 27, 1895	80.00	22.50	950.00	(6)		
J35	10¢ deep rose, Sept. 24, 1894	80.00	12.50	850.00	(6)		
J36	30¢ deep claret, Apr. 27, 1895	185.00	50.00				
J37	50¢ deep claret, Apr. 27, 1895	450.00	120.00				
	Issues of 1895-97, Design of J33, Wmkd. (191)						
J38	1¢ deep claret, Aug. 29, 1895	5.00	.30	190.00	(6)		
J39	2¢ deep claret, Sept. 14, 1895	5.00	.20	190.00	(6)		
J40	3¢ deep claret, Oct. 30, 1895	30.00	1.00	425.00	(6)		
J41	5¢ deep claret, Oct. 15, 1895	32.50	1.00	450.00	(6)		
J42	10¢ deep claret, Sept. 14, 1895	35.00	2.00	550.00	(6)		
J43	30¢ deep claret, Aug. 21, 1897	250.00	22.50	3,750.00	(6)		
J44	50¢ deep claret, Mar. 17, 1896	165.00	20.00	2,250.00	(6)		
	Issues of 1910-12, Design of J33, Wmkd. (190)						
J45	1¢ deep claret, Aug. 30, 1910	17.50	2.00	400.00	(6)		
J46	2¢ deep claret, Nov. 25, 1910	17.50	.15	350.00	(6)		
J47	3¢ deep claret, Aug. 31, 1910	325.00	15.00	3,850.00	(6)		
J48	5¢ deep claret, Aug. 31, 1910	55.00	3.50	600.00	(6)		
J49	10¢ deep claret, Aug. 31, 1910	70.00	7.50	1,150.00	(6)		
J50	50¢ deep claret, Sept. 23, 1912	550.00	65.00	6,500.00	(6)		
	Issues of 1914-15, Design of J33, Perf. 10						
J52	1¢ carmine lake	35.00	7.50	550.00	(6)		
J53	2¢ carmine lake	25.00	.20	350.00	(6)		
J54	3¢ carmine lake	375.00	16.50	4,500.00	(6)		
J55	5¢ carmine lake	22.50	1.50	285.00	(6)		
J56	10¢ carmine lake	35.00	1.00	675.00	(6)		
J57	30¢ carmine lake	125.00	12.00	2,350.00	(6)		
J58	50¢ carmine lake	5,000.00	350.00	36,000.00	(6)		
	Issues of 1916, Design of J33, Unwmkd.						
J59	1¢ rose	900.00	150.00	7,250.00	(6)		
J60	2¢ rose	75.00	7.00	800.00	(6)		
	Issues of 1917, Design of J33, Perf. 11						
J61	1¢ carmine rose	1.50	.08	40.00	(6)		
J62	2¢ carmine rose	1.25	.05	35.00	(6)		
J63	3¢ carmine rose	7.50	.08	100.00	(6)		
J64	5¢ carmine	7.50	.08	95.00	(6)		
J65	10¢ carmine rose	10.00	.20	125.00	(6)		
J66	30¢ carmine rose	50.00	.40	525.00	(6)		
J67	50¢ carmine rose	65.00	.12	750.00	(6)		

Please detach at perforation.

NO POSTAGE
NECESSARY IF
MAILED IN THE
UNITED STATES

OFFICIAL BUSINESS
Penalty for Private Use $300

BUSINESS REPLY MAIL
First Class, Permit No. 73026, Washington, D.C.

United States Postal Service
Philatelic Sales Division
Washington, DC 20265-9980

Want to know about all the stamps and products your U.S. Postal Service offers?

Item #862
Price $5.00

*You can "sign up" to receive a **FREE** copy of the Philatelic Catalog. This bimonthly catalog will keep you up-to-date on the currently available stamp issues and philatelic products ... give you the opportunity to have stamps, postal cards, collecting kits and more delivered right to your home! When you order from it, you will automatically receive copies for the balance of the year.*

*Your Philatelic Catalog is **FREE** when you send in this card. Neatly print your name and address below and drop this card in the mail. No postage necessary.*

Information which you provide will be protected and only disclosed in accordance with the Privacy Act of 1974.

Mr./Mrs./Ms.

Initials   Last Name

Street address
(Include P.O. Box, Apt. No., R.D. Route, etc. where appropriate)

City   State   ZIP CODE

Please Print Legibly

Please detach at perforation.

	Issue of 1925, Design of J33	Un	U	PB/LP	#	FDC	Q
J68	½¢ dull red, Apr. 13	.50	.06	11.00	(6)		

Issues of 1930-31, Design of J69

J69	½¢ Figure of Value	3.50	.70	35.00	(6)		
J70	1¢ carmine	2.50	.15	27.50	(6)		
J71	2¢ carmine	3.50	.15	40.00	(6)		
J72	3¢ carmine	25.00	1.00	240.00	(6)		
J73	5¢ carmine	20.00	1.50	225.00	(6)		
J74	10¢ carmine	45.00	.50	400.00	(6)		
J75	30¢ carmine	120.00	1.00	1,000.00	(6)		
J76	50¢ carmine	140.00	.30	1,150.00	(6)		

Design of J78

| J77 | $1 carmine | 30.00 | .06 | 275.00 | (6) | | |
| J78 | $5 "FIVE" on $ | 40.00 | .12 | 375.00 | (6) | | |

Issues of 1931-56, Design of J69, Perf. 11x10½

J79	½¢ dull carmine	1.25	.08	22.50	(4)		
J80	1¢ dull carmine	.15	.05	2.00	(4)		
J81	2¢ dull carmine	.15	.05	2.00	(4)		
J82	3¢ dull carmine	.25	.05	3.00	(4)		
J83	5¢ dull carmine	.35	.05	4.00	(4)		
J84	10¢ dull carmine	1.10	.05	8.50	(4)		
J85	30¢ dull carmine	8.50	.08	45.00	(4)		
J86	50¢ dull carmine	9.50	.06	57.50	(4)		

Design of J78

| J87 | $1 scarlet | 40.00 | .20 | 300.00 | (4) | | |

Issues of 1959, June 19, Design of J88 and J98, Perf. 11x10½

J88	½¢ Figure of Value	1.25	.85	125.00	(4)		
J89	1¢ carmine rose	.05	.05	.50	(4)		
J90	2¢ carmine rose	.06	.05	.60	(4)		
J91	3¢ carmine rose	.07	.05	.70	(4)		
J92	4¢ carmine rose	.08	.05	1.25	(4)		
J93	5¢ carmine rose	.10	.05	.75	(4)		
J94	6¢ carmine rose	.12	.05	1.40	(4)		
J95	7¢ carmine rose	.14	.06	1.60	(4)		
J96	8¢ carmine rose	.16	.05	1.75	(4)		
J97	10¢ carmine rose	.20	.05	1.25	(4)		
J98	30¢ Figure of Value	.70	.05	5.50	(4)		
J99	50¢ carmine rose	1.10	.05	6.50	(4)		

Design of J101

| J100 | $1 carmine rose | 2.00 | .05 | 10.00 | (4) | | |
| J101 | $5 Outline Figure of Value | 8.00 | .15 | 40.00 | (4) | | |

Issues of 1978-85, Design of J88

J102	11¢ carmine rose, Jan. 2, 1978	.22	.05	1.10	(4)		
J103	13¢ carmine rose, Jan. 2, 1978	.26	.05	1.30	(4)		
J104	17¢ carmine rose, June 10, 1985	.34	.05	1.70	(4)		

Official Postage Stamps

O7 O14 O18 O34 O44 O52

O57 O76 O91 O93

O71

O95 O101 O114 O121 O127

O128 O129 O129A O130 O132

O133 O135 O136 O138 O139

Official Stamps

The franking privilege having been abolished as of July 1, 1873, these stamps were provided for each of the departments of Government for the prepayment on official matter.

These stamps were supplanted on May 1, 1879 by penalty envelopes and on July 5, 1884 were declared obsolete.

Designs are as follows: Post Office officials, figures of value and department name; all other departments, various portraits and department names.

Issues of 1873, Perf. 12
Printed by the Continental Bank Note Co. Thin, Hard Paper, Department of Agriculture: Yellow

		Un	U
O1	1¢ Franklin	60.00	30.00
O2	2¢ Jackson	40.00	13.50
O3	3¢ Washington	35.00	3.50
O4	6¢ Lincoln	45.00	12.50
O5	10¢ Jefferson	100.00	47.50
O6	12¢ Clay	130.00	70.00
O7	15¢ Webster	100.00	47.50
O8	24¢ Winfield Scott	115.00	55.00
O9	30¢ Hamilton	150.00	85.00

Executive Dept.: Carmine

		Un	U
O10	1¢ Franklin	225.00	85.00
O11	2¢ Jackson	150.00	70.00
O12	3¢ Washington	175.00	65.00
O13	6¢ Lincoln	275.00	140.00
O14	10¢ Jefferson	250.00	150.00

Dept. of the Interior: Vermilion

		Un	U
O15	1¢ Franklin	15.00	2.25
O16	2¢ Jackson	12.00	1.50
O17	3¢ Washington	20.00	1.50
O18	6¢ Lincoln	15.00	1.50
O19	10¢ Jefferson	12.50	3.50
O20	12¢ Clay	20.00	2.50
O21	15¢ Webster	37.50	7.25
O22	24¢ W. Scott	27.50	5.50
O23	30¢ Hamilton	37.50	5.75
O24	90¢ Perry	90.00	12.50

Dept. of Justice: Purple

		Un	U
O25	1¢ Franklin	35.00	17.50
O26	2¢ Jackson	60.00	20.00
O27	3¢ Washington	60.00	7.00
O28	6¢ Lincoln	55.00	10.00
O29	10¢ Jefferson	65.00	25.00

		Un	U
O30	12¢ Clay	45.00	12.00
O31	15¢ Webster	100.00	47.50
O32	24¢ W. Scott	275.00	120.00
O33	30¢ Hamilton	250.00	85.00
O34	90¢ Perry	375.00	175.00

Navy Dept.: Ultramarine

		Un	U
O35	1¢ Franklin	30.00	10.00
O36	2¢ Jackson	20.00	8.00
O37	3¢ Washington	25.00	3.00
O38	6¢ Lincoln	20.00	4.50
O39	7¢ Stanton	150.00	60.00
O40	10¢ Jefferson	30.00	10.00
O41	12¢ Clay	40.00	8.25
O42	15¢ Webster	70.00	22.50
O43	24¢ W. Scott	70.00	30.00
O44	30¢ Hamilton	60.00	12.50
O45	90¢ Perry	275.00	80.00

Post Office Dept.: Black

		Un	U
O47	1¢ Figure of Value	7.25	3.00
O48	2¢ Figure of Value	7.00	2.50
O49	3¢ Figure of Value	2.50	.75
O50	6¢ Figure of Value	7.00	1.65
O51	10¢ Figure of Value	32.50	16.50
O52	12¢ Figure of Value	20.00	3.75
O53	15¢ Figure of Value	22.50	6.50
O54	24¢ Figure of Value	30.00	8.25
O55	30¢ Figure of Value	30.00	7.00
O56	90¢ Figure of Value	45.00	11.00

Dept. of State: Green

		Un	U
O57	1¢ dark green Franklin	40.00	10.00
O58	2¢ dark green Jackson	85.00	25.00
O59	3¢ bright green Washington	35.00	7.50
O60	6¢ bright green Lincoln	30.00	7.50
O61	7¢ dark green Stanton	60.00	15.00
O62	10¢ dark green Jefferson	45.00	12.50
O63	12¢ dark green Clay	75.00	27.50
O64	15¢ dark green Webster	65.00	15.00
O65	24¢ dark green W. Scott	150.00	75.00
O66	30¢ dark green Hamilton	135.00	60.00

	1873 continued, Perf. 12	Un	U
O67	90¢ dark green Perry	300.00	120.00
O68	$2 green & black		
	Seward	550.00	250.00
O69	$5 gr. & blk. Seward	4,250.00	2,000.00
O70	$10 gr. & blk. Seward	2,750.00	1,300.00
O71	$20 gr. & blk. Seward	2,250.00	1,100.00
	Treasury Dept.: Brown		
O72	1¢ Franklin	12.00	1.75
O73	2¢ Jackson	18.00	1.75
O74	3¢ Washington	10.00	1.00
O75	6¢ Lincoln	17.50	1.00
O76	7¢ Stanton	40.00	11.00
O77	10¢ Jefferson	40.00	3.50
O78	12¢ Clay	40.00	1.50
O79	15¢ Webster	35.00	3.25
O80	24¢ W. Scott	165.00	55.00
O81	30¢ Hamilton	60.00	3.25
O82	90¢ Perry	65.00	3.00
	War Dept.: Rose		
O83	1¢ Franklin	57.50	3.25
O84	2¢ Jackson	52.50	5.00
O85	3¢ Washington	47.50	1.00
O86	6¢ Lincoln	225.00	4.00
O87	7¢ Stanton	50.00	30.00
O88	10¢ Jefferson	17.50	3.00
O89	12¢ Clay	50.00	2.00
O90	15¢ Webster	12.00	1.20
O91	24¢ W. Scott	12.50	1.75
O92	30¢ Hamilton	15.00	1.50
O93	90¢ Perry	40.00	10.00

Issues of 1879
Printed by the American Bank Note Co.
Soft, Porous Paper,
Dept. of Agriculture: Yellow

		Un	U
O94	1¢ Franklin, issued		
	without gum	*1,350.00*	—
O95	3¢ Washington	170.00	30.00
	Dept. of the Interior: Vermilion		
O96	1¢ Franklin	120.00	65.00
O97	2¢ Jackson	2.50	.75
O98	3¢ Washington	2.00	.60
O99	6¢ Lincoln	3.00	1.00
O100	10¢ Jefferson	30.00	17.50
O101	12¢ Clay	60.00	30.00
O102	15¢ Webster	135.00	70.00
O103	24¢ W. Scott	1,100.00	—

	Dept. of Justice: Bluish Purple	Un	U
O106	3¢ Washington	45.00	17.50
O107	6¢ Lincoln	100.00	60.00
	Post Office Dept.: Black		
O108	3¢ Figure of Value	7.50	1.40
	Treasury Dept.: Brown		
O109	3¢ Washington	25.00	2.50
O110	6¢ Lincoln	45.00	17.50
O111	10¢ Jefferson	60.00	15.00
O112	30¢ Hamilton	700.00	135.00
O113	90¢ Perry	725.00	135.00
	War Dept.: Rose Red		
O114	1¢ Franklin	1.75	.75
O115	2¢ Jackson	2.75	1.00
O116	3¢ Washington	2.75	.65
O117	6¢ Lincoln	2.50	.70
O118	10¢ Jefferson	20.00	6.00
O119	12¢ Clay	15.00	1.75
O120	30¢ Hamilton	45.00	25.00

Official Postal Savings Mail, Perf. 12
These stamps were used to prepay postage on official correspondence of the Postal Savings Division of the Post Office Department. Discontinued Sept. 23, 1914.

	Issues of 1911, Wmkd. (191)		
O121	2¢ Official Postal Savings	9.00	1.10
O122	50¢ Official Postal Svgs.	100.00	32.50
O123	$1 Official Postal Savings	95.00	9.50
	Wmkd. (190)		
O124	1¢ Official Postal Savings	4.00	1.00
O125	2¢ Official Postal Savings	30.00	3.50
O126	10¢ Official Postal Savings	8.50	1.00
	Penalty Mail Issues, Unwmkd.		
O127	1¢, Jan. 12, 1983	.05	—
O128	4¢, Jan. 12, 1983	.08	—
O129	13¢, Jan. 12, 1983	.26	—
O129A	14¢, May 15, 1985	.28	—
O130	17¢, Jan. 12, 1983	.34	—
O132	1.00, Jan. 12, 1983	2.00	—
O133	5.00, Jan. 12, 1983	10.00	—
	Coil Stamps, Perf. 10 Vertically		
O135	20¢, Jan. 12, 1983	1.00	.40
O136	22¢, May 15, 1985	.44	—
O137 not assigned.			
	Perf. 11		
O138	(14¢) D Stamp, Feb. 4, 1985	.50	—
	Coil Stamp, Perf. 10 Vertically		
O139	(22¢) D Stamp, Feb. 4, 1985	1.75	—

Confederate States of America

1

2

3

5

5

6

8

9

11

11

13

14

General Issues, All Imperf.			
Issues of 1861: Lithographed,			
Unwatermarked		Un	U
1	5¢ Jefferson Davis	195.00	110.00
2	10¢ Thomas Jefferson	250.00	200.00
Issues of 1862			
3	2¢ Andrew Jackson	600.00	725.00
4	5¢ blue J. Davis (6)	125.00	105.00
5	10¢ Thomas Jefferson	900.00	625.00
Typographed			
6	5¢ J. Davis		
	(London print)	12.00	20.00
7	5¢ blue (6) (local print)	16.00	17.00
Issue of 1863, Engraved			
8	2¢ Andrew Jackson	67.50	*285.00*

		Un	U
Thick or Thin Paper			
9	10¢ Jefferson Davis	800.00	650.00
10	10¢ blue (9), (with		
	rectangular frame)	3,500.00	1,750.00
Prices of #10 are for copies showing parts of lines on at least two sides of frame.			
11	10¢ Jefferson Davis,		
	die A	13.00	15.00
12	10¢ blue J. Davis,		
	die B (11)	14.00	16.00
Dies A and B differ in that B has an extra line outside its corner ornaments.			
13	20¢ George Washington	47.50	*275.00*
Issue of 1862, Typographed			
14	1¢ John C. Calhoun		
	(This stamp was never		
	put in use.)	135.00	—

PR1   PR2   PR3

Newspaper Stamps
Issue of 1865, Perf. 12
Printed by the National Bank Note Co.,
Thin, Hard Paper, No Gum, Unwmkd.,

	Colored Borders	Un	U
PR1	5¢ Washington	175.00	—
PR2	10¢ Franklin	85.00	—
PR3	25¢ Lincoln	85.00	—

White Border, Yellowish Paper

PR4	5¢ light blue (PR1)	40.00	30.00

Reprints of 1875
Printed by the Continental Bank Note Co.,
Hard, White Paper, No Gum

PR5	5¢ dull blue (PR1),		
	white border	75.00	—
PR6	10¢ dark bluish green,		
	(PR2), colored border	45.00	—
PR7	25¢ dark carmine		
	(PR3), colored border	70.00	—

Issue of 1880
Printed by the American Bank Note Co.,
Soft, Porous Paper, White Border

PR8	5¢ dark blue (PR1)	135.00	—

Issue of 1875
Printed by the Continental Bank Note Co.,
Thin, Hard Paper

PR9-PR15: "Statue of Freedom" (PR15)

PR9	2¢ black	9.00	9.00
PR10	3¢ black	12.50	12.50
PR11	4¢ black	10.50	10.50
PR12	6¢ black	15.00	15.00
PR13	8¢ black	20.00	20.00
PR14	9¢ black	47.50	47.50
PR15	10¢ Statue of Freedom	20.00	17.50

PR16-PR23: "Justice" (PR18)

PR16	12¢ rose	47.50	35.00
PR17	24¢ rose	60.00	40.00
PR18	36¢ rose	65.00	45.00
PR19	48¢ rose	120.00	75.00
PR20	60¢ rose	60.00	45.00
PR21	72¢ rose	145.00	100.00
PR22	84¢ rose	235.00	120.00
PR23	96¢ rose	130.00	100.00
PR24	$1.92 Ceres	150.00	110.00
PR25	$3 "Victory"	200.00	125.00
PR26	$6 Clio	325.00	150.00
PR27	$9 Minerva	425.00	185.00

		Un	U
PR28	$12	500.00	250.00
PR29	$24 "Peace"	500.00	275.00
PR30	$36 "Commerce"	550.00	325.00
PR31	$48 red brown Hebe		
	(PR78)	700.00	425.00
PR32	$60 violet Indian		
	Maiden (PR79)	700.00	375.00

Special Printing, Hard, White Paper,
Without Gum

PR33-PR39: Statue of Freedom (PR15)

PR33	2¢ gray black	60.00	—
PR34	3¢ gray black	65.00	—
PR35	4¢ gray black	80.00	—
PR36	6¢ gray black	110.00	—
PR37	8¢ gray black	130.00	—
PR38	9¢ gray black	150.00	—
PR39	10¢ gray black	185.00	—

PR40-PR47: "Justice" (PR18)

PR40	12¢ pale rose	210.00	—
PR41	24¢ pale rose	275.00	—
PR42	36¢ pale rose	375.00	—
PR43	48¢ pale rose	425.00	—
PR44	60¢ pale rose	500.00	—
PR45	72¢ pale rose	650.00	—
PR46	84¢ pale rose	675.00	—
PR47	96¢ pale rose	800.00	—
PR48	$1.92 dark brown		
	Ceres (PR24)	*2,400.00*	—
PR49	$3 vermilion "Victory"		
	(PR25)	*5,000.00*	—
PR50	$6 ultra. Clio (PR26)	*6,000.00*	—
PR51	$9 yel. Minerva		
	(PR27)	*11,000.00*	—
PR52	$12 bl. grn. Vesta		
	(PR28)	*10,000.00*	—
PR53	$24 dark gray violet		
	"Peace" (PR29)	—	—
PR54	$36 brown rose		
	"Commerce" (PR30)	—	—
PR55	$48 red brown Hebe		
	(PR78)	—	—
PR56	$60 violet Indian		
	Maiden (PR79)	—	—

All values of this issue #PR33 to PR56 exist
imperforate but were not regularly issued.

Issue of 1879, Perf. 12, Printed by the American Bank Note Co., Soft, Porous Paper

		Un	U
PR57-PR62: Statue of Freedom (PR15)			
PR57	2¢ black	4.00	3.50
PR58	3¢ black	5.00	4.50
PR59	4¢ black	5.00	4.50
PR60	6¢ black	10.50	9.00
PR61	8¢ black	10.50	9.00
PR62	10¢ black	10.50	9.00
PR63-PR70: "Justice" (PR18)			
PR63	12¢ red	30.00	20.00
PR64	24¢ red	30.00	18.50
PR65	36¢ red	120.00	85.00
PR66	48¢ red	90.00	50.00
PR67	60¢ red	60.00	50.00
PR68	72¢ red	160.00	100.00
PR69	84¢ red	120.00	75.00
PR70	96¢ red	80.00	55.00
PR71	$1.92 pale brown		
	Ceres (PR24)	65.00	50.00
PR72	$3 red vermilion		
	"Victory" (PR25)	65.00	50.00
PR73	$6 blue Clio (PR26)	120.00	85.00
PR74	$9 org. Minerva (PR27)	70.00	50.00
PR75	$12 yellow green		
	Vesta (PR28)	110.00	75.00
PR76	$24 dark violet		
	"Peace" (PR29)	145.00	100.00
PR77	$36 Indian red		
	"Commerce" (PR30)	185.00	120.00
PR78	$48 Hebe	250.00	150.00
PR79	$60 Indian Maiden	275.00	150.00

All values of the 1879 issue except #PR63 to PR66 and PR68 to PR70 exist imperforate but were not regularly issued.

Issue of 1893 Special Printing

PR80	2¢ intense black Statue of Freedom (PR15)	150.00	—

Issue of 1885

PR81	1¢ black Statue of Freedom (PR15)	6.00	4.00

		Un	U
PR82-PR89: "Justice" (PR18)			
PR82	12¢ carmine	20.00	10.00
PR83	24¢ carmine	22.50	15.00
PR84	36¢ carmine	35.00	17.50
PR85	48¢ carmine	45.00	30.00
PR86	60¢ carmine	70.00	40.00
PR87	72¢ carmine	80.00	45.00
PR88	84¢ carmine	165.00	100.00
PR89	96¢ carmine	120.00	85.00

All values of the 1885 issue exist imperforate but were not regularly issued.

Issue of 1894 Printed by the Bureau of Engraving and Printing, Soft Wove Paper

PR90-PR94: Statue of Freedom (PR90)			
PR90	1¢ Statue of Freedom	35.00	—
PR91	2¢ intense black	35.00	—
PR92	4¢ intense black	45.00	—
PR93	6¢ intense black	750.00	—
PR94	10¢ intense black	85.00	—
PR95-PR99: "Justice" (PR18)			
PR95	12¢ pink	375.00	—
PR96	24¢ pink	350.00	—
PR97	36¢ pink	2,500.00	—
PR98	60¢ pink	2,500.00	—
PR99	96¢ pink	3,750.00	—
PR100	$3 scarlet "Victory" (PR25)	5,000.00	—
PR101	$6 pl. blue Clio (PR26)	5,750.00	3,000.00

Issue of 1895, Unwmkd. PR102-PR105: Statue of Freedom (PR116)

PR102	1¢ black	20.00	6.00
PR103	2¢ black	21.00	6.00
PR104	5¢ black	30.00	10.00
PR105	10¢ black	65.00	30.00
PR106	25¢ carmine "Justice" (PR118)	90.00	30.00
PR107	50¢ carmine "Justice" (PR119)	200.00	85.00
PR108	$2 scarlet "Victory" (PR120)	225.00	55.00
PR109	$5 ultra. Clio (PR121)	325.00	135.00

PR15

 PR18

 PR24

 PR25

 PR26

 PR27

 PR28

 PR29

 PR30

PR78

 PR79

 PR90

 PR116

 PR118

 PR119

 PR120

 PR121

 PR122

 PR123

 PR124

 PR125

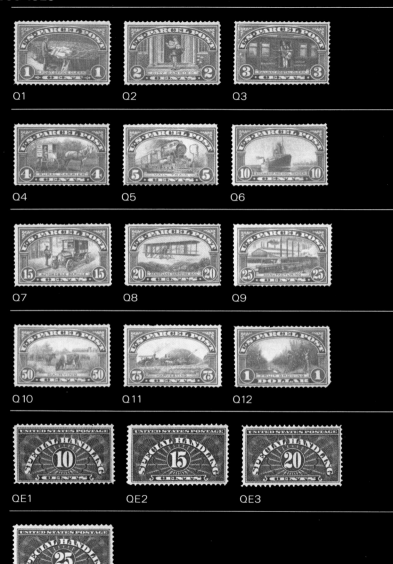

Q1

Q2

Q3

Q4

Q5

Q6

Q7

Q8

Q9

Q10

Q11

Q12

QE1

QE2

QE3

QE4

1895 continued, Perf. 12		Un	U
PR110	$10 green Vesta		
	(PR122)	300.00	150.00
PR111	$20 slate "Peace"		
	(PR123)	600.00	275.00
PR112	$50 dull rose		
	"Commerce" (PR124)	625.00	275.00
PR113	$100 purple Indian		
	Maiden (PR125)	700.00	325.00

Issue of 1895-97
Wmkd. (191), Yellowish Gum

PR114-PR117: Statue of Freedom (PR116)

PR114	1¢ black	2.50	2.00
PR115	2¢ black	2.50	1.50
PR116	5¢ black	5.00	3.00
PR117	10¢ black	2.50	2.00
PR118	25¢ "Justice"	4.00	3.75
PR119	50¢ "Justice"	5.00	3.50
PR120	$2 "Victory"	7.50	9.50
PR121	$5 Clio	20.00	25.00
PR122	$10 Vesta	17.50	25.00
PR123	$20 "Peace"	18.50	27.50
PR124	$50 "Commerce"	20.00	27.50
PR125	$100 Indian Maiden	25.00	35.00

In 1899 the Government sold 26,989 sets of these stamps, but, because the stock of the high values was not sufficient to make up the required number, the $5, $10, $20, $50 and $100 were reprinted. These are virtually indistinguishable from earlier printings.

Parcel Post Stamps

Issued for the prepayment of postage on parcel post packages only.

Beginning July 1, 1913 these stamps were valid for all postal purposes.

Issue of 1912-13, Wmkd. (190)		Un	U
Q1	1¢ Post Office Clerk,		
	Nov. 27, 1912	4.00	.90
Q2	2¢ City Carrier,		
	Nov. 27, 1912	4.50	.70
Q3	3¢ Railway Postal Clerk,		
	Apr. 5, 1913	10.00	5.00
Q4	4¢ Rural Carrier,		
	Dec. 12, 1912	25.00	2.00
Q5	5¢ Mail Train,		
	Nov. 27, 1912	25.00	1.25
Q6	10¢ Steamship and Mail Tender,		
	Dec. 9, 1912	40.00	1.75
Q7	15¢ Automobile Service, Dec. 16, 1912	65.00	9.00
Q8	20¢ Aeroplane Carrying Mail, Dec. 16, 1912	140.00	17.50
Q9	25¢ Manufacturing,		
	Nov. 27, 1912	80.00	4.50
Q10	50¢ Dairying,		
	Mar. 15, 1913	210.00	35.00
Q11	75¢ Harvesting,		
	Dec. 18, 1912	80.00	30.00
Q12	$1 Fruit Growing,		
	Jan. 3, 1913	400.00	20.00

Special Handling Stamps

For use on parcel post packages to secure the same expeditious handling accorded to First-class mail matter.

Issue of 1925-29, Design of QE3, Perf. 11			
QE1	10¢ Special Handling	1.50	.90
QE2	15¢ Special Handling	1.65	.90
QE3	20¢ Special Handling	2.00	1.75
QE4	25¢ Special Handling	20.00	7.50
QE4a	25¢ deep green	25.00	4.50

Souvenir Pages

With First Day Cancellations

The Postal Service offers Souvenir Pages for new stamps. The series began with a page for the Yellowstone Park Centennial stamp issued March 1, 1972. The pages feature one or more stamps tied by the first day cancel, technical data and information on the subject of the issue. More than just collectors' items, Souvenir Pages make wonderful show and conversation pieces. Souvenir Pages are issued in limited editions.

1972

1	Yellowstone Park, FDC with Eagle 1971 Watermark,	$150.00
1a	Same with Parsons Wmk.	$175.00
1b	Same without any Wmk.	$150.00
1c	Yellowstone Park with Washington, DC First Day cancel and Eagle 1971 Watermark,	$600.00
1d	Same without any Wmk.	$200.00
1A	Family Planning (ASDA) with Eagle 1971 Watermark,	$600.00
1Aa	Same without any Wmk.	$500.00
2	Cape Hatteras, with Eagle 1971 Wmk.	$150.00
2a	Same with Parsons Wmk.	$175.00
2b	Same without any Wmk.	$150.00
3	Fiorello La Guardia, with Eagle 1971 Wmk.	$150.00
3a	Same with Parsons Wmk.	$250.00
3b	Same without any Wmk.	$150.00
4	City of Refuge, with 1971 Eagle Wmk.	
4a	Same with Parsons Wmk.	$175 00
4b	Same without any Wmk.	$150.00
5	Wolf Trap Farm, with 1971 Eagle Wmk. (No star before (GPO #),	$50.00
5a	Same with 1972 Eagle Wmk.	$50.00
5b	Wolf Trap Farm with Star and Parsons Wmk.beforeGPO#,	$60.00
6	Colonial Craftsman, (4),	$40.00
7	Mount McKinley,	$50.00
8	Olympic Games, (4),	$25.00

8E	Olympic Games with Broken Red Circle on 6¢ stamp,	$600.00
9	PTA,	$15.00
10	Wildlife Conservation, (4),	$15.00
11	100th Anniversary of Mail Order,	$15.00
11E	Mail Order with Double-Tailed Cat on stamp,	$400.00
12	Osteopathic Medicine,	$15.00
13	Tom Sawyer,	$15.00
14	Benjamin Franklin,	$15.00
15	Christmas, (2),	$20.00
16	Pharmacy,	$12.00
17	Stamp Collecting,	$12.00

1973

18	Eugene O'Neill Coil, with 1972 Eagle Wmk. and U.S. GPO # 1972-0-491-478,	$25.00
18E	Same with 1973 Eagle Wmk. and U.S. GPO # 1973-0-509-757,	$600.00
19	Love,	$20.00
20	Pamphleteer,	$12.00
21	George Gershwin,	$12.00
22	Posting a Broadside,	$10.00
22E	Same with 1976 Eagle Watermark,	$400.00
23	Copernicus,	$10.00
24	Postal Service Employees (10),	$12.00
25	Harry S. Truman,	$10.00
26	Post Rider,	$10.00
27	Amadeo Gianninni	$10.00
28	Boston Tea Party, (4),	$12.00
29	Progress in Electronics, (4),	$12.00
30	Robinson Jeffers,	$7.00
31	Lyndon B. Johnson,	$7.00
32	Henry O. Tanner,	$7.00
33	Willa Cather,	$7.00
34	Colonial Drummer,	$8.00
35	Angus Cattle,	$7.00
36	Christmas, (2),	$12.00
37	13¢ Airmail sheet stamp,	$5.00

38	10¢ Crossed Flags,	$5.00
39	Jefferson Memorial,	$5.00
40	13¢ Airmail Coil,	$5.00

1974

41	Mount Rushmore Airmail,	$5.00
41a	Mount Rushmore with Wmk.	$40.00
42	ZIP Code,	$5.00
42E	ZIP Code, date error,	$600.00
43	Statue of Liberty Airmail,	$5.00
43a	Statue of Liberty with Wmk.	$50.00
44	Elizabeth Blackwell,	$5.00
45	VFW 75th Anniversary	$5.00
46	Robert Frost,	$5.00
47	EXPO '74,	$5.00
48	Horse Racing,	$5.00
49	Skylab with Wmk.	$8.00
49a	Skylab without Wmk.	$30.00
50	Universal Postal Union, (8),	$10.00
51	Mineral Heritage, (4),	$8.00
52	Kentucky Settlement,	$5.00
53	Continental Congress, (4)	$8.00
54	Chautauqua,	$5.00
55	Kansas Wheat,	$5.00
56	Energy Conservation,	$5.00
57	6.3¢ Bulk Rate, (2),	$5.00
58	Sleepy Hollow,	$5.00
59	Retarded Children,	$5.00
60	Christmas, (3),	$9.00

1975

61	Benjamin West,	$5.00
62	Pioneer,	$8.00
63	Collective Bargaining,	$5.00
64	Sybil Ludington,	$5.00
65	Salem Poor,	$5.00
66	Haym Salomon,	$5.00
67	Peter Francisco,	$5.00
68	Mariner,	$8.00

69	Lexington & Concord,	$5.00
70	Paul Laurence Dunbar,	$5.00
71	D.W. Griffith,	$5.00
72	Bunker Hill,	$5.00
73	Military Services, (4),	$9.00
74	Apollo Soyuz, (2),	$9.00
75	International Women's Year,	$5.00
76	Postal Service Bicentennial, (4),	$8.00
77	World Peace Through Law,	$5.00
78	Banking & Commerce, (2),	$5.00
79	Christmas, (2),	$6.00
80	Francis Parkman, (4),	$4.00
81	Freedom of the Press,	$4.00
82	Old North Church,	$4.00
83	Flag & Independence Hall, (2),	$4.00
84	Freedom to Assemble, (2),	$4.00
85	Liberty Bell Coil,	$4.00
86	American Eagle & Shield,	$4.00

1976

87	Spirit of '76, (3),	$7.00
87E	Spirit of '76 with error cancellation,	$600.00
88	25¢ & 31¢ Airmails, (2),	$5.00
89	Interphil 76,	$5.00
90	Fifty State Flag Series, (5 pages),	$60.00
91	Freedom to Assemble Coil, (2),	$4.00
92	Telephone Centennial,	$4.00
93	Commercial Aviation,	$4.00
94	Chemistry,	$4.00
95	7.9¢ Bulk Rate, (2),	$4.00
96	Benjamin Franklin,	$4.00
97	Bicentennial SS, (4 pages),	$60.00
97E	31¢ Souvenir Sheet with missing 31¢ values,	$600.00
98	Declaration of Independence, (4),	$8.00
99	Olympics, (4),	$9.00
100	Clara Maass,	$4.00
101	Adolph S. Ochs,	$4.00
102	Christmas, (3),	$6.00
103	77¢ Bulk Rate, (2),	$4.00

1977

104	Washington at Princeton,	$4.00
105	$1 Vending Machine Booklet Pane, perf. 10, (8),	$30.00
106	Sound Recording	$4.00
107	Pueblo Pottery, (4),	$5.00
108	Lindbergh Flight,	$5.00
109	Colorado Statehood,	$4.00
110	Butterfly, (4),	$5.00
111	Lafayette,	$4.00
112	Skilled Hands, (4),	$5.00
113	Peace Bridge,	$4.00
114	Herkimer at Oriskany,	$4.00

115	1st Civil Settlement,	$4.00
116	Articles of Confederation,	$4.00
117	Talking Pictures,	$4.00
118	Surrender at Saratoga,	$4.00
119	Energy, (2),	$4.00
120	Christmas, Mailbox, (2),	$4.00
121	Christmas, Valley Forge, (2),	$4.00
122	Petition for Redress Coil, (2),	$4.00
123	Petition for Redress sheet stamp, (2 items),	$4.00
124	1¢, 2¢, 3¢ (2), 4¢ Americana,	

1978

125	Carl Sandburg	$4.00
126	Indian Head Penny,	$4.00
127	Captain Cook, Anchorage cancel, (2),	$5.00
128	Captain Cook, Honolulu cancel, (2),	$5.00
129	Harriet Tubman,	$4.00
130	American Quilt, (4),	$5.00
131	16¢ Statue of Liberty,	$4.00
132	Lighthouse,	$4.00
133	American Dance, (4),	$5.00
134	French Alliance,	$4.00
135	Dr. Papanicolaou,	$4.00
136	"A" Stamps, (2),	$4.00
137	Jimmie Rodgers,	$4.00
138	CAPEX '78, (SS),	$8.00
139	Oliver Wendell Holmes,	$4.00
140	Photography,	$4.00
141	Fort McHenry Flag, (2),	$4.00
142	George M. Cohan,	$4.00
143	Rose Booklet single,	$4.00
144	8.4¢ Bulk Rate,	$4.00
145	Viking Missions,	$5.00
146	Remote Oupost,	$4.00
147	American Owls, (4),	$5.00
148	Wright Brothers, (2),	$5.00
149	American Trees,	$5.00
150	Christmas, Hobby Horse,	$4.00
151	Christmas, della Robbia,	$4.00
152	$2 Kerosene Lamp,	$12.00

1979

153	Robert F. Kennedy,	$4.00
154	Martin Luther King, Jr.,	$4.00
155	International Year of the Child,	$4.00
156	John Steinbeck,	$4.00
157	Albert Einstein,	$4.00
158	Octave Chanute, (2),	$5.00
159	Pennsylvania Toleware, (4),	$5.00
160	American Architecture, (4),	$5.00

161	Endangered Flora, (4),	$5.00
162	Seeing Eye Dogs,	$4.00
163	$1 Americana,	$10.00
164	Special Olympics,	$4.00
165	$5 Americana,	$30.00
166	Country Schoolhouse,	$6.00
167	10¢ Olympic, (2),	$5.00
168	50¢ Americana,	$6.00
169	John Paul Jones,	$4.00
170	15¢ Olympic, (4),	$8.00
171	Christmas, Gerard David Madonna,	$4.00
172	Christmas, Santa Claus,	$4.00
173	3.1¢ Non-Profit Coil,	$5.00
174	31¢ Olympics,	$8.00
175	Will Rogers,	$4.00
176	Vietnam Veterans,	$4.00
177	Wiley Post, (2),	$5.00

1980

178	W. C. Fields,	$4.00
179	Winter Olympics, (4),	$8.00
180	Windmills Booklet, (10),	$8.00
181	Benjamin Banneker,	$3.50
182	Letter Writing, (6),	$5.00
183	1¢ Americana, (2 items),	$3.50
184	Frances Perkins,	$3.50
185	Dolley Madison,	$3.50
186	Emily Bissell,	$3.50
187	3.5¢ Non-Profit Coil,	$5.00
188	Helen Keller/ Anne Sullivan,	$3.50
189	Veterans Administration,	$3.50
190	General Bernardo de Galvez,	$3.50
191	Coral Reefs, (4),	$4.50
192	Organized Labor,	$3.50
193	Edith Wharton,	$3.50
194	American Education,	$3.50
195	Indian Masks, (4),	$4.50
196	American Architecture, (4),	$4.50
197	Philip Mazzei Airmail,	$4.00
198	Christmas, Art Masterpiece	$4.00
199	Christmas, Season's Greetings,	$4.00
200	Sequoyah,	$3.50
201	28¢ Scott Airmail,	$3.50
202	35¢ Curtiss Airmail,	$4.00

1981

203	Everett Dirksen,	$3.50
204	Whitney M. Young,	$3.50
205	"B" Sheet & Coil, (3),	$3.50
206	"B" Booklet, (8),	$4.50
207	Freedom of Conscience, Sheet & Coil, (3),	$3.50
208	Flowers Block, (4),	$4.00
209	Flag Sheet & Coil, (3),	$3.50
210	18¢ Flag Booklet, (8),	$4.50
211	American Red Cross,	$3.50
212	George Mason,	$3.50

213	Savings and Loans,	$3.50
214	Wildlife Booklet,	
	(10),	$6.00
215	Surrey Coil, (2),	$3.50
216	Space Achievement,	
	(8),	$10.00
217	Rachel Carson,	$3.50
218	Dr. Charles Drew,	$3.50
219	Professional	
	Management,	$3.50
220	Electric Auto Coil,	
	(2),	$3.50
221	Wildlife Habitats,	
	(4),	$4.00
222	International Year	
	of Disabled,	$3.50
223	Edna St. Vincent	
	Millay,	$3.50
224	Alcoholism,	$3.50
225	Architecture, (4),	$4.00
226	Babe Zaharias,	$3.50
227	Bobby Jones,	$3.50
228	Frederic	
	Remington,	$3.50
229	"C" Sheet/Coil,	
	(3),	$3.50
230	"C" Booklet, (10),	$5.00
231	18¢/20¢ Hoban,	
	(2),	$3.50
232	Yorktown, (2),	$3.50
233	Christmas,	
	Contemporary	$3.50
234	Christmas,	
	Traditional	$3.50
235	John Hanson,	$3.50
236	Fire Pumper Coil,	
	(2),	$4.00
237	U.S. Desert Plants,	
	(4),	$4.00
238	9.3¢ Coil, (3),	$3.50
239	Flag Sheet Coil,	
	(3),	$3.50
240	Flag Booklet, (8),	$4.50

1982

241	Sheep Booklet,	
	(10),	$5.00
242	Dr. Ralph Bunche,	$3.00
243	Chief Crazy Horse,	$3.00
244	Robert Millikan,	$3.00
245	Franklin Roosevelt,	$3.00
246	Love,	$3.00
247	5.9¢ Non-Profit,	
	(4),	$3.00
248	George	
	Washington,	$3.00
249	10.9¢ Bulk Rate	
	Coil, (2),	$3.00
250	Birds & Flowers Series,	
	(5 pages),	$40.00
250a	Birds & Flowers with	
	all 10½ x 11	
	Perfs.,	$70.00
250b	Birds & Flowers with	
	all 11 x 11 Perfs.,	$75.00
251	Netherlands,	$3.00
252	Library of	
	Congress,	$3.00
253	Consumer Coil,	
	(2),	$3.00
254	World's Fair, (4),	$3.50
255	Horatio Alger,	$3.00
256	Locomotive Coil,	
	(2 items),	$3.00
257	Aging Together,	$3.00
258	Barrymore Family,	$3.00
259	Dr. Mary Walker,	$3.00
260	Peace Garden,	$3.00
261	America's Libraries,	$3.00

262	Jackie Robinson,	$4.00
263	Stagecoach Coil,	
	(3 items),	$3.00
264	Touro Synagogue,	$3.00
265	Wolf Trap,	$3.00
266	Architecture, (4),	$3.50
267	Francis of Assisi,	$3.00
268	Ponce de Leon,	$3.00
269	Christmas,	
	Contemporary, (4),	$4.00
270	Christmas,	
	Traditional,	$3.00
271	Kitten & Puppy,	$3.00
272	Igor Stravinsky,	
	(2 items),	$3.00

1983

273	Official Mail,	
	(7 stamps, 5 pgs.),	$30.00
274	Science & Industry,	$2.50
275	Sleigh Coil, (4),	$3.00
276	Sweden/USA	
	Treaty,	$2.50
277	Handcar Coil,	
	(3 items),	$3.00
278	Balloon, (4),	$4.00
279	Civilian Conservation	
	Corps.,	$2.50
280	40¢ Olympics	
	Airmail, (4),	$5.00
281	Joseph Priestley,	$2.50
282	Voluntarism,	$2.50
283	The Concord,	$2.50
284	Physical Fitness,	$2.50
285	Brooklyn Bridge,	$2.50
286	Tennessee Valley	
	Authority,	$2.50
287	Carl Schurz, (5),	$2.50
288	Medal of Honor,	$2.50
289	Scott Joplin,	$2.50
290	Thomas H.	
	Gallaudet,	$2.50
291	28¢ Olympics	
	Airmail, (4),	$4.00
292	Pearl Buck, (4),	$2.50
293	Babe Ruth,	$4.00
294	Nathaniel	
	Hawthorne,	$2.50
295	Henry Clay, (7),	$2.50
296	13¢ Olympics, (4),	$4.00
297	$9.35 Eagle,	$150.00
297A	$9.35 Eagle Booklet	
	Pane of 3,	$200.00
298	Omnibus,	
	(3 items),	$3.00
299	Treaty of Paris,	$2.50
300	Civil Service,	$2.50
301	Metropolitan	
	Opera,	$2.50
302	Inventors, (4),	$3.50
303	Dorothea Dix,	
	(3 items),	$2.50
304	Streetcars, (4),	$3.50
305	Motorcycle Coil,	
	(4),	$3.00
306	Christmas,	
	Contemporary,	$2.50
307	Christmas,	
	Traditional,	$2.50
308	35¢ Olympics	
	Airmail, (4),	$4.50
309	Martin Luther,	$2.50
310	Flag Booklet, (10),	$5.00

1984

311	Alaska Statehood,	$2.50
312	Winter Olympics,	
	(4),	$4.00
313	FDIC,	$2.50

314	Harry S. Truman,	$2.50
315	Love,	$2.50
316	Carter G. Woodson,	$2.50
317	Railroad Caboose	
	Coil, (2),	$3.00
318	Soil and Water	
	Conservation,	$2.50
319	Credit Union Act,	$2.50
320	Lillian M. Gilbreth,	$2.50
321	Orchids, (4),	$4.00
322	Hawaii Statehood,	$2.50
323	Baby Buggy Coil,	
	(3),	$3.00
324	National Archives,	$2.50
325	Summer Olympics,	
	(4),	$4.00
326	Louisiana World	
	Exposition,	$2.50
327	Health Research,	$2.50
328	Douglas Fairbanks,	$2.50
329	Jim Thorpe,	$3.50
330	Richard Russell,	
	(2),	$2.50
331	John McCormack,	$2.50
332	St. Lawrence	
	Seaway,	$2.50
333	Migratory Bird Hunting	
	and Conservation	
	Stamp Act,	$3.00
334	Roanoke Voyages,	$2.50
335	Herman Melville,	$2.50
336	Horace Moses,	$2.50
337	Smokey Bear,	$3.00
338	Roberto Clemente,	$3.50
339	Dr. Frank Laubach,	$2.50
340	Dogs, (4),	$3.50
341	Crime Prevention,	$2.50
342	Family Unity,	$2.50
343	Eleanor Roosevelt,	$2.50
344	Nation of Readers,	$2.50
345	Christmas,	
	Santa Claus,	$2.50
346	Christmas,	
	Traditional,	$2.50
347	Hispanic	
	Americans,	$2.50
348	Vietnam Veterans	
	Memorial,	$2.50

1985

349	Jerome Kern,	$2.50
350	Abraham Baldwin,	
	(3),	$2.50
351	"D" Sheet & Coil,	
	(3),	$2.50
352	"D" Booklet, (10),	$5.00
353	Non. Penalty Mail	
	sheet & coil, (3),	$2.50
354	Alden Partridge,	
	(2),	$2.50
355	Alfred Verville	
	Airmail,	$2.50
356	Lawrence & Elmer	
	Sperry Airmail,	$2.50
357	Transpacific	
	Airmail,	$2.50
358	Chester Nimitz,	$2.50
359	Mary McLeod	
	Bethune,	$2.50
360	Grenville Clark,	$2.50
361	Sinclair Lewis, (2),	$2.50
362	Duck Decoys, (4),	$3.00
363	Iceboat, (2),	$3.00
364	Winter Special	
	Olympics,	$2.50
365	Flag over Capitol,	
	sheet & coil, (3),	$2.50
366	Flag Booklet, (5),	$3.00

367	Stanley Steamer coil, (2),	$3.00	415	Father Edward J. Flanagan, (3 items),	$2.50	444
368	Seashells Booklet, (10),	$5.00	416	Dog Sled Coil, (2),	$3.00	

367	Stanley Steamer coil, (2),	$3.00	**415**	Father Edward J. Flanagan, (3 items),	$2.50
368	Seashells Booklet, (10),	$5.00	**416**	Dog Sled Coil, (2),	$3.00
369	Love,	$2.50	**417**	John Harvard,	$2.50
370	Oil Wagon coil, (3),	$3.00	**418**	Navajo Art, (4),	$3.50
371	Pushcart coil, (3),	$3.00	**419**	Dr. Paul Dudley White, (3),	$3.50
372	John J. Audubon,	$2.50			
373	Express Mail,	$50.00	**420**	Dr. Bernard Revel,	$3.50
373A	Eagle Booklet, (3),	$100.00	**421**	T.S. Eliot,	$2.50
374	Tricycle coil, (4),	$3.00	**422**	Woodcarved Figurines, (4),	$3.50
375	Rural Electrification Administration,	$2.50	**423**	Christmas, Contemporary,	$2.50
376	14¢ and 22¢ Penalty Mail sheet & coil, (4),	$2.50	**424**	Christmas, Traditional,	$2.50
377	AMERIPEX '86,	$2.50	**425**	RFD Truck Coil,	$3.00
378	Sylvanus Thayer, (3),	$2.50	**426**	Bread Wagon Coil,	$3.00
379	School bus coil, (7),	$3.00		**1987***	
			427	Tow Truck Coil,	$3.00
380	Stutz Bearcat coil, (2),	$3.00	**428**	Michigan Statehood,	$2.50
381	Abigail Adams,	$2.50	**429**	Pan American Games,	$2.50
382	Buckboard coil, (5),	$3.00	**430**	1987 Love,	$2.50
383	Ambulance coil, (3),	$3.00	**431**	Tractor Coil,	$3.00
384	Frederic Bartholdi,	$2.50	**432**	Julia Ward Howe Regular,	$2.50
385	Henry Knox, (3),	$2.50	**433**	Jean Baptiste Pointe Du Sable,	$2.50
386	Korean War Veterans,	$2.50	**434**	Enrico Caruso,	$2.50
387	Social Security Act,	$2.50	**435**	Mary Lyon Regular,	$2.50
388	Father Serra Airmail,	$2.50	**436**	2¢ Re-engraved Locomotive Coil,	$3.00
389	Veterans, World War I,	$2.50	**437**	Girl Scouts,	$3.00
390	Walter Lippmann, (4),	$2.50	**438**	Canal Boat Coil,	$3.00
391	American Horses, (4),	$3.50	**439**	Special Occasions Booklet, (10),	$6.00
392	Public Education,	$2.50	**440**	United Way,	$2.50
393	Youth, (4),	$3.50	**441**	Flag-Fireworks Regular,	$2.50
394	Help End Hunger,	$2.50	**442**	Flag Coil with Pre- phosphored Paper,	$2.50
395	Letters, (2),	$2.50	**443**	American Wildlife, (5 pages),	$30.00
396	Christmas, Contemporary,	$2.50			
397	Christmas, Traditional,	$2.50			
398	Washington coil, (2),	$2.50			

444	Delaware Statehood,	$2.50
445	U.S./Morocco Diplomatic Relations,	$2.50
446	William Faulkner,	$2.50
447	Lacemaking, (4),	$3.00
448	$5 Bret Harte,	$15.00
449	Pennsylvania Statehood,	$2.50
450	Constitution Booklet, (5),	$12.00
451	New Jersey Statehood,	$2.50
452	Constitution,	$2.50
453	Certified Public Accountants,	$2.50
454	Locomotive Booklet, (5),	$15.00
455	Christmas, Contemporary,	$2.50
456	Christmas, Traditional,	$2.50

*Numbers and pricing for 1987 issues subject to change.

Prices are courtesy of Charles D. Simmons, a stamp dealer specializing in Souvenir Pages.

1986

399	Arkansas Statehood,	$2.50
400	Jack London,	$2.50
401	Stamp Collecting Booklet, (4),	$4.50
401E	Stamp Booklet with Missing Colors,	$600.00
402	Love,	$2.50
403	Sojourner Truth,	$2.50
404	Hugo L. Black, (5),	$2.50
405	Republic of Texas,	$2.50
406	William J. Bryan,	$5.00
407	Fish Booklet, (5),	$4.50
408	Public Hospitals,	$2.50
409	Duke Ellington,	$2.50
410	Presidents SS, (4),	$25.00
411	Polar Explorers, (4),	$3.50
412	Belva Ann Lockwood, (2),	$2.50
413	Margaret Mitchell, (3 items),	$2.50
414	Statue of Liberty,	$2.50

Fish Commemorative Stamp Booklet

FIRST DAY OF ISSUE

American Commemorative Panels

The Postal Service offers American Commemorative Panels for each new commemorative stamp and special Christmas stamp issued. The series first began September 20, 1972 with the issuance of the Wildlife Commemorative Panel and will total 298 panels by the end of 1987. The panels feature stamps in mint condition complemented by reproductions of steel line engravings and stories behind the commemorated subject.

1972
1 Wildlife, $15.00
2 Mail Order, $13.00
3 Osteopathic Medicine, $15.00
4 Tom Sawyer, $13.00
5 Pharmacy, $15.00
6 Christmas 1972, $18.00
7 'Twas the Night Before Christmas, $18.00
8 Stamps, $13.00
1973
9 Love, $16.00
10 Pamphleteers, $14.00
11 George Gershwin, $15.00
12 Posting of the Broadside, $14.00
13 Copernicus, $14.00
14 Postal People, $14.00
15 Harry S. Truman, $17.00
16 Post Rider, $14.00
17 Boston Tea Party, $42.00
18 Electronics, $14.00
19 Robinson Jeffers, $14.00
20 Lyndon B. Johnson, $17.00
21 Henry O. Tanner, $14.00
22 Willa Cather, $14.00
23 Drummer, $17.00
24 Angus Cattle, $14.00
25 Christmas, 1973, $18.00
26 Christmas, Needlepoint Noel, $18.00
1974
27 Veterans, $15.00
28 Robert Frost, $15.00
29 EXPO '74, $17.00
30 Horse Racing, $17.00
31 Skylab, $23.00
32 Universal Postal Union, $17.00
33 Mineral Heritage, $20.00
34 Fort Harrod, $15.00
35 Continental Congress, $17.00
36 Chautauqua, $15.00

37 Kansas Wheat, $15.00
38 Energy Conservation, $15.00
39 Sleepy Hollow, $15.00
40 Retarded Children, $15.00
41 Christmas, Currier & Ives, $22.00
42 Christmas, Angel Altarpiece, $22.00
1975
43 Benjamin West, $16.00
44 Pioneer, $25.00
45 Collective Bargaining, $16.00
46 Contributors to the Cause, $16.00
47 Mariner, $25.00
48 Lexington & Concord, $18.00
49 Paul Laurence Dunbar, $16.00
50 D. W. Griffith, $16.00
51 Bunker Hill, $18.00
52 Military Uniforms, $18.00
53 Apollo Soyuz, $25.00
54 World Peace Through Law, $16.00
55 International Women's Year, $16.00
56 Postal Bicentennial, $20.00
57 Banking and Commerce, $18.00
58 Christmas, A Treasured Tradition, $23.00
59 Christmas, Madonna, $23.00
1976
60 Spirit of '76, $25.00
61 Interphil 76, $24.00
62 State Flags, $40.00
63 Centennial of the Telephone, $18.00
64 Commercial Aviation, $25.00
65 Chemistry, $18.00
66 Benjamin Franklin, $20.00
67 Declaration of Independence, $20.00

68 Olympics, $22.00
69 Clara Maass, $19.00
70 Adolph S. Ochs, $19.00
71 Christmas, Currier Winter Pastime, $25.00
72 Christmas, Copley Nativity, $25.00
1977
73 Washington at Princeton, $24.00
74 Sound Recording, $36.00
75 Pueblo Indian Art, $135.00
76 Solo Transatlantic Flight, $135.00
77 Colorado Statehood, $30.00
78 Butterflies, $34.00
79 Lafayette, $30.00
80 Skilled Hands, $30.00
81 Peace Bridge, $30.00
82 Herkimer at Oriskany, $30.00
83 Civil Settlement, $30.00
84 Articles of Confederation, $30.00
85 Talking Pictures, $30.00
86 Surrender at Saratoga, $30.00
87 Energy Conservation & Development, $30.00
88 Christmas, Washington at Valley Forge, $36.00
89 Christmas, Rural Mailbox, $50.00
90 Carl Sandburg, $18.00
91 Captain Cook, $28.00
92 Harriet Tubman, $18.00
93 American Quilts, $27.00
94 American Dance, $22.00
95 French Alliance, $23.00
96 Dr. George Papanicolaou, $18.00

97	Jimmie Rodgers,	$24.00
98	Photography,	$18.00
99	George M. Cohan,	$24.00
100	Viking Missions,	$60.00
101	American Owls,	$60.00
102	American Trees,	$60.00
103	Christmas, Madonna and Child,	$25.00
104	Christmas, Hobby Horse,	$25.00

1979

105	Robert F. Kennedy,	$18.00
106	Martin Luther King, Jr.,	$16.00
107	International Year of the Child,	$16.00
108	John Steinbeck,	$16.00
109	Albert Einstein,	$18.00
110	Pennsylvania Toleware,	$16.00
111	American Architecture,	$16.00
112	Endangered Flowers,	$18.00
113	Seeing Eye Dogs,	$18.00
114	Special Olympics,	$24.00
115	John Paul Jones,	$16.00
116	15¢ Olympic Games,	$24.00
117	Christmas, Gerard David Madonna	$25.00
118	Christmas, Santa Claus,	$25.00
119	Will Rogers,	$18.00
120	Vietnam Veterans,	$22.00
121	10¢, 31¢ Olympic Games,	$24.00

1980

122	W.C. Fields,	$15.00
123	Winter Olympics,	$22.00
124	Benjamin Banneker,	$15.00
125	Frances Perkins,	$15.00
126	Emily Bissell,	$15.00
127	Helen Keller/ Anne Sullivan,	$15.00
128	Veterans Administration,	$15.00
129	General Bernardo de Galvez,	$15.00
130	Coral Reefs,	$20.00
131	Organized Labor,	$15.00
132	Edith Wharton,	$15.00
133	Learning Never Ends,	$15.00
134	Northwest Indian Masks,	$22.00
135	American Architecture,	$15.00
136	Christmas, Stained Glass Window,	$23.00

| 137 | Christmas, Contemporary, | $23.00 |

1981

138	Everett Dirksen,	$14.00
139	Whitney Moore Young,	$14.00
140	American Flowers,	$17.00
141	American Red Cross,	$15.00
142	Savings & Loans,	$14.00
143	Space Achievement,	$20.00
144	Professional Management,	$14.00
145	Preservation of Wildlife Habitats,	$19.00
146	Int'l. Year Disabled Persons,	$14.00
147	Edna St. Vincent Millay,	$14.00
148	American Architecture,	$14.00
149	Babe Zaharias/Bobby Jones,	$17.00
150	James Hoban,	$14.00
151	Frederic Remington,	$14.00
152	Battle of Yorktown/ Virginia Capes,	$14.00
153	Christmas, "Teddy Bear,"	$20.00
154	Christmas, Madonna and Child,	$20.00
155	John Hanson,	$15.00
156	U.S. Desert Plants,	$17.00

1982

157	Roosevelt,	$22.00
158	Love,	$25.00
159	G. Washington,	$22.00
160	State Birds & Flowers,	$25.00
161	The Netherlands,	$22.00
162	Library of Congress,	$22.00
163	World's Fair,	$25.00
164	Horatio Alger,	$22.00
165	Aging Together,	$22.00
166	The Barrymores,	$25.00
167	Dr. Mary Walker,	$22.00
168	International Peace Garden,	$25.00
169	America's Libraries,	$22.00
170	Jackie Robinson,	$25.00
171	Touro Synagogue,	$22.00
172	American Architecture,	$22.00
173	Wolf Trap,	$22.00
174	Francis of Assisi,	$22.00
175	Ponce de Leon,	$22.00
176	Christmas, Tiepolo Madonna and Child,	$25.00

| 177 | Christmas, Season's Greetings, | $25.00 |
| 178 | Kitten & Puppy, | $25.00 |

1983

179	Science and Industry,	$12.00
180	Sweden/USA Treaty,	$12.00
181	Ballooning,	$16.00
182	Civilian Conservation Corps,	$12.00
183	Olympics (40¢),	$14.00
184	Joseph Priestley,	$12.00
185	Voluntarism,	$10.00
186	The Concord,	$12.00
187	Physical Fitness,	$10.00
188	Brooklyn Bridge,	$12.00
189	Tennessee Valley Authority,	$12.00
190	Medal of Honor,	$16.00
191	Scott Joplin,	$16.00
192	Olympics (28¢),	$16.00
193	Babe Ruth,	$18.00
194	Nathaniel Hawthorne,	$12.00
195	Olympics (13¢),	$16.00
196	Treaty of Paris,	$12.00
197	Civil Service,	$12.00
198	Metropolitan Opera,	$12.00
199	American Inventors,	$12.00
200	Streetcars,	$14.00
201	Christmas, Traditional,	$16.00
202	Christmas, Season's Greetings,	$16.00
203	Olympics (35¢),	$16.00
204	Martin Luther,	$14.00

1984

205	Alaska Statehood,	$10.00
206	Winter Olympics,	$14.00
207	FDIC,	$10.00
208	Love,	$12.00
209	Carter G. Woodson,	$10.00
210	Soil and Water Conservation,	$10.00
211	Credit Union Act of 1934,	$10.00
212	Orchids,	$14.00
213	Hawaii Statehood,	$12.00
214	National Archives,	$10.00
215	Summer Olympics,	$14.00
216	Louisiana World Exposition,	$12.00
217	Health Research,	$10.00
218	Douglas Fairbanks,	$10.00
219	Jim Thorpe,	$12.00
220	John McCormack,	$10.00
221	St. Lawrence Seaway,	$12.00

222	Preserving Wetlands,	$14.00	**250**	Public Education,	$8.00	
223	Roanoke Voyages,	$10.00	**251**	Youth,	$8.00	
224	Herman Melville,	$10.00	**252**	Help End Hunger,	$8.00	
225	Horace Moses,	$10.00	**253**	Christmas, Contemporary,	$12.00	
226	Smokey Bear,	$12.00	**254**	Christmas, Traditional,	$12.00	
227	Roberto Clemente,	$12.00		**1986**		

222 Preserving Wetlands, $14.00
223 Roanoke Voyages, $10.00
224 Herman Melville, $10.00
225 Horace Moses, $10.00
226 Smokey Bear, $12.00
227 Roberto Clemente, $12.00
228 Dogs, $12.00
229 Crime Prevention, $10.00
230 Family Unity, $10.00
231 Christmas, Traditional, $12.00
232 Christmas, Season's Greetings, $12.00
233 Eleanor Roosevelt, $10.00
234 Nation of Readers, $10.00
235 Hispanic Americans, $10.00
236 Vietnam Veterans Memorial, $14.00
1985
237 Jerome Kern, $8.00
238 Mary McLeod Bethune, $8.00
239 Duck Decoys, $10.00
240 Winter Special Olympics, $10.00
241 Love, $10.00
242 Rural Electrification Administration, $8.00
243 AMERIPEX '86, $12.00
244 Abigail Adams, $8.00
245 Frederic Auguste Bartholdi, $10.00
246 Korean War Veterans, $10.00
247 Social Security Act, $8.00
248 World War I Veterans, $10.00
249 American Horses, $10.00

250 Public Education, $8.00
251 Youth, $8.00
252 Help End Hunger, $8.00
253 Christmas, Contemporary, $12.00
254 Christmas, Traditional, $12.00
1986
255 Arkansas Statehood, $8.00
256 Stamp Collecting, $10.00
257 Love, $10.00
258 Sojourner Truth, $8.00
259 Republic of Texas, $8.00
260 Fish, $10.00
261 Public Hospitals, $8.00
262 Duke Ellington, $8.00
263 U.S. Presidents' Sheet #1, $10.00
264 U.S. Presidents' Sheet #2, $10.00
265 U.S. Presidents' Sheet #3, $10.00
266 U.S. Presidents' Sheet #4, $10.00
267 Polar Explorers, $9.00
268 Statue of Liberty, $10.00
269 Navajo Art, $9.00
270 T.S. Eliot, $8.00
271 Woodcarved Figurines, $9.00
272 Christmas, Traditional, $10.00
273 Christmas, Contemporary, $10.00
1987*
274 Michigan Statehood, $8.00
275 Pan American Games, $8.00
276 Love, $8.00

277 Jean Baptiste Du Sable, $8.00
278 Enrico Caruso, $8.00
279 Girl Scouts, $8.00
280 Special Occasions, $8.00
281 United Way, $8.00
282 #1 American Wildlife, $10.00
283 #2 American Wildlife, $10.00
284 #3 American Wildlife, $10.00
285 #4 American Wildlife, $10.00
286 #5 American Wildlife, $10.00
287 Delaware Statehood, $8.00
288 New Jersey Statehood, $8.00
289 U.S./Morocco Diplomatic Relations, $8.00
290 William Faulkner, $8.00
291 Lacemakers, $8.00
292 Constitution Booklet, $8.00
293 Constitution, $8.00
294 Certified Public Accountants, $8.00
295 Locomotives, $8.00
296 Christmas, Traditional, $10.00
297 Christmas, Contemporary, $9.00
298 Pennsylvania Statehood, $8.00

*1987 issues subject to change.

Prices are courtesy of the American Society of Philatelic Pages and Panels, an organization specializing in Commemorative Panels.

Souvenir Cards

These cards were issued as souvenirs of the philatelic gatherings at which they were distributed by the United States Postal Service, its predecessor the United States Post Office Department or the Bureau of Engraving and Printing. They were not valid for postage.

The forerunner of the souvenir cards is the 1938 Philatelic Truck souvenir sheet which the Post Office Department issued and distributed in various cities visited by the Philatelic Truck. It shows the White House, printed in blue on white paper. Issued with and without gum. Price with gum, $80, without gum, $10.

Values are for uncancelled cards; cards bearing USPS cancels are valued approximately $1 higher.

**United States Post Office
& United States Postal Service**

1960 Barcelona, 1st International Philatelic Congress, Mar. 26-Apr. 5. Enlarged vignette, Landing of Columbus from No. 231. Printed in black. 400.00

1968 EFIMEX, International Philatelic Exhibition, Nov. 1-9, Mexico City. Card of 1. No. 292, inscribed in Spanish. 6.00

1970 PHILYMPIA, London International Stamp Exhibition, Sept. 18-26. Card of 3. Nos. 548-550. 4.50

1971 EXFILIMA '71, 3rd Inter-American Philatelic Exhibition, Nov. 6-14, Lima, Peru. Card of 3, Nos. 1111 and 1126, Peru No. 360. Card inscribed in Spanish. 3.50

1972 BELGICA '72, Brussels International Philatelic Exhibition, June 24-July 9, Brussels, Belgium. Card of 3 Nos. 914, 1026 and 1104. Card inscribed in Flemish and French. 350
OLYMPIA PHILATELIC MUNCHEN '72, Aug. 18-Sept. 10, Munich, Germany. Card of 4, Nos. 1460-1462 and C85. Card inscribed in German. 3.75
EXFILBRA '72, 4th Inter-American Philatelic Exhibition, Aug. 26-Sept. 2, Rio de Janeiro, Brazil. Card of 3. No. C14, Brazil Nos. C18-C19. Card inscribed in Portuguese. 3.50
NATIONAL POSTAL FORUM VI, Aug. 28-30, Washington, D.C. Card of 4. No. 1396. 3.50

1973 IBRA '73 Internationale Briefmarken Aussteilung, May 11-20, Munich, Germany. With one No. C13. 4.00
APEX '73, International Airmail Exhibition, July 4-7, Manchester, England. Card of 3, Newfoundland No. C4, U.S. No. C3a and Honduras No. C12. 3.50
POLSKA '73, Swiatowa Wystawe Filatelistyczna, Aug. 19-Sept. 2, Poznan, Poland. Card of 3, No. 1488 and Poland Nos. 1944-1945. Card inscribed in Polish. 4.00
POSTAL PEOPLE CARD, Card of 10 (#1489-1498) distributed to Postal Service employees. Not available to public. 14x11." 75.00 (est.)

1974 HOBBY, The Hobby Industry Association of America Convention and Trade Show, February 3-6, Chicago, Illinois. Card of 4, Nos. 1456-1459. 4.00
INTERNABA, International Philatelic Exhibition, June 7-16, Basel, Switzerland. Card of 8, strip of Nos. 1530-1537. Card inscribed in 4 languages. 4.00
STOCKHOLMIA '74, International frimarksustailning, September 21-29, Stockholm, Sweden. Card of 3 No. 836, Sweden Nos. 300 and 765. Card inscribed in Swedish. 4.50
EXFILMEX '74 UPU, Philatelic Exposition Inter-Americana, October 26-November 3, Mexico City, Mexico. 2 No. 1157 and Mexico No. 910. Card inscribed in Spanish and English. 4.50

1975 ESPANA '75, World Stamp Exhibition, Apr. 4-13, Madrid, Spain. Card of 3 Nos. 233, 1271 and Spain No. 1312. Card inscribed in Spanish. 4.00
ARPHILA '75, June 6-16, Paris, France. Card of 3, Nos. 1187, 1207 and France No. 1117. Card inscribed in French. 3.50

1976 WERABA '76, Third International Space Stamp Exhibition, April 1-4, Zurich, Switzerland. Card of 2. Nos. 1434 and 1435 se-tenant. 4.00
BICENTENNIAL EXPOSITION on Science and Technology, May 30-Sept. 6, Kennedy Space Center, Fla. Card of 1, No. C76. 5.50
COLORADO STATEHOOD CENTENNIAL, August 1. Card of 3. Nos. 743, 288 and 1670. 5.00
HAFNIA '76, International Stamp Exhibition, Aug. 20-29, Copenhagen, Denmark. Card of 2. No. 5 and Denmark No. 2. Card inscribed in Danish and English. 5.00
ITALIA '76, International Philatelic Exhibition, Oct. 14-24, Milan, Italy. Card of 3. No. 1168 and Italy Nos. 578 and 601. Card inscribed in Italian. 4.00
NORDPOSTA '76, North German Stamp Exhibition, Oct 30-31, Hamburg, Germany. Card of 3. No. 689 and Germany Nos. B366 and B417. Card inscribed in German. 4.00

1977 AMPHILEX '77, International Philatelic Exhibition, May 26-June 5, Amsterdam, Netherlands. Card of 3. No. 1027 and Netherlands Nos. 41 and 294. Card inscribed in Dutch. 4.50

SAN MARINO '77, International Philatelic Exhibition, Aug. 28-Sept. 4, San Marino. Card of 3. Nos. 1-2 and San Marino No. 1. Card inscribed in Italian. 5.00

1978 ROCPEX '76, International Philatelic Exhibition, Mar. 20-29, Taipei, Taiwan. Card of 6. Nos. 1706-1709 and Taiwan Nos. 1812 and 1816. Card inscribed in Chinese. 4.00

NAPOSTA '78, Philatelic Exhibition, May 20-25, Frankfurt, Germany. Card of 3. Nos. 555, 563 and Germany No. 1216. Card inscribed in German. 4.00

1979 BRASILIANA '79, International Philatelic Exhibition, Sept. 15-23. Rio de Janeiro, Brazil. Card of 3. Nos. C91-C92 (C92a) and Brazil No. A704. Card inscribed in Portuguese. 4.00

JAPEX '79, International Philatelic Exhibition, Nov. 2-4, Tokyo, Japan. Card of 2. Nos. 1158 and Japan No. A674. Card inscribed in Japanese. 4.00

1980 LONDON '80—IPEX, May 6-14, London, England. Card of 1 U.S. 2¢ 1907 No. 329. Card inscribed in English. 4.00

NORWEX '80—IPEX, June 13-22, Oslo, Norway. 1975 Norway stamp and two 1925 Nos. 620-621 (Norse-American issue). Card inscribed in Norwegian. 4.00

ESSEN '80—IPEX, Nov. 15-19, Essen, West Germany. Card of 2. 1954 West German and NO. 1014 Gutenberg Bible. Card inscribed in German. 4.00

1981 WIPA '81, May 22-31, Vienna, Austria. Card of 2. 1967 Austria and No. 1252 American Music.

NSCM, National Stamp Collecting Month. Oct. 1981. Issued to call attention to special month for stamp collectors. Card of 2. Nos. 245 and 1918. Card inscribed in English. 4.00

PHILATOKYO '81, International Philatelic Exhibition, Oct. 9-18, Tokyo, Japan. Card of 2. Nos. 1531 and Japan No. 800. Card inscribed in Japanese. 4.00

NORDPOSTA '81, North German Stamp Exhibition, Nov. 7-8, Hamburg, Germany. Card of 2. Nos. 923 and Germany 9NB133. Card inscribed in German. 4.00

1982 CANADA '82, International Philatelic Youth Exhibition, May 20-24, Toronto, Ontario, Canada. Card of 2. 1869 U.S. Eagle and Shield and 1859 Canadian Beaver. 4.00

PHILEXFRANCE '82, June 11-21, Paris, France. Card of 2. 1978 U.S. French Alliance and 1976 French commemoration of American Bicentennial. 4.00

ESPAMER '82, Oct. 12-17, San Juan, Puerto Rico. Card of 3. Nos. 810 and 1437 and the U.S. Ponce de Leon 1982 issue. 4.00

NSCM, National Stamp Collecting Month, October. Issued to call attention to special month for stamp collectors. Card of 1. No. C3a. 4.00

1983 Sweden/U.S., March 24, Philadelphia, PA. Card of 3. U.S. Nos. 958 and 2036, Sweden No. 1453. 4.00

German/U.S., April 29, Germantown, PA. Card of 2. U.S. No. 2040 and German No. 1397. 4.00

TEMBAL '83, May 21-29, Basil, Switzerland. Card of 2, in German. U.S. No. C71 and Switzerland No. 3L1. 4.00

BRASILIANA '83, July 29-August 7, Rio de Janeiro, Brazil. Card of 2, in Portuguese. U.S. No. 1 and Brazil No. 1. 4.00

BANGKOK '83, August 4-13, Bangkok, Thailand. Card

of 2, in Thai. U.S. No. 210 and Thailand No. 1. 4.00

NSCM, National Stamp Collecting Month. Card of 1. U.S. No. 293. 4.00

Memento, in conjunction with USPS participation at major international philatelic exhibitions during '83-'84, Tribute to Stamp Collectors Worldwide.

1984 ESPANA '84, International Exhibition, April 27-May 6, Madrid, Spain. Card of 2, in Spanish. U.S. No. 233, Spain 1930 issue of 40-centimo tribute to Christopher Columbus. 2.00

SALON DER PHILATELIE, International Philatelic Exhibition, June 19-26, Hamburg, Federal Republic of Germany. Card of 2, in English, French and German. U.S. No. C66. German 1949 issue honoring Heinrich von Stephan, initiator of the first UPU Congress.

AUSIPEX '84, Sept. 21-30, Melbourne, Australia. U.S. No. 290 and Western Australian 1854 1-penny Swan River Settlement. 2.00

NSCM '84, National Stamp Collecting Month, Oct. 1-31. U.S. No. 2104. 2.00

PHILAKOREA '84, Oct. 22-31, Seoul, Korea. U.S. No. 741 and 1975 Korean Mount Sorak National Park. 2.00

1985 Memento, U.S. Second International Philatelic memento card honors George Washington. First distribution at STAMPEX '85 in London, England, February 26.

OLYMPHILEX '85, March 18-24, Lausanne, Switzerland. U.S. No. C106 and 1984 Swiss 80-centime for home of the International Olympic Committee. 2.00

ISRAPHIL '85, May 14-22, Tel Aviv, Israel. U.S. No. 566 and Israeli 1950 22-prutot Struggle for Free Immigration. 2.00

ARGENTINA '85, International Philatelic Exhibition, July 5-14, Buenos Aires, Argentina. Card of 2, in Spanish. U.S. No. 1737 and Argentine No. B27.

MOPHILA '85, Philatelic Exhibition, Sept. 11-15, Hamburg, Federal Republic of Germany. Card of 2, in German. U.S. No. 296 and German No. B595. 2.00

ITALIA '85, Oct. 25-Nov. 3, Rome, Italy. In Italian. U.S. No. 1107 and Italian No. 830.

1986 Memento '86, features Statue of Liberty Centennial, first distributed at STAMPEX '86 in London, March 4-9.

STOCKHOLMIA '86, August 28-September 7, for Sweden's International Philatelic Exhibition. Illustrated stamp designs honor 350th Anniversary of Sweden's Postal System.

1954 POSTAGE STAMP DESIGN EXHIBITION, National Philatelic Museum, Mar. 13, Philadelphia. Card of 4. Monochrome views of Washington, D.C. Inscribed: "Souvenir sheet designed, engraved and printed by members, Bureau, Engraving and Printing/Reissued by popular request." 625.00

1966 SIPEX, 6th International Philatelic Exhibition, May 21-30, Washington, D.C. Card of 3. Multicolored views of Washington D.C. Inscribed "Sixth International Philatelic Exhibition/Washington, D.C./Designed, Engraved, and Printing by Union Members of Bureau of Engraving and Printing." 210.00

1969 SANDIPEX, San Diego Philatelic Exhibition, July 16-20, San Diego, Cal. Card of 3. Multicolored views of Washington, D.C. Inscribed: "Sandipex—San Diego 200th Anniversary—1769-1969." 80.00
ASDA National Postage Stamp Show, Nov. 21-23, 1969, New York. Card of 4. No. E4. 30.00

1970 INTERPEX, Mar. 13-15, New York. Card of 4. Nos. 1027, 1035, C35 and C38. 65.00
COMPEX, Combined Philatelic Exhibition of Chicagoland, May 29-31, Chicago. Card of 4. No. C18. 20.00
HAPEX, American Philatelic Society Convention, Nov. 5-8, Honolulu, Hawaii. Card of 3. Nos. 799, C46 and C55. 25.00

1971 INTERPEX, Mar. 12-14, New York. Card of 4. No. 1193. Background includes Nos. 1331-1332, 1371 and C76. 5.00
WESTPEX, Western Philatelic Exhibition, Apr. 23-25, San Francisco. Card of 4. Nos. 740, 852, 966 and 997. 4.50
NAPEX '71, National Philatelic Exhibition, May 21-23, Washington, D.C. Card of 3. Nos. 990, 991, 992. 4.50
TEXANEX '71, Texas Philatelic Association and American Philatelic Society conventions, Aug. 26-29, San Antonio, Tex. Card of 3. Nos. 938, 1043 and 1242. 4.50
ASDA National Postage Stamp Show, Nov. 19-21, New York. Card of 3. Nos. C13-C15. 4.50
ANPHILEX '71, Anniversary Philatelic Exhibition, Nov. 26-Dec. 1, New York. Card of 2. Nos. 1-2. 4.50

1972 INTERPEX, Mar 17-19, New York. Card of 4. No. 1173. Background includes Nos. 976, 1434-1435 and C69. 4.00
NOPEX, Apr. 6-9, New Orleans. Card of 4. No. 1020. Background includes Nos. 323-327. 3.50
SEPAD '72, Oct. 20-22, Philadelphia. Card of 4. No. 1044. 3.50
ASDA National Postage Stamp Show, Nov. 17-19, New York. Card of 4. Nos. 883, 863, 868 and 888. 3.00
STAMP EXPO, Nov. 24-26, San Francisco. Card of 4. No. C36. 3.00

1973 INTERPEX, March 9-11, New York. Card of 4. No. 976. 4.00
COMPEX '73, May 25-27, Chicago. Card of 4. No. 245. 4.00
NAPEX '73, Sept. 14-16, Washington, D.C. Card of 4. No. C3. Background includes Nos. C4-C6. 3.50
ASDA National Postage Stamp Show, Nov. 16-18, New York. Card of 4. No. 908. Foreground includes Nos. 1139-1144. 4.00
STAMP EXPO NORTH, Dec. 7-9, San Francisco. Card of 4. No. C20. 4.00

1974 MILCOPEX, March 8-10, Milwaukee, Wisconsin. Card of 4. No. C43. Background depicts U.P.U. monument at Berne, Switzerland. 5.00

1975 NAPEX '75, May 9-11, Washington, D.C. Card of 4. No. 708. 14.00
INTERNATIONAL WOMEN'S YEAR. Card of 3. Nos. 872, 878 and 959. Reproduction of 1886 dollar bill. 35.00
ASDA National Postage Stamp Show, Nov. 21-23, New York. Bicentennial series. Card of 4. No. 1003. "...and maintain the liberty which we have derived from our ancestors." 57.50

1976 INTERPHIL '76, Seventh International Philatelic Exhibition, May 29-June 6, Philadelphia. Bicentennial series. Card of 4. No. 120. "that all men are created equal." 9.50
STAMP EXPO '76, June 11-13, Los Angeles. Bicentennial series. Card of 4. Nos. 1351, 1352, 1345 and 1348 se-tenant vertically. "when we assumed the soldier, we did not lay aside the citizen." 6.50

1977 MILCOPEX, Milwaukee Philatelic Society, Mar. 4-6, Milwaukee. Card of 2. Nos. 733 and 1128. 5.00
ROMPEX '77, Rocky Mountain Philatelic Exhibition, May 20-22, Denver. Card of 4. No. 1001. 4.00
PURIPEX '77, Silver Anniversary Philatelic Exhibit, Sept. 2-5, San Juan, Puerto Rico. Card of 4. No. 801. 5.00
ASDA National Postage Stamp Show, Nov. 15-20, New York. Card of 4. No. C45. 4.50

1978 CENJEX '78, Federated Stamp Clubs of New Jersey, 30th annual exhibition, June 23-25, Freehold, N.J. Card of 9. Nos. 646, 680, 689, 1086, 1716 and 4 No. 785. 5.00

1980 NAPEX '80, July 4-6, Washington, D.C. Card of 4. No. 573. 5.00
ASDA National Postage Stamp Show, Sept. 25-28, New York. Card of 4. No. 962. 5.00

1981 STAMP EXPO '81, South International Stamp Collectors Society, Mar. 20-22, Anaheim, Cal. Card of 4. No. 1287. 5.00

1982 MILCOPEX, March 5-7, Milwaukee, Wisconsin. Card of 4. No. 1136. 5.00
ESPAMER '82, Oct. 12-17, San Juan, Puerto Rico. Card of 1. No. 244. 5.00

1983 TEXANEX-TOPEX '83, June 17-19, San Antonio, Texas. Card of 2. Nos. 776 and 1660. 5.00
NORTHEASTERN '83, Oct. 21-23, Boston, Mass. Card of 2. Nos. 718 and 719. 5.00

1984 STAMP EXPO '84 SOUTH, April 27-29, Los Angeles, California. Card of 4. U.S. Nos. 1791-1794. 3.00
ESPANA '84, April 27-May 6, Madrid, Spain. Card of 4. U.S. No. 241 as a block of 4. 3.00
COMPEX '84, May 25-27, Rosemont, Illinois. Card of 4. U.S. No. 728 as a block of 4. 3.00

1985 MILCOPEX '85, March 1-3, Milwaukee, WI. Card of block of 4 of U.S. No. 880. 4.00
NAPEX '85, June 7-9, Arlington, VA.

1986 AMERIPEX '86, May 22-June 1, Rosemont, IL. Celebrates 100th anniversary of organized stamp collecting. Card consists of 1¢ Franklin, No. 134, issue of 1870, 20¢ Treaty of Paris, U.S. No. 2052, issues of 1983, 8¢ Stamp Collecting, No. 1474, issue of 1972. 4.00

1987 CAPEX '87, June 13-21, for international philatelic exhibition in Toronto, Ontario, Canada. Stamp illustrations feature 1923 U.S. definitive Bison (without denomination) and the 1981 Canadian commemorative picturing Vancouver Island Marmot. Card inscribed in English and French.
HAFNIA '87, October 16-25, Copenhagen, Denmark. Card features illustrations of seagoing vessels in honor of HAFNIA.

 CAPEX'87

Toronto, Ontario, Canada
June 13-21, 1987

 Canada 17

The United States issued this Buffalo stamp in 1923. It was the first U.S. regular issue to feature American Wildlife.

Ce timbre représentant un bison a été émis par les États-Unis en 1923. Il s'agit du premier timbre courant américain ayant pour sujet un animal sauvage.

The U.S. Postal Service is pleased to issue this souvenir card, featuring American Wildlife, in honor of CAPEX '87.

L'Administration postale des États-Unis est heureuse d'émettre cette carte-souvenir sur la faune américaine, en l'honneur de CAPEX '87.

This stamp was issued by Canada in 1981 as part of its Endangered Wildlife series. It depicts the Vancouver Island Marmot.

Ce timbre a été émis par le Canada en 1981 dans le cadre d'une série consacrée aux espèces menacées d'extinction. Il reproduit une marmotte de l'île de Vancouver.

© UNITED STATES POSTAL SERVICE 1987

Subject Index

IMPORTANT NOTE: This Index covers all issues from the 1893 Columbian Exposition issues (#230) through 1987. Listings in italic typeface refer to Definitive or Regular issues. The numbers listed next to the stamp description are the Scott numbers, and the numbers in parenthesis are the numbers of the pages on which the stamps are illustrated..

312

313

316

317

318